P9-BZI-934

HISTORICAL MAPS OF CIVIL WAR BATTLEFIELDS

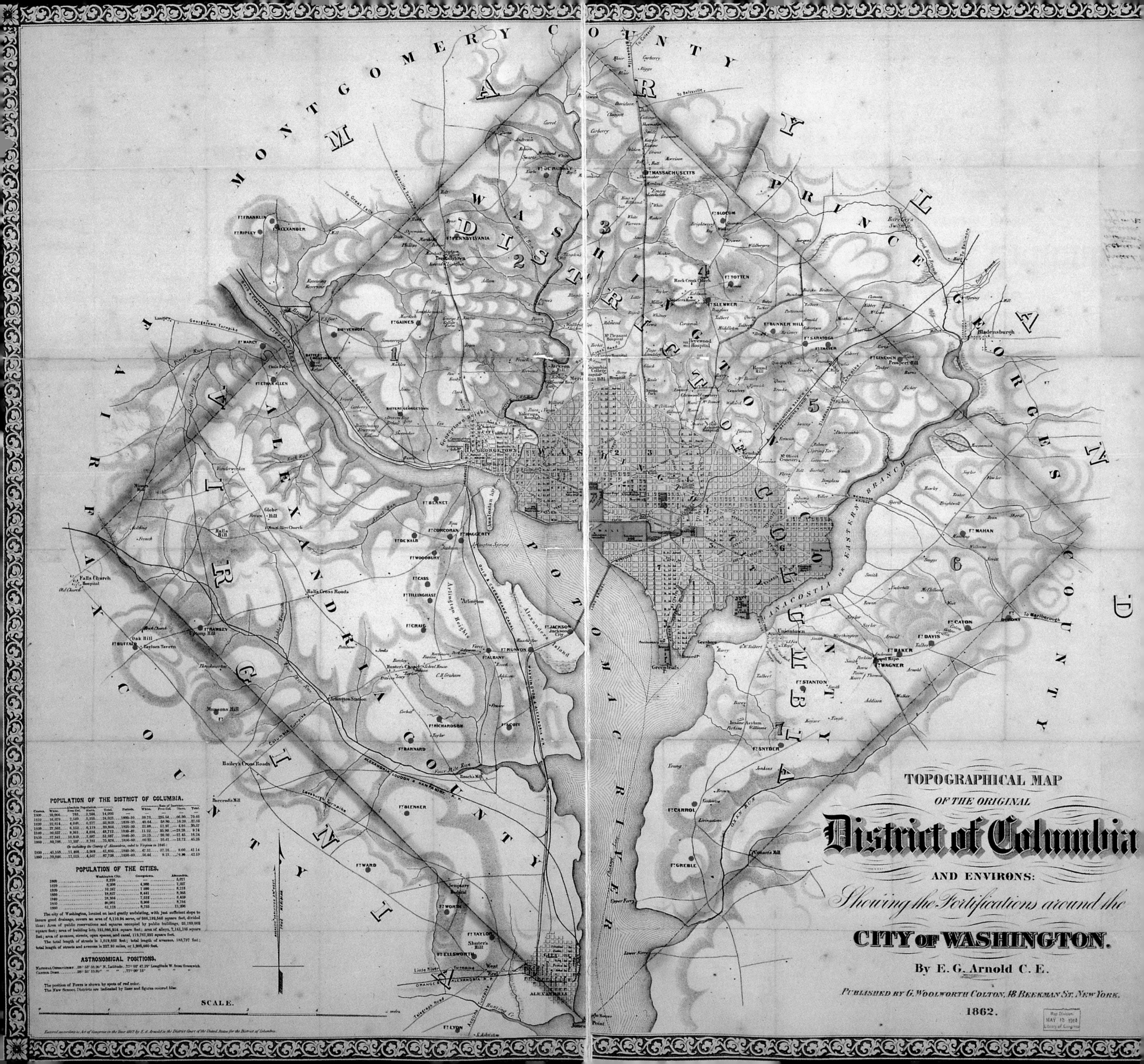
TOPOGRAPHICAL MAP
OF THE ORIGINAL
District of Columbia
AND ENVIRONS:
Showing the Fortifications around the
CITY OF WASHINGTON.
By E. G. Arnold C. E.
PUBLISHED BY G. WOOLWORTH COLTON, 18 BEEKMAN ST. NEW YORK.
1862.
MONTGOMERY COUNTY
MARYLAND
PRINCE GEORGES COUNTY
FAIRFAX COUNTY
VIRGINIA
ALEXANDRIA COUNTY
WASHINGTON COUNTY
DISTRICT OF COLUMBIA
POTOMAC RIVER
ANACOSTIA OR EASTERN BRANCH
POPULATION OF THE DISTRICT OF COLUMBIA.
POPULATION OF THE CITIES.
ASTRONOMICAL POSITIONS.
SCALE.
Bladensburgh
Georgetown
Alexandria
Falls Church
Balls Cross Roads
Bailey's Cross Roads
Arlington
Arlington Heights
Hunter's Chapel
Glebe Hill
Munsons Hill
Uniontown
Greenleafs Point
Rock Creek Church
Georgetown Turnpike
Columbia Turnpike
Four Mile Run
FT. MASSACHUSETTS
FT. SLOCUM
FT. TOTTEN
FT. SLEMMER
FT. BUNKER HILL
FT. SARATOGA
FT. LINCOLN
FT. MAHAN
FT. STANTON
FT. DAVIS
FT. BAKER
FT. WAGNER
FT. CATON
FT. SNYDER
FT. CARROLL
FT. GREBLE
FT. DE RUSSY
FT. PENNSYLVANIA
FT. GAINES
FT. FRANKLIN
FT. ALEXANDER
FT. RIPLEY
FT. MARCY
FT. ETHAN ALLEN
FT. BENNET
FT. CORCORAN
FT. HAGGERTY
FT. DE KALB
FT. WOODBURY
FT. CASS
FT. TILLINGHAST
FT. CRAIG
FT. ALBANY
FT. RUNYON
FT. JACKSON
FT. SCOTT
FT. RICHARDSON
FT. BARNARD
FT. BLENKER
FT. RAMSEY
FT. BUFFALO
FT. WARD
FT. WORTH
FT. TAYLOR
FT. ELLSWORTH
FT. LYON

HISTORICAL MAPS OF CIVIL WAR BATTLEFIELDS

MICHAEL SHARPE

PRC

Acknowledgments

Teddy Nevill of TRH Pictures did the research and procured all the maps for this book from the Library of Congress and the National Archives.

This edition first published in 2000 by
PRC Publishing Ltd,
Kiln House, 210 New Kings Road, London SW6 4NZ

ISBN 1 85648 584 6

Printed and bound in Italy

CONTENTS

*INTRO*DUCTION

Less than a century after its declaration of independence, the United States of America found itself embroiled in a bitterly divisive and damaging civil war, which had economic, political, and social ramifications that are still felt today. The war of 1863–65 pitted the Union of Northern States against the Confederacy of the Southern, and has been described as the first modern war. In its battles, tactics, and weaponry we can see elements of both the Napoleonic age and the new machine age, which held portents of future wars, not least the world war of 1914–18. At least 600,000 Americans lost their lives fighting for constitutional principles, sectional differences, economic self-interest, and moral righteousness. As a defining moment in United States history, the Civil War has no equal.

Origins of the Conflict

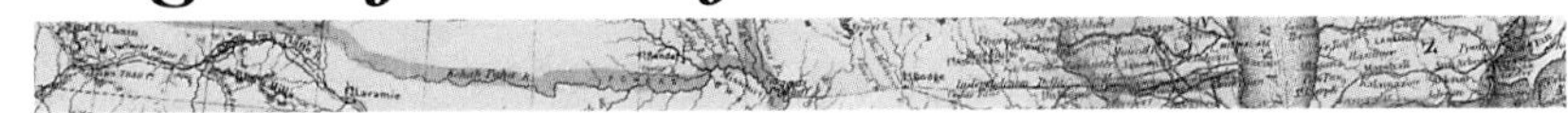

After the Constitution was adopted by all of the states in 1789, uniting them into one nation, differences between the states had been worked out through compromises. Less than a century later, by 1861 the differences between the Northern States (which included those of the midwest and west) and the Southern States had become so great that compromise would no longer work.

One area of conflict concerned the tariff that had to be paid on imported goods. In 1828 Northern businessmen helped get the "Tariff Act" passed. It raised the prices of manufactured products from Europe, which were sold mainly in the South. Ostensibly, the purpose of the law was to encourage the South to buy products from the North, but it angered Southerners, who now had to pay more for the goods they wanted from Europe or pay more to get goods from the North. Though most of tariff laws had been changed by the time of the Civil War, it was still a cause for considerable resentment.

Additionally, in the years preceding the war, the focus of political power in the Union Government, centered on Washington D.C., was changing. The Northern and Midwestern States were becoming increasingly powerful as their populations increased, while the Southern States were losing influence. Just as the original thirteen colonies had fought for their independence almost 100 years earlier, the Southern States felt a growing need for freedom from central Union authority. This centered on a demand for states' rights, based on the premise that each state

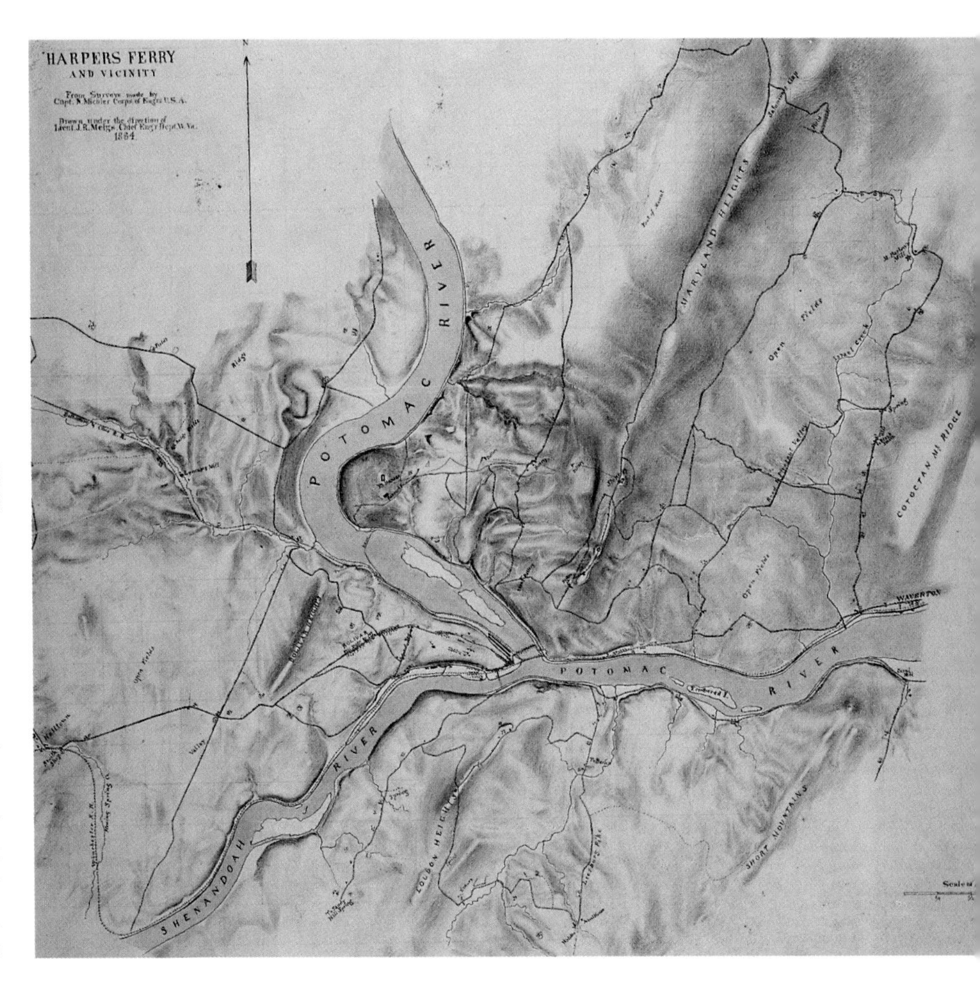

Above: An 1864 map of the confluence of the Potomac and Shenandoah rivers at Harpers Ferry, drawn under the direction of Lt. John Meigs of the Department of West Virginia. Until its abandonment on April 18, 1861, Harpers Ferry had been the site of the U.S. Arsenal and Armory. On the night of October 16, 1859, the abolitionist John Brown seized the armory and held it until the 18th when Marines under Robert E. Lee stormed it. Brown was hanged and became a martyr for a cause that would escalate into war two years later.

should exercise autonomous control over its laws. The rights issue prompted early calls in the Southern States for secession from the Union.

Perhaps the most emotional source of conflict was slavery. Cotton was the dominant industry in the agrarian South and it depended largely on slave labor. In the liberal North, slave ownership was viewed with abhorrence, loudly expressed through the Press. In the South, culturally and politically wholly different to its Northern neighbors, slavery had been a part of the way of life for well over 200 years and was, in theory, upheld within the Constitution, which guaranteed the right to own property and protected against seizure of property. Slaves were regarded as property. Inevitably, the Southern States resented what they viewed as an attempt to undermine their economy and culture, so hastening the drift to secession.

In 1860, Abraham Lincoln was elected President. His anti-slavery stance and promise to keep the new western territories free from slavery was taken by some Southern politicians as a direct challenge to their liberty, and on December 20, 1860, a secession convention met in South Carolina and adopted an Ordinance of Secession from the Union. Mississippi, Florida, Alabama, Georgia, Louisiana, and Texas quickly followed suit. These states sent delegates to Montgomery, Alabama and on February 8, 1861, adopted a provisional constitution for the newly formed Confederate States of America. Jefferson Davis was chosen as the President for a six-year term of office. The Constitution by which the permanent government of the Confederate States of America was formed was reported by the committee and adopted by the Provisional Congress on March 11, 1861, to be submitted to the states for ratification. All states ratified it and conformed to its requirements without delay. The Constitution varied in very few particulars from the Constitution of the United States, preserving carefully the fundamental principles of popular representative democracy and confederation of co-equal states.

The War Begins

The first clash of the war came after a demand for the surrender of Fort Sumter, in Charleston, South Carolina on April 11, 1861. The Union commander, Major Robert Anderson, refused. At 4.30 a.m. on April 12, 1861, the first shot of the war was fired from a Confederate artillery battery. Artillery exchanges continued through April 13, when terms of capitulation were finally agreed. The fort was evacuated by steamer at noon on April 14. The following day Lincoln issued a proclamation calling for 75,000 militia to serve for 90 days to put down "combinations too powerful to be suppressed" by the ordinary mechanism of government.

The proclamation by Lincoln served to polarize the yet uncommitted states into action. Virginia, North Carolina, Arkansas, and Tennessee severed their ties with the Union, unwilling to supply troops to fight against their sister Southern States. The border states of Maryland, Missouri, and Kentucky, while providing soldiers to both armies, were kept under Union control.

The newly created Confederacy faced a huge problem. Eleven states had left the Union; 22 remained. The population of the Confederate States was about nine million, almost one-third of whom were slaves. The Union States could count 22 million individuals and had a steady stream of immigrants. The South had only two main east-west railroad lines and limited ability to manufacture locomotives or rolling stock. Most of the known deposits of coal, iron ore, and copper were in the North, together with about 92 percent of the country's industrial capacity. The Navy remained loyal to the Union and most of the merchant shipping was Northern-owned. If the South was to achieve victory, it would be against long odds.

Bull Run Creek

With Virginia having cast its lot with the South, the Confederate capital was moved from Montgomery, Alabama to Richmond, Virginia, barely 100 miles from Washington, D.C. The area of Maryland and Virginia between the two capitals would see some of the bloodiest fighting during the war.

In the spring of 1861, Lincoln, seeing that his 90-day volunteers' terms of enlistment would soon be expiring, placed Brigadier-General Irvin McDowell at the head of the 30,000 men then in Washington and ordered an advance toward the Confederate capital. Although McDowell was unhappy with the untrained state of his troops, he proposed moving against Beauregard's concentration of about 22,000 Confederate troops near Manassas, Virginia. Delays in the advance allowed

Beauregard time to reinforce his position with some 9,000 troops under Brigadier-General Joseph E. Johnston, who had succeeded in giving a Union "holding force" the slip, and moved his command by rail from the Shenandoah Valley to Manassas. On July 21, 1861, the two amateur armies clashed across Bull Run Creek. Although McDowell's attack plan was initially successful, a stubborn stand by Thomas J. ("Stonewall") Jackson's brigade allowed Johnston's late-arriving reinforcements to turn the tide for the Confederates. McDowell ordered a retreat, which soon became a rout. The inexperienced Confederates, however, were in no shape to pursue the beaten Federals; the Union army, now more a disorganized mob, retreated back to Washington.

War in the West

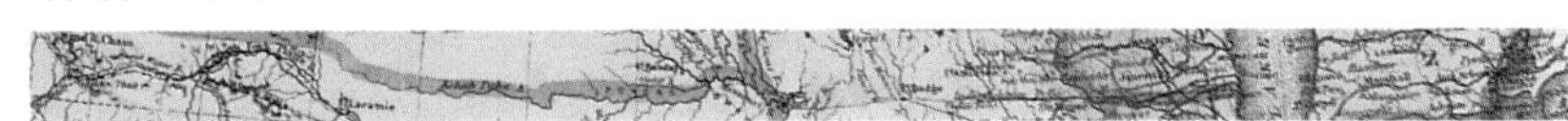

Kentucky, cut through by the strategically important Mississippi River, had already declared its neutrality. Although both sides hesitated to violate that neutrality, Confederate Major-General Leonidas Polk moved to occupy Columbus on September 4, 1861, prompting the state to declare in favor of the Union, although unbeknown to Polk, Grant had planned to occupy the city on the following day.

General Albert Johnston, regarded by many as the South's finest general, arrived to take command of the Western Department in mid-September, 1861. His new command numbered but 20,000 troops, most of them raw and ill-equipped, between the Appalachian Mountains to the east and the Mississippi River. In the Trans-Mississippi Theater, the Confederate victory at Wilson's Creek, Missouri on August 10, 1861, was achieved despite a complete lack of co-operation between Southern Generals Price and McCulloch.

To correct these shortcomings, Johnston immediately appealed for more troops and appointed Major-General Earl Van Dorn as the ranking general over both Price and McCulloch for the new year. Brigadier-General Felix Zollicoffer was ordered to occupy the Cumberland Gap with a command of raw recruits to bolster Johnston's weak right flank.

Even with these measures however, the Union forces opposing Johnston could have easily advanced right over his makeshift defenses. Johnston kept them at bay by a combination of bluff and bluster. The theatrics were successful to a point, but were gradually exposed on his right flank, primarily because of Zollicoffer's inexperience. Brigadier-General Crittenden was subsequently sent east to assume command of the right wing and found Zollicoffer camped on the wrong (north) side of the unfordable Cumberland River. He was facing Brigadier-General George H. Thomas's Union command, twice as large as his own. Although Crittenden ordered a move back to the south bank, in early January Zollicoffer was still to be found on the north side of the river. To compound problems, the Union forces were starting to advance. Suddenly realising his desperate circumstances, Zollicoffer launched a dawn attack on the Union encampment at Mill Springs, Kentucky during a rain-soaked, dreary, January day. The attack failed and Zollicoffer was killed when he mistakenly rode into the Union lines; most of his command managed to escape to the south bank of the river.

Johnston's right flank had collapsed, but it did not prove to be his undoing. Thomas subsequently advanced toward Nashville, but the onset of winter in this barren region stopped him about 60 miles short of his objective.

In February 1862, Johnston's defensive line began to come apart. His Achilles' heel proved to be the Cumberland and Tennessee rivers, which ran into the heart of Confederate territory. Although the Tennessee plunged deep into his rear, Johnston's immediate concern was the Cumberland, which curved past Clarksville, Tennessee (the site of the South's second largest ironworks) and Nashville, his base of supply. If Union gunboats were allowed to freely ply this river, his railroad bridges would be quickly destroyed and his supply situation rendered untenable.

In response, Fort Henry and Fort Donelson were built on the Tennessee and Cumberland, respectively, to block the rivers and prevent just this type of disaster. The forts were constructed at a point where the rivers were only 12 miles apart. Fort Henry was badly sited, on low ground subject to flooding and dominated by high ground across the river. Johnston's engineer arrived in late November 1861 and noticed the problem immediately, but by mid-January he had still not arrived at a solution. Fort Henry fell to Flag Officer Foote's Union ironclad fleet and the rising flood waters on February 6, 1862. Fort Donelson was sited rather better, and Foote's fleet lost a heavy artillery duel with its gunners. Union troops, under Grant, assaulted and took Fort Donelson on February 16, 1862, together with about 15,000 Southern troops.

Johnston accepted that he could no longer hold Nashville. He left Nathan Bedford Forrest in charge of the rear-guard and fell back to Murfreesboro. Major-General Buell, still advancing cautiously, did not reach the now undefended city of Nashville until February 23. With the fall of Nashville, Major-General Polk's position at Columbus, Kentucky was rendered untenable. He abandoned his fortifications and fell back. Some 7,000 Southern troops were sent to New Madrid and the fortress at Island No. 10 to block the Mississippi River. Another 10,000 were moved to the railroad junction at Humboldt, Tennessee, from which they could be rapidly deployed.

In the Mississippi Theater, the Confederacy was suffering further setbacks. General Van Dorn had been defeated at Pea Ridge, Arkansas on March 7–8 by Union forces under Brigadier-General Curtis, effectively losing the state of Missouri. Brigadier-General Sibley's New Mexico campaign, aimed at gaining California and access to Pacific ports, came to an abrupt end following the battle at Glorieta on March 28. New Madrid, on the Mississippi River, fell to Union forces on March 13, although Island No. 10 held out until April 7.

On April 6, 1862, the largest battle so far was fought near Shiloh Church, a Methodist meeting house in West Tennessee. Grant's Army of the Tennessee, numbering some 48,000 men, had camped near Pittsburg Landing on the Tennessee River, awaiting the arrival of General Buell's Army of the Ohio with another 30,000 troops, so they could make a combined advance on Corinth, Mississippi. Johnston and Beauregard, commanding the 44,000 men of the Confederate Army of the Mississippi, realized that they could not hope to challenge a united Union force, and advanced north from Corinth for a quick strike at Grant. Johnston would undoubtedly have preferred to await the arrival of Van Dorn's Trans-Mississippi command with another 15,000 men, but time was not on his side.

The Confederate attack on the morning of April 6 caught Grant napping. The Confederate defeats at Forts Henry and Donelson, and their subsequent evacuation of Nashville, had led Grant to believe the Southern forces were a spent force. He had not ordered the fortification of his camps at Shiloh, nor had he organized for adequate reconnaissance. The initial Southern attacks overran many of the Union camps and rapidly pushed toward Pittsburg Landing. However, as the initial shock wore off, the veteran troops among the Union forces began to stiffen their resistance. Prentiss's stand in the Sunken Road bought Grant the time he needed to cobble together a final defensive line covering Pittsburg Landing. Fortunately for Grant, Johnston was killed in the attack and the resulting command confusion meant that the Confederates were not able to consolidate their forces for a final push against the Landing before evening. That afternoon and night, the lead elements of the Army of the Ohio began to arrive and take position. The Union armies began a general advance on the morning of April 7, and the now outnumbered Confederates were forced to withdraw back to Corinth. Casualties numbered about 13,000 Union and 10,000 Confederate.

The Peninsula Campaign

Following the Union fiasco at Bull Run, Major-General George B. McClellan replaced McDowell as commander of the Union forces. He forged the Union Army of the Potomac into a fine fighting force, but was slow to move the army southward. After repeated urging by the Lincoln government, McClellan decided to move against Richmond via the Yorktown Peninsula in March.

For the Southern commanders, the defense of the Peninsula presented a major predicament, compounded by the fact that in the Virginia theater their 70,000 troops faced at least 200,000 Union men.

The task was handed to Major-General John Bankhead Magruder, who, despite inadequate resources, set to work with customary zeal. He had a long defensive line constructed with Yorktown serving as its left flank. A secondary line was built some ten miles back from the first, just in front of Williamsburg. General Robert E. Lee, military advisor to President Davis at that time, was afraid these lines might be outflanked, and on his advice, a third line was constructed about ten miles in front of Richmond, with flanks anchored on the Chickahominy and James Rivers.

Magruder used his meager resources to their maximum effect, and by bluff and feint, gave McClellan cause for hesitation in attacking. To compound his problems, on April 4 he learned that Fort Monroe, with a 12,000-man Union garrison, had been taken from his command authority and that McDowell's 38,000-man corps, which he had been expecting as reinforcements, was to be kept near Washington for its defense.

Finally, he also learned that a stop had been put to additional Union recruiting efforts.

Based on these developments, McClellan opted to lay a siege. By early May he had set up 15 ten-gun batteries of 13-inch siege mortars. General Joseph E. Johnston, now in command of Confederate field forces, balked at the prospect of bombardment, and ordered evacuation of Yorktown on May 3, leaving behind some 56 heavy siege guns of his own with ammunition, which McClellan added to his plentiful stocks. On May 5, the Confederate rearguard engaged the Union advance elements in the Battle of Williamsburg, and Johnston pulled back even closer to Richmond.

On May 16 Lee received intelligence that McDowell and some 40,000 Union troops would be moving south toward the Confederate capital. Disaster threatened. With McClellan poised to the east, Johnston could not move to intercept McDowell without risking the loss of Richmond. Conversely, if Johnston did not act, then McDowell would be free to move against the city. His counter-punch was masterful. Knowing that President Lincoln was always particularly concerned about any threat to his capital, and invariably given to overreaction, he ordered "Stonewall" Jackson to make an aggressive show in the Shenandoah Valley and threaten Washington, D.C.

After engaging a Union force at Front Royal on May 23, Jackson pushed General Nathanial Banks from his supply depot at Winchester on May 25. Besides netting some 3,000 prisoners, 9,000 small arms, and tons of supplies, the operation prompted Lincoln to order McDowell to halt his advance on Richmond and to try to intercept Jackson. Recognizing a chance to trap Jackson, Lincoln then ordered Fremont's command from the west to take Harrisonburg and close the southern end of the Shenandoah Valley.

Jackson, however, remained stoic. Realizing the danger of his current position, he determined to make good his escape and take all the captured Union supplies with him. By a hair's breadth, Jackson broke through the closing jaws of the Union trap, fighting at Cross Keys on June 8 and at Port Republic on June 9. Thus, with only 17,000 men, Jackson neutralized the threat to Richmond by a Union army four times the size.

Jackson's splendid leadership galvanized Johnston, whose 70,000 Southern troops faced 100,000 Union troops outside Richmond. The rain-swollen Chickahominy River presented a possible avenue for attack. McClellan, against his better judgment, had been ordered to split his own army across this river. Johnston saw that a rapid attack on the Union wing on the south side of the river would give the Confederates a local numerical superiority and a good chance for success.

The plan Johnston formulated was simple; a straightforward advance east along parallel roads to attack Keyes in front of Seven Pines. In the event, rain and mud threw the advance into disarray and at the end of the day, the Confederates could only claim the capture of ten artillery pieces and 6,000 rifles. They had inflicted 5,000 casualties on the Union troops, but had suffered 6,000 themselves. Moreover, Johnston was badly wounded and had to be relieved of command. He was succeeded by Robert E. Lee, who had established a fine reputation as a tactician. He predicted that McClellan would use his engineering expertise and superior firepower to move slowly forward from one entrenched position to the next until he finally took Richmond. Lee set about reinforcing his defenses. To his advantage, rain fell continuously for the next 10 days and McClellan's heavy artillery train was immobilized. The Confederates effectively neutralized any attempt to bring them up by rail, using their own 32-pounder artillery piece mounted on a railroad car to smash the railroad.

Lee pulled reinforcements from every quarter until he could muster a force of about 85,000 men. He planned to leave some 30,000 south of the Chickahominy in newly constructed entrenchments to hold McClellan's 75,000-strong force there, and use the remaining 55,000 Southern troops to crush the 30,000 Union troops on the north bank. By defeating and destroying a large portion of this force, Lee would be free to capture McClellan's supply base and thereby force him out into the open. During June 12–15, J. E. B. Stuart's cavalry reconnoitered the Union army dispositions. With Jackson currently returning from the Shenandoah Valley and due to arrive on June 25, Lee planned his attack on June 26.

McClellan was by now convinced that he faced an army of some 200,000 Confederate troops, a belief that had a profound effect on his decisions during the confusing series of battles known as the "Seven Days." The Confederates, after some minor fighting on June 25, moved north out of Richmond on June 26. Mechanicsville was taken easily, but an attempt to move east across Beaver Dam Creek was stopped by

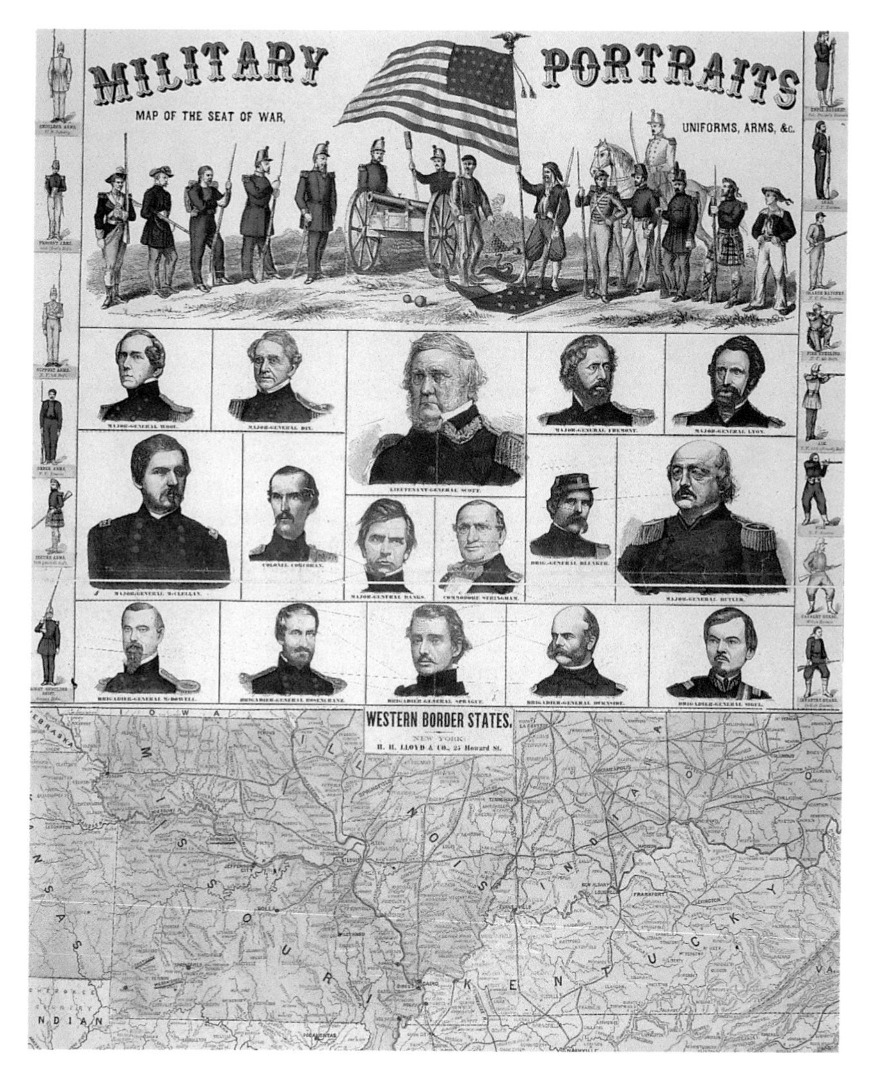

Above: Map of the western border states with portraits of Union military leaders —Generals Wool, Dix Scott, Fremont, Lyon, McClellan, Banks, Blenker, Butler, McDowell, Rosecrans, Sprague, Burnside, and Sigel, Colonel Corcoran, and Commodore Stringham. Illustrations at the top show early volunteers and those on the borders depict drill.

Union forces in strong defensive positions. Jackson's force, which was to have turned the flank of the position, had still not arrived.

On the morning of June 27, the Beaver Dam Creek position was finally won, though only because of an ordered Union retreat to a prepared position on Turkey Hill behind the Boatswain's Swamp Creek. Here Fitz-John Porter's command of 35,000 Union troops was protected by a triple line of entrenchments with artillery support and marshy ground to their front. When Jackson's troops finally arrived that evening, the position was carried, but only at heavy cost to the Confederacy.

On Saturday, June 28, Lee realized that McClellan was falling back on the James River, and revised his earlier plans to try to catch the Union troops on either side of White Oak Swamp. The following day, Magruder was ordered to link up with Jackson and attack the retreating Union forces. The Confederates were badly handled in a clash at Savage Station, primarily because Jackson again failed to show up on time; however, in retreat, McClellan was forced to abandon much of his supplies.

On Monday, the sixth of the "Seven Days," the lack of co-operation that had hampered earlier Confederate operations emerged again among the pursuers. Huger decided to cut an alternate road through the thick forest when he found his designated road blocked by felled trees. Holmes's command ran into a naval bombardment. Jackson, who had difficulty in crossing the White Oak Swamp Creek, showed no inclination toward haste. Only Longstreet's and A. P. Hill's Union troops were engaged, at Glendale, costing the lives of some 3,300 Confederates.

On July 1, the last of the "Seven Days," Lee discovered that McClellan had taken position on Malvern Hill to protect the last leg of his retreat. This position was held by a formidable force led by Porter and Keyes with two divisions each, more than 100 artillery pieces, and a further four divisions in reserve. Lee attempted to bring his artillery to bear, but it soon became apparent that he was out-gunned. No satisfactory alternative approach could be found, and confusion in orders prompted a series of unco-ordinated Confederate assaults that cost another 5,500 Southern casualties. Again, Jackson failed to arrive in time to assist in the battle.

Lee's had achieved his objective of relieving Richmond from McClellan's forces, but at a very high cost—some 20,614 casualties, compared to Union losses of 15,849.

2nd Bull Run, Antietam, and Fredericksburg

On June 26, 1862, John Pope received command of the newly created Union Army of Virginia, formed by the consolidation of the commands of McDowell, Banks, and Fremont. By July 12, this army had moved south to a point that threatened Richmond's access to the Shenandoah Valley. Although McClellan was still threatening the Confederate capital, Lee sent reinforcements to Jackson with orders to "suppress" Pope. By August 3, McClellan was evacuating the Peninsula, thus removing the dual threat to Lee and allowing him the opportunity to concentrate on Pope exclusively. The opposing armies maneuvered through mid-August, and by August 22 were facing each other across the Rappahannock River near Sulphur Springs, Virginia. Pope's lines were too strong for a frontal attack, so Lee directed forces around Pope's unsecured flanks to cut his supply lines. The first raid in Pope's rear, by Stuart's cavalry, failed to seriously damage his supply line, but did net Pope's payroll of $350,000 and the headquarters' copy of all the week's dispatches. The second raid was carried out by Jackson's "foot cavalry" —so called because of the rapidity with which they moved long distances—which neutralized Bristoe Station and Manassas Station and destroyed Union supplies distributed over almost a square mile.

Despite these setbacks, Pope still believed he was in a position to destroy Lee. Lee had split his army and the Union troops were in position between Lee's two wings with forces capable of destroying either one. Pope hurried his command to Manassas hoping to smash Jackson's wing, only to discover that he had vanished. Eventually Jackson was discovered and attacked at Sudley Mountain, near the site of the First Battle of Bull Run. Jackson grimly held his position through August 29, and on August 30, Longstreet's wing of Lee's army arrived and turned the tide of battle. During the late afternoon, after Pope had committed his last reserves, Longstreet launched a massive assault into the flank of the Union army, routing it from the field. Pope suffered some 16,000 casualties, lost 30 artillery pieces, 20,000 small arms, and mountains of other supplies; he was relieved of command on September 2.

Although Lee had gained another stunning victory, he was unclear as to the best way to press his advantage. His forces could not stay in northern Virginia, but retreat would negate the advantages of his recent victory. He decided to invade Maryland, where he hoped to gain support from the local populace, and also saw an opportunity to sway foreign opinion with another victory on Northern soil. He felt confident that the Army of the Potomac was still demoralized from its recent defeats and McClellan, if remaining true to form, would react slowly. However, the Army of the Potomac was not demoralized; on the contrary, it was still full of fight. Nor did Maryland welcome the Confederates with open arms, and worst of all, McClellan secured a copy of Lee's entire plan of operations for the Maryland campaign in advance.

Pre-warned by an informer that McClellan had a copy of his orders, Lee hastened to concentrate his Army of Northern Virginia, now split into five segments, to defend himself from the attack he knew McClellan would be planning. With reinforcements from Longstreet, D. H. Hill was able to hold McClellan's army at bay at Turner's Gap in South Mountain long enough for Lee to form a defensive position on September 15 at Sharpsburg, Maryland, behind Antietam Creek. The 12,500-man Union garrison at Harpers Ferry surrendered that same day. On September 16, McClellan was facing, at most, some 18,000 Confederates in line of battle. If he had attacked, almost certainly he would have crushed this small force. He did not, and instead spent the day planning and investigating the terrain; all the time, Confederate reinforcements were arriving.

McClellan finally attacked the next day. Though Confederate reinforcements, in the form of the divisions of McLaws, Anderson, and A. P. Hill, arrived throughout the day, McClellan at no time faced odds worse than two to one in his favor. Believing faulty intelligence estimates of Lee's strength, McClellan was unwilling to fully commit his army to the attack for fear of a Confederate trap. The result was a bloody seesaw battle in which Lee's outnumbered Confederates fought McClellan's army to a draw.

Lee retreated the following night and, despite repeated urgings, McClellan failed to press forward in pursuit of Lee's forces. Antietam proved to be the bloodiest single day of the war, with over 23,000 casualties. Although a tactical failure for McClellan, strategically it was a victory, since the Confederates had to retreat.

Despite urging from Lincoln, McClellan could not be induced to advance, and during the period of October 10–12, Stuart's cavalry went on the rampage in Union territory, causing the government much embarrassment. McClellan was sacked and replaced by Ambrose E. Burnside.

Major-General Burnside was reluctant to accept command of the Army of the Potomac, feeling that he was not competent to hold such a position. Ultimately, he was overruled and forced to accept the assignment. Burnside's modesty soon proved correct.

His opening offensive began well; stealing a march on Lee and moving rapidly down the Rappahannock River, he planned to cross over to Fredericksburg on December 19, 1862. However, the pontoon bridges he had ordered failed to arrive on time, giving Lee the opportunity to entrench in excellent defensive terrain on the south bank covering the crossing. It was clear that any attempt to assault Lee's lines would be futile—to all except Burnside. After crossing the river, his assault troops ran into a murderous barrage of fire and were cut down before they even came near the Confederate positions. Luckily for the Federals, Lee did not have sufficient strength to launch a counterattack and Union heavy artillery was able to protect the retreat of the surviving troops. After the disaster at Fredericksburg, in late January 1863 Lincoln replaced Burnside with "Fighting Joe" Hooker as commander of the Army of the Potomac.

Bragg's Kentucky Campaign

With the fall of Corinth, Mississippi at the end of May 1862 and the defeat on June 6 of the Confederate fleet defending Memphis, the Mississippi River was opened to Union gunboats as far south as Vicksburg.

The Union command organization underwent major changes during this period. At the end of June Pope was ordered east to his fateful encounter at the Second Battle of Bull Run, relinquishing his command to Major-General Rosecrans. On July 11 Hallack was made commander-in-chief of all Union armed forces, east and west, and went to Washington, D.C. Grant, still shaken by the Shiloh campaign, was given Rosecrans's army and other forces in the theater, totaling some 75,000 troops.

Buell's forces, having been ordered to march on Chattanooga, Tennessee, and under constant pressure from Washington and Confederate cavalry and guerrilla attacks on his supply lines, slowly crawled forward. On August 12, 1862, John Hunt Morgan's cavalry destroyed an 800-foot-long tunnel on the Louisville & Nashville Railroad and cut off Buell from his base of supply at Louisville, Kentucky. This, combined with intelligence that Bragg was advancing north, led Buell to conclude he must fall back to protect Nashville.

General Bragg, now in command of Confederate forces in the theater, determined to go over on the offensive to recover both Tennessee and Kentucky. His campaign began favorably as Confederate forces in East Tennessee, under the control of General Kirby Smith and in co-operation with Bragg, moved north into Kentucky with 12,000 troops. On August 30, at Richmond, Kentucky, they met the 7,000 Union troops, most of them new recruits, who were defending the city. In a one-sided battle, Smith suffered only about 450 casualties while the Federals lost 206 killed, 844 wounded, and 4,303 captured or missing. Lexington, Kentucky was captured by Smith's forces, unopposed, the following day.

By September 13, Bragg had advanced as far as Glasgow, Kentucky, which placed him between Buell, now at Bowling Green, and Smith at Lexington. Bragg's forces then moved north to the Green River and forced the surrender of the 4,000-man Union garrison at Munfordsville. In response, Buell advanced his forces northward to Louisville and began a movement to the southeast towards the suspected location of Bragg's troops. The two armies met outside Perryville, Kentucky on October 8, 1862. Bragg, who was outnumbered three to one, ordered an attack on the Union left wing, routing the troops under General McCook. On the opposite flank, Joe Wheeler's 1,200 Confederate cavalry immobilized Crittenden's corps of 22,500 troops, but no decisive victory was gained and Bragg decided to retreat southward. Buell's pursuit was ponderous, and Bragg arrived safely back in Knoxville on October 22. Two days later Lincoln, unhappy with the turn of events, ordered Buell to turn over his command to Major-General Rosecrans.

Further west, on September 20, Grant came close to trapping Major-General Sterling Price's command of Trans-Mississippi troops at Iuka, Mississippi, about 20 miles east of Corinth. Confusion among the Confederate high commanders, Price and Van Dorn, then prompted Van Dorn to assault Corinth, thinking it now only lightly defended. A Confederate force of about 22,000 men advanced to the attack on October 3, 1862. However, Corinth was far from lightly defended. A double ring of fortifications—the outer ring of which had been built by the Confederates themselves before evacuating the town earlier that year—was held by an equal number of Union troops backed by artillery. Corinth saw some of the most vicious fighting of the war; despite

breaking through to the town, the Confederate forces were outflanked and a Union counterattack quickly drove them back out with heavy losses. A second attack on October 4 produced no tangible gains, and Van Dorn ordered a retreat. Almost trapped by Rosecrans's pursuit and a converging Union column ordered out by Grant, Van Dorn's forces suffered well over 4,000 casualties to Union losses of 2,500. The western flank of Bragg's offensive campaign had suddenly collapsed.

Following his recent appointment of Rosecrans, Lincoln sought a renewed offensive, but despite repeated urging the new commander delayed his movement from Nashville until the end of December. Then, having learned that one of Bragg's divisions had been detached to Vicksburg and that Forrest's and Morgan's cavalry commands were on raids elsewhere, he moved his Army of the Cumberland to the southeast. The opposing armies collided on December 31 just north of Murfreesboro at Stones River.

The opposing commanders had planned attacks on the right flank, but Bragg was quicker to the draw and the Union army was quickly forced onto the back heel. Hardee's and Polk's corps wheeled the Union troops back at the Round Forest, bending the line by almost 90 degrees—but it had not broken and, apparently bolstered by a meeting of his officers that night, Rosecrans decided not to retreat, despite having suffered some 12,000 casualties to Bragg's 9,000.

In the opposing camp Bragg's losses had negated the possibility of an assault on Rosecrans's new position, and so Bragg waited, hoping Rosecrans would make the logical decision and retreat. On January 2, with the Union troops still in position, Bragg ordered an ill-advised assault on the Union left flank. Despite some initial success, the troops were ripped apart by the Union artillery, costing Bragg another 1,700 casualties. Finally conceding defeat, he retreated during the night of January 3 to Tullahoma, Tennessee. Although his army was too battered to attempt a pursuit, Rosecrans could claim Stones River as a Union victory.

The Chancellorsville Campaign

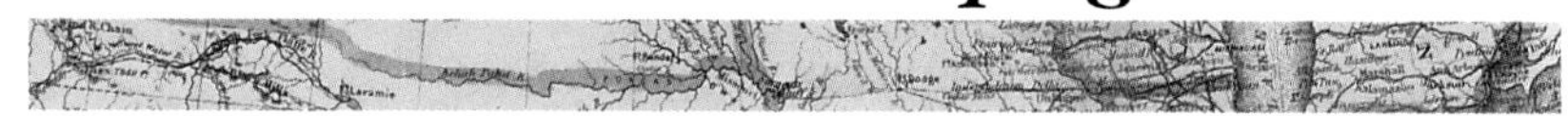

On January 25, 1863, Lincoln appointed "Fighting Joe" Hooker to the command of the Army of the Potomac. Hooker's first priority was to improve the welfare and morale of the discouraged troops. To counter the Southern cavalry he reorganized his mounted troops into a single corps of 11,500 men under the command of Brigadier-General George Stoneman.

Hooker's command numbered some 130,000 troops and 412 artillery pieces, more than twice the strength of Lee in infantry, cavalry, and artillery, which he intended to use in a pincer movement against Lee. Each Union wing would be almost the size of Lee's entire command. As half of the army crossed the Rappahannock River below Fredericksburg, the other would cross upstream and move against Lee's rear, while the Union cavalry would make diversionary attacks behind the lines.

Bad weather halted any movement until late April. Then, after watching Sedgwick's men consolidating their bridgehead below Fredericksburg, Lee decided that the main threat was Hooker's flanking column and moved the bulk of his army towards Hooker, leaving Major-General Jubal Early with about 10,000 men to contain Sedgwick.

On May 1, while still inside the tangle of the Wilderness, Hooker suddenly had an attack of nerves and halted his advance, ordering his men into a defensive posture. Had he at this point advanced to more open country, his superior numbers would have given him a distinct advantage, especially with respect to his artillery.

With Hooker paused in the Wilderness, Lee and Jackson conceived a bold but risky counterattack. Lee divided his forces once again and sent Jackson's corps on a long march to turn Hooker's unprepared right flank. Late in the afternoon of May 2, Jackson slammed into Hooker's flank, routing the Union XI Corps. Tragically for the Confederacy, Jackson was accidentally shot by his own men after the initial assault and died of pneumonia eight days later.

On May 3, in an attempt to come to the aid of Hooker, Sedgwick attacked and broke through Early's defensive line, but was halted again near Bank's Ford and Salem Church. The following day Lee launched a counterattack, but could not drive Sedgwick from his position. Later that night, Hooker's nerve failed him again, and he ordered a full retreat of the Army of the Potomac.

Despite the fact that Hooker's army had escaped, it is likely that, had Lee actually continued to assault the Union army in its prepared defenses, he could very well have destroyed his own army. Hooker was defeated more by his own loss of nerve than by Lee and Jackson. He would be relieved of command of the army in mid-June.

The Vicksburg Campaign

Vicksburg, a heavily fortified city controlling the middle stretch of the Mississippi River, was situated atop high, unscalable bluffs from where its batteries could dominate the river below, threatening destruction on Union gunboats attempting to pass. Directly to the north was the vast Yazoo Delta, impassable to a large body of troops, and 100 miles downstream the fortress at Port Hudson prevented Union naval forces from moving upstream.

Grant planned a two-pronged advance on Vicksburg, landing Major-General Sherman to the north of Vicksburg while he moved south down the railroad through Grenada. The plan was a costly failure, largely due to the harrying of Forrest's and Van Dorn's cavalry. A raid in December 1862 cut to shreds Grant's supply lines in Tennessee, and during the same period a second raid destroyed the Union supply depot at Holly Springs, Mississippi. With his existing supplies denied him, and no way of bringing in more, Grant was forced to retreat to Memphis. To the north Sherman's attempt to land troops at Chickasaw Bluffs was repulsed with heavy losses.

Grant refused to be discouraged by these setbacks and kept at work toward his objective of Vicksburg. Efforts were made to construct a canal across the tongue of land in front of Vicksburg to divert the river channel and bypass the city's artillery batteries, but these were abandoned when a dam gave way, causing significant damage to the Union camps.

Next he tried to move the fleet via a circuitous route through Lake Providence, about 50 miles north of Vicksburg, but found the route through the bayous to the Red River blocked by cypress trees and flood debris.

A third project again aimed at exploiting the complex river system around Vicksburg, moving via the Yazoo Pass, a bayou just south of Helena, Arkansas. However, after successfully moving into the Tallahatchie River system, the Union fleet was blocked by a Confederate fort.

A fourth attempt was made, utilizing the bayous to reach the Sunflower River which flowed into the Yazoo River above Haines Bluff, but underwater vegetation fouled the Union fleet's paddle wheels, and they were forced to abandon this idea.

The final project involved the construction just below Duckport of a second canal that would allow the passage of light draft vessels; falling river levels scuppered this project.

Still no closer to his goal, but bolstered by two gunboats that had run the gauntlet of the batteries at Port Hudson, Grant set to work on his final plan. He requested and received agreement from Admiral Porter to try to run his ships past the Vicksburg artillery batteries. On April 16, under the blanket of a dark, moonless sky, the ships stole past the Vicksburg guns. Only one transport vessel was lost, and there were no casualties among the Union personnel. On April 20, more transport vessels were run past Vicksburg, with the loss of another transport and six of twelve supply barges.

To try to deceive the Confederates as to his true line of operations, Grant ordered Sherman to make diversionary attacks at Haines Bluff and a harassing cavalry raid by Colonel R. H. Grierson; these succeeded in distracting Pemberton's attention. Grant had initially intended to cross the Mississippi at Grand Gulf on April 28, but found Confederate forces too strong at that point. He moved the landing point to Bruinsburg and crossed without opposition on April 30.

Grant's diversions had forced Pemberton to disperse the Confederate army, and he was unable to rapidly field sufficient forces to contain Grant's bridgehead. Although a Confederate task force under Brigadier-General John Bowen met and briefly held Grant's advance elements at Port Gibson on May 1, he was forced to retreat for lack of reinforcements. Emboldened, Grant implemented a bold new operational strategy. Informed that General Johnston was assembling an army in central Mississippi to come to Pemberton's support, Grant decided to move inland and interpose himself between the two Confederate forces, thereby abandoning his river-based line of communications. Pemberton meanwhile, despite urgings by Johnston to immediately concentrate his own forces and move against Grant's bridgehead, pulled the Confederate defenders back into the vicinity of Vicksburg.

On May 12, Grant began moving the Union army of about 44,000 troops toward the interior of Mississippi. This force met and defeated a small task force under Brigadier-General Maxey Gregg at Raymond that same day, and two days later broke up the concentration of Johnston's forces at Jackson. The Confederates abandoned the important railhead and supply depot and escaped to the north.

Pemberton was again ordered by Johnston to move out of Vicksburg, to strike Grant's rear and link up with his own relief forces. Fatally, he delayed until May 15. Marching out of Vicksburg with the intention of cutting Grant's now non-existent supply line, Pemberton changed his mind again on May 16 and decided to obey Johnston's orders by attempting to link up with him at Brownsville. By now, however, Grant had already made contact with his lead division near Champion Hill.

Grant rapidly moved his forces to the west toward Vicksburg, having left Sherman with two divisions in Jackson to complete the destruction of railroad tracks and stores. With 29,000 men to oppose almost 23,000 in Pemberton's command, Grant fought a series of desperate battles, with key positions changing hands several times, before the Confederates were finally forced to retreat towards Vicksburg. Pemberton attempted to stand at the Big Black River, but his forces were again routed and driven into the Vicksburg defenses, enabling Grant to re-establish contact with the Union fleet on the Yazoo River on May 18.

Grant began his assault on the city on May 18, and attacked again on May 22. The Confederate defenders put up a stiff resistance, and after suffering heavy losses, Grant laid siege, with the intention of starving the garrison into submission. Johnston rapidly built up a relief force (which, combined with Pemberton's forces, at one point would have outnumbered the besieging Union troops) but co-ordinating his assault with an attempted breakout by Pemberton proved impossible, and on June 15 Johnston notified the Confederate authorities that he considered the defense of Vicksburg untenable.

By the end of June, the privations brought on by the siege were beginning to tell on the defenders of Vicksburg, and on July 4, Pemberton formally surrendered his army of 2,166 officers and 27,230 enlisted men, 172 cannon and 60,000 small arms. Five days later another 7,000 Confederate troops surrendered to Major-General Nathanial Banks at Port Hudson, Louisiana. The Mississippi River was once again open to the sea and under Union control, effectively splitting the Confederacy in half.

The Gettysburg Campaign

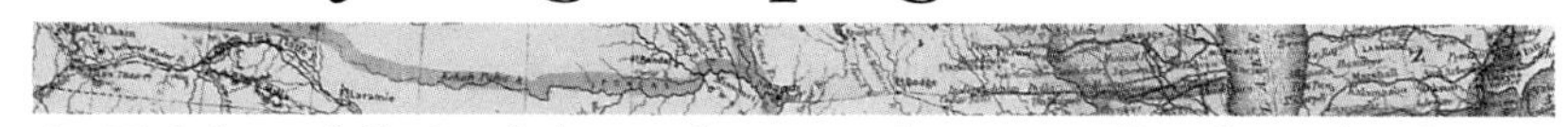

As Vicksburg fell, Confederate forces in the east suffered another heavy defeat, when General Robert E. Lee failed to break the center of the Union line at Gettysburg. Lee, the commander of the Confederate Army of Northern Virginia, had recently defeated the Union Army of the Potomac at the Battle of Chancellorsville. However, although Chancellorsville had been a decisive victory for the Confederacy, Lee himself knew that all he had really accomplished was to buy a little more time, for although the Federals had been repelled from much of Virginia, which contained the all-important capital of the Confederacy at Richmond, Lee knew it would only be a matter of time before the powerful Union armies moved south again.

Faced with the prospect of another defensive battle for Richmond, Lee took the initiative and went on the attack, despite a significant inferiority in numbers. His military instincts, and the knowledge that his Confederate army was short of supplies, including food, clothing, and shoes, convinced him to make a thrust into Pennsylvania, where vital supplies could be had. Another potential benefit was the possibility of gaining foreign recognition for the Confederacy, and strengthening the position of the Northern Democrats, who were in favor of making peace with the South.

Once he had overcome skeptics within the Confederate Cabinet, and the Confederate President, Jefferson Davis, Lee was granted permission to undertake his northern campaign. He divided the Army of Northern Virginia into three corps, keeping Longstreet in command of I Corps, and promoted Lieutenant-Generals Richard S. Ewell and Ambrose Powell Hill to the command of II and III Corps respectively. Though both these commanders had been successful, and would go on to further successes, neither was as skillful a soldier as "Stonewall" Jackson, who had been lost to the Confederacy at Chancellorsville.

Together with his exceptional cavalry commander, J. E. B. Stuart, for the upcoming campaign Lee could count on a highly skilled group of officers, little afflicted by personal differences. In marked contrast to this was the powerful Union Army of the Potomac, which had only been under Major-General George Gordon Meade since June 28. Meade had little time to come to terms with his new responsibilities. His army was large, well-clothed, and well-armed; however, in two years it had fought six battles and incurred five defeats. During this period, his veterans had served under five commanders, each of them markedly inferior to his Southern counterpart. The men in the ranks displayed no air of being a defeated army, however, and bolstered by their divisional commanders

—men like Sedgwick, Sickles, Hancock, Reynolds, and Slocum—they somehow forged a pride and cohesion, something that had been a trademark of the Southern forces from the beginning.

The invasion of the North began on June 15, when lead elements of Ewell's Corps crossed the Potomac River near Shepherdstown into Maryland. Notionally still loyal to the Union, the state had provided several combat units to Lee's army. On June 19, the Confederates moved into Pennsylvania and now threatened the cities of Baltimore and Washington.

Knowing that Meade would have to respond, Lee had no clear idea of where exactly he wished to fight the decisive battle. Ewell had executed a well-organized capture of three Union garrisons near Winchester, Virginia, although Stuart had been rocked by a surprise advance of the Union cavalry resulting in the Battle of Brandy Station on June 9, the largest cavalry fight of the war. With his reputation tarnished, Stuart set off on one of his lightning raids to redeem his reputation, and while he was off on this enterprise, he left Lee's army virtually blind.

Gettysburg, the scene of the coming battle, was a small, prosperous farming town that also contained a shoe factory. When Major-General Henry Heth, leading one of Hill's divisions, asked if he could use his superior numbers to collect some shoes, he ran into a large Union force. On the following day, July 1, 1863, Heth's brigades and two dismounted Union cavalry brigades under the command of John Buford engaged on the ridges to the northwest of Gettysburg, first on Herr Ridge, then in and around McPherson Woods. The Union cavalry commander, Buford, had correctly estimated Confederate intentions and placed his dismounted troopers to delay the initial Southern advance.

At this time the rest of the Army of the Potomac was spread out, heading for a defensive line along a river known as Pipe Creek. Of the Confederate forces, Ewell's Corps was still well to the north of Gettysburg, and Longstreet's was a day's march to the west. Stuart's whereabouts were unknown.

The Northern cavalry was quickly outnumbered and Buford urgently sent for help from Major-General John Reynolds, on his left wing. When Reynolds arrived, he could see the dismounted cavalrymen being pushed back. He sent an urgent message to General Meade, informing him that the enemy was advancing in strong force on Gettysburg. It was only when the Confederates recognized some of the veteran regiments of Reynolds's corps that they realized for sure that they had run into the Army of the Potomac and were not engaged with Pennsylvania militia. During the fighting Reynolds was killed and Abner Doubleday took over his command.

By around midday, the Union forces controlled McPherson Woods, Seminary Ridge, the southern end of Oak Ridge, Barlow Knoll, and the town of Gettysburg itself. A major Confederate drive on the town was stalled, and the fight along Oak Ridge see-sawed back and forth as both sides were alternately repulsed by massed musketry or short-range artillery fire.

At about 2.30 in the afternoon, Lee arrived to observe the fighting. He ordered an attack on the front and flank of XI Corps that routed them from their positions on Oak Ridge and Barlow Knoll back into Gettysburg. Another attack on I Corps troops defending Seminary Ridge drove them back into Gettysburg and onto Cemetery Ridge.

Fortunately for the Federals, one of their divisions, under the highly capable and inspiring Major-General Hancock, had been left on Cemetery Hill to construct defenses. Hancock arrived on the field to the sight of Union forces streaming out of Gettysburg and onto Cemetery Hill. He quickly decided to form a defensive line based on Cemetery Hill, with additional divisions deployed on Culps Hill on the right, and a left flank extending down Cemetery Ridge as far as the Round Tops.

Noting the confusion in the Union ranks, General Lee was anxious to take advantage. Hill's troops were exhausted from the fighting, and Longstreet's were still some distance away, leaving only Ewell's men. Lee's style of issuing orders was at times a little vague, and the discretionary phrasing of his order confused his subordinate. By the time Ewell finally realized that he had been ordered to take Culps Hill, the opportunity had already gone; the Union divisions were already dug-in.

Meade, at his headquarters in Taneytown, was persuaded by Hancock not to pull back to Pipe Creek, and that Gettysburg was the place to make the fight. Meade subsequently ordered all remaining corps of the Army of the Potomac to concentrate there and himself started out for Cemetery Ridge.

The fighting around the town died down the evening of July 1. With Lee and Meade now both on the field by early the following morning, the stage had been set for the biggest battle yet of the Civil War.

Lee planned to launch an attack on the Union left, around the Peach Orchard and the Wheatfield. The attacks were to fall in echelon from right to left, with Ewell to co-ordinate an attack on Culps Hill if the opportunity arose. Unfortunately for the plan, the attacking divisions were slow to move into place and, when they were finally in the position Lee had wanted them, the situation had changed. The once weak Union line along the Emmitsburg Road had been reinforced, prompting Confederate divisional commanders to suggest that the attack should move further to the right and focus on Little Round Top. Neither Lee nor Longstreet could be persuaded; in hindsight this was possibly their single greatest tactical error. The commanding height of Little Round Top would have allowed Confederate artillery to enfilade almost the entire Union line.

In the opening exchanges, a Confederate regiment under Colonel Oates actually captured the feature known as Big Round Top. Like many of his fellow officers, Oates was convinced that the Round Tops held the key to the battlefield. The 20th Maine Infantry Regiment of the Union army held onto the summit of Little Round Top in a bitter slugging match with the 15th Alabama Infantry Regiment, ensuring that the Union left flank remained securely anchored.

The main Southern assault against the Union left first pushed the Union troops out of the Peach Orchard, and then the Wheatfield and a rocky hill known as the Devil's Den. Furious fighting characterized this assault, and losses were heavy. Fortunately for the Union, Meade's line allowed rapid reinforcement of threatened sectors. Little Round Top was quickly reinforced by V Corps, and VI Corps moved to seal the gap between the Round Tops and the more elevated sections of Cemetery Ridge to the north. As dusk fell the Union troops strengthened their prepared defensive positions along Cemetery Ridge and the Round Tops.

Even the terrible slaughter of the second day paled in comparison to the events on the third day of the battle. Lee, desperate for a decisive victory, and perhaps suffering from the effects of the heart ailment that eventually killed him, made a series of uncharacteristically poor decisions. Having failed to breach the Union flanks, he decided to attack their center, although such a move had already been anticipated by his counterpart. It was decided that the attack would focus on a copse of trees in the center of Cemetery Ridge.

Preceded by a massive artillery bombardment of the ridge, Pickett's division would spearhead the main assault of 15,000 Southern infantry, to storm and capture the Union center. A diversionary attack on Culps Hill was to be made to prevent Meade from shifting troops to reinforce his center. Longstreet, knowing that the attack stood no chance of success, made one last entreaty to General Lee to call off the attack, but failed.

At 1 p.m. the Confederate artillery opened fire, but many of their shots were long, falling into and creating more damage to units being held in reserve behind the lines than to the front-line troops. After an hour of artillery exchanges, the Union gunners reduced their fire, choosing to conserve their ammunition and give the impression that they had been put out of action. The Confederate artillery commander then advised Pickett that this was the moment to advance. When Pickett sought permission from Longstreet to do so, all he could do was nod. Soon after the Union guns fell silent, more than 12,000 veteran Southern infantry moved to the attack.

In their path were about 5,700 Union men, posted in defense of the half-mile front that was the focus of the attack of the divisions of Pickett, Pettigrew, and Trimble. The Southern ranks moved forward in line abreast; as they moved forward they calmly filled the gaps being blown in their lines by the Union artillery and continued to advance.

Of the 12,000 men who went forward in "Pickett's Charge," less than 5,000 returned. Lee shouldered the entire responsibility for the failure of the assault. More lives were lost when a pointless cavalry charge, ordered by Union Brigadier-General Judson Kilpatrick, on the Confederate right flank was met with a storm of fire.

Expecting Meade to launch a counterattack, Lee ordered his army into a defensive posture. None came, and Lee decided to retreat back into Virginia, so ending the Battle of Gettysburg. Meade, suspecting Lee of trying to set a trap for him, was slow to pursue. By August 4, the two armies were back where they had started at the beginning of the campaign.

The Tullahoma Campaign

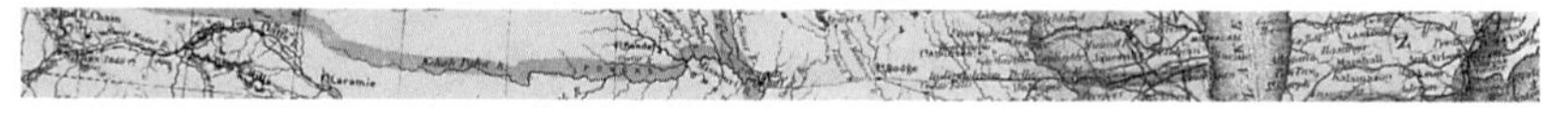

In the Western Theater, for the six months following the Battle of Stones River, Bragg and Rosecrans had eyed each other warily in Middle

Tennessee. Unfazed by the repeated urgings of politicians in Washington, Rosecrans refused to budge from Murfreesboro until he felt sufficiently strong. When it finally came, on June 24, his advance was swift and skillful. As forces under Crittenden and Granger made diversionary movements to the east and west, Rosecrans drove his main force straight ahead toward Manchester, Tennessee. His advance passed through rough country with several defended passes to overcome, but he successfully broke through Confederate forces at Hoover's Gap. With Rosecrans now squarely on the flank of Hardee's corps, Bragg had no choice but to fall back on his supply base at Tullahoma and make preparations to defend against an attack by the Union forces.

On arriving at Manchester on June 27, however, Rosecrans again deceived Bragg, moving southeast around Bragg's right flank instead of southwest. He thereby threatened the railroad that was Bragg's line of supply. With Union forces threatening from the north, and after suffering another raid on his railroad lines by Wilder's "Lightning" brigade, Bragg decided to yield Middle Tennessee to Rosecrans and retreated across the Tennessee River.

For the cost of few casualties, Rosecrans had masterminded Union occupation of all of Middle Tennessee and taken more than 1,600 prisoners. The Washington authorities, elated with the dual successes at Gettysburg and Vicksburg, urged Rosecrans to advance again. He moved forward again on August 16 in a co-ordinated movement against Knoxville with Major-General Burnside's forces. Burnside's opponent, Major-General Simon Bolivar Buckner, pulled out of Knoxville and Burnside entered unopposed on September 3, cutting the only direct Confederate rail link between Richmond and Chattanooga. Burnside then moved against the Southern forces guarding the Cumberland Gap, and took 2,500 prisoners. Contrary to orders, he then decided to rest his troops, instead of supporting Rosecrans's move against Chattanooga.

His support would have been gratefully received. The most obvious route for Rosecrans's advance on Chattanooga was to the north, but Bragg had it well defended. To deceive Bragg that this was the route he intended to use, Rosecrans sent three brigades ahead to create the impression that a large force was preparing to cross the river on the route north. The ruse worked; Bragg moved reinforcements to cover the anticipated movement, and some 50 miles south, at Bridgeport, the main body of the Union army crossed the Tennessee River virtually unopposed.

Rosecrans then split his army into three columns. Crittenden's corps was sent directly north to Chattanooga. McCook's corps was ordered to take a southern detour through Winston Gap, and Thomas's corps moved straight through the middle. Once more, Bragg had been completely outmaneuvered, and was forced to quickly evacuate Chattanooga.

Believing the stories of fake "deserters" sent out by Bragg to spread the story that the Confederate army was completely demoralized and in full retreat, Rosecrans began to overextend himself. In fact, Bragg was looking for Rosecrans to do exactly that, so he would open himself up for a counterpunch. With the Union army split into three widely separated columns, it appeared the opportunity might present itself to defeat each one in turn. In the event delays and disorganization within Bragg's own army meant that opportunities to crush Thomas and then Crittenden were wasted.

Realizing the danger his own army was in, Rosecrans desperately tried to reunite the widely separated columns. By September 18, he had been successful in concentrating most of his forces east of the ridge near the Rossville Gap, about seven or eight miles east of Chattanooga on the banks of Chickamauga Creek, scene of one of the most bitterly fought battles of the war.

Chickamauga and Chattanooga

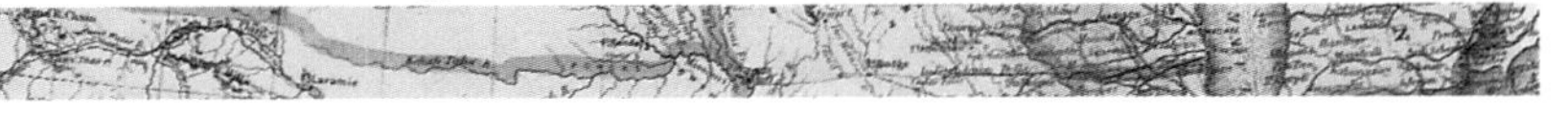

During late August, Bragg's Army of Tennessee had received reinforcements, bolstering his strength to about 65,000 men. Rosecrans had approximately the same number under his command. Chickamauga was one of the few large battles of the war fought with approximately equal numbers on both sides.

The heavily wooded battlefield left little room for maneuvering, but finally, on September 20, confusion in orders left a gaping hole in Rosecrans's right flank through which Longstreet stormed with four divisions. Almost half of the Union army was routed and hastily beat a retreat towards Chattanooga. Total disaster was averted by the stand of Thomas's corps on Snodgrass Hill, which successfully held the left wing long enough to organize an orderly retreat.

It was a significant, but costly, Confederate victory. Although Union losses had exceeded 16,000, the Southern army had lost more than

18,000 casualties. As Union troops consolidated their defensive positions in Chattanooga, Bragg occupied the heights overlooking the city, and confidently waited for the Unions to either leave or starve.

Indeed, the situation did look rather ominous for the Union forces. With the Confederate Army of Tennessee controlling the heights of Missionary Ridge and Lookout Mountain, the only Union supply line was a thin and vulnerable wagon route through the mountains, totally inadequate to supply a large army.

Bragg's own supply situation, while not as serious as that faced by Union troops, was also problematic. Additionally, Bragg was experiencing increasing insubordination among his staff, which was only partly resolved by sacking Lieutenant-General Polk and D. H. Hill. Major-General Nathan Bedford Forrest was so enraged that he threatened to kill Bragg, prompting the Confederate President to give him an independent command.

In the wake of the Chickamauga disaster, heads also rolled in the Union camp, including McCook and Crittenden, two of Rosecrans's corps commanders. Lincoln realized that the Union must continue to hold Chattanooga, and detached Major-General Hooker and 20,000 men from the Army of the Potomac and five divisions under Sherman from the west as reinforcements. Soon, the Union army inside Chattanooga would outnumber Bragg's besiegers.

For a month after Chickamauga, Rosecrans held onto his command, after which Major-General George Thomas, the only Union corps commander to escape any blame for Chickamauga, took over. At the same time Grant was put in charge of the newly created Military Division of the Mississippi, consisting of the Departments of the Cumberland, Ohio, and Tennessee.

Arriving in Chattanooga on October 23, Grant found the Union army on the verge of starvation. Thomas and his chief engineer, "Baldy" Smith, quickly devised a plan to reopen their supply line, using a small fleet of flat assault boats to float downstream to seize Brown's Ferry. The boats would then be converted into a pontoon bridge and additional troops would cross, take Raccoon Mountain to the west, and secure a new Union supply line.

In the early hours of October 27, 1,500 Union troops men floated silently downstream on 60 wooden boats and captured the Confederate pickets at Brown's Ferry unawares. Hooker arrived from Bridgeport with another two divisions to secure the bridgehead, thus opening the famous "Cracker Line." As supplies poured into Chattanooga, Bragg was forced to accept that his strategy of starving out the Union army had failed.

By the end of November, he had detached Longstreet to try to retake Knoxville from Burnside. Grant seized his moment. With both Hooker's and Sherman's troops now available, as well as Thomas's Army of the Cumberland, he planned to attack Bragg's position on Missionary Ridge. Sherman would hit Bragg's right flank and Hooker would attack his left. Thomas's men would make a showing against the center to prevent reinforcements from being sent to either of the flanks. In the event, Sherman's three divisions were fought to a standstill by Cleburne's division. Hooker made some inroads on the left, but it was Thomas who seized the initiative, attacked directly up the front of the ridge to split Bragg's army in half, and won the day. Forced from their supposedly impregnable position, Bragg's troops were sent streaming south into Georgia.

At Knoxville, Longstreet had come up against extremely strong entrenched positions and failed to find any weaknesses. However on November 27, after learning of Bragg's defeat at Chattanooga, Longstreet decided that he must launch an assault, first to ease the pressure on Bragg's retreat, and second to ease his own withdrawal.

On the morning of November 29, Longstreet's troops advanced. They soon ran into trouble; poor reconnaissance and planning meant that the soldiers became trapped in a nine-foot ditch with no scaling ladders, and as some attempted to climb out, they were raked with artillery volleys. When Longstreet called off the attack, he had lost 813 casualties whereas losses to the Union totaled only 13.

Reports that Sherman was headed his way with six divisions prompted Longstreet to abandon the attack and take his command back to Virginia to rejoin Lee. Davis relieved the discredited Bragg and placed the Army of Tennessee temporarily in the command of Lieutenant-General Hardee in its winter camp at Dalton, Georgia.

The Red River Campaign

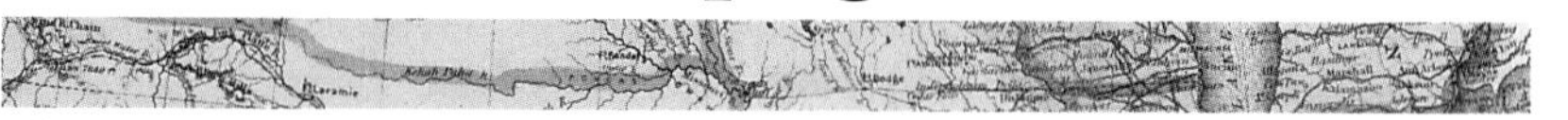

The capture of Port Hudson in July 1863 gave control of the lower Mississippi River to the Union and released the troops of the Department of the Gulf for employment elsewhere. Major-General Nathaniel Banks, their commander, saw an expedition against Mobile, Alabama as the most effective means of rendering support to the proposed operations against Bragg at Chattanooga, which was the highest priority of the Union forces in the Western Theater.

The authorities in Washington, however, directed Banks to move his forces against the Confederates in Texas, as much a symbolic as a strategic target. In September 1863 a Union attempt to move against Sabine Pass, one of the main routes into the state, ended in dismal failure. A second attempt to reach the Sabine River by an overland march was terminated because of anticipated supply difficulties. Banks thereafter resorted to naval operations to reduce the Texas Gulf Coast ports. Between November and December 1863, Brownsville, Corpus Christi, and Fort Esperanza were occupied by Union forces. By the beginning of 1864, the only major port in Texas still in Confederate hands was Galveston—and in early January Banks began operations against it.

Only days into the Galveston operation, Banks was directed to resume the delayed Red River operation against Shreveport, Louisiana with his forces bolstered by Steele's Union forces in Arkansas, detachments of Sherman's command in Mississippi, and gunboat support from Farragut under the command of Admiral Porter.

Restricted to the few weeks in late March and April when spring rains swell the depth of the Red River, allowing navigation above Alexandria, Louisiana, Banks planned to open his operation in mid-March, although he was decidedly unhappy that his rendezvous points with Sherman and Steele were many miles behind Confederate lines. Commanding the Confederate troops in the Trans-Mississippi Theater was General Edmund Kirby Smith, who could muster about 25,000 men. Major-General Richard Taylor, son of former President Zachary Taylor, was placed in command of Confederate field forces.

Sherman's detachment, under the command of Major-General A. J. Smith, arrived at Alexandria, Louisiana on March 18. Banks's command arrived a week later. On March 27, Banks received new orders from General Grant that required him to conclude operations against Shreveport by April 25, because of the need for troops for operations against Atlanta and Mobile in May. Banks considered calling off the campaign, but decided that the Confederates would not be able to make a strong defense of Shreveport and pressed on.

By April 3, the Red River had risen enough to allow Banks's transports and thirteen of the smaller gunboats to pass the rapids above Alexandria. The Confederates were still not fully concentrated and were gathered about 40 miles northwest of the city. Taylor, the Confederate field commander, awaited the arrival of two divisions from Sterling Price's forces, under the command of Brigadier-General Thomas Churchill before moving against the Federals.

Leaving about 5,000 men to protect his rear, on April 6 Banks advanced with a force of about 24,000 men toward Mansfield. His advance elements encountered Taylor's army of about 16,000 about two miles south of Mansfield on April 8. The battle began in earnest at about 4.00 p.m. Union troops were sent forward to assault the Confederate positions without proper support for their flanks, allowing the Southern forces to put them to flight after two hours of bitter fighting. Under a counterattack, the Union divisions of Landram and Cameron fell apart. Only the timely arrival of Emory's division saved the Union forces from disaster.

During the night, Banks withdrew to Pleasant Hill, about nine miles southwest of the Confederates. Taylor was eager to complete the destruction of the Union army and put his tired troops on the road in pursuit. By 1.00 p.m. on April 9 they had reached the vicinity of Pleasant Hill, and were given two hours' rest while Taylor devised a plan of attack. He planned to assault the Union left, using Walker's and Mouton's divisions in the center to pin the Union defenders down, while his Confederate cavalry was to move around the Union right to cut off Banks's expected retreat route.

Churchill's assault, when it came, did not go deep enough into the Union flank, leaving Taylor's own flank exposed to a counterattack by the Union reserve. The Confederate assault was repulsed with heavy loss. Banks withdrew during the night and when Kirby Smith reached the battlefield in the morning, he left Taylor with Mouton's division and the cavalry (about 5,200 troops) to continue to harass Banks withdrawal while taking the remainder to move against Steele in Arkansas. With time against him, Banks abandoned his attempt to capture Shreveport, knowing that he could expect no help from Steele and that he must soon return Sherman's troops.

At the end of May the Union troops finally escaped back down the Red River. The Red River Campaign had proved a complete failure for the Union. Banks was relieved of command and Kirby Smith fired Taylor.

Lee and Meade

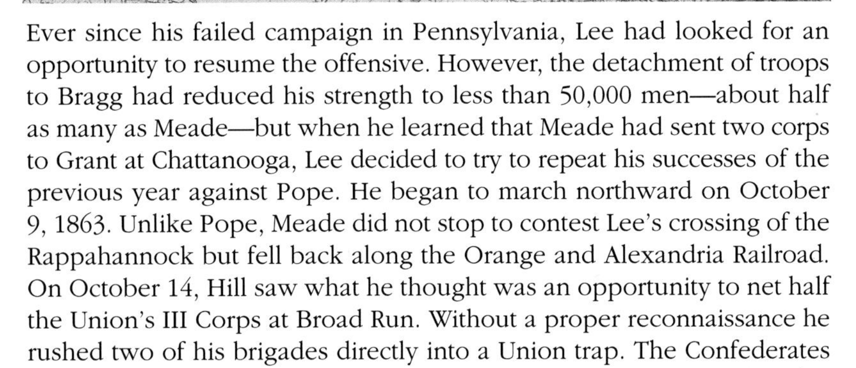

Ever since his failed campaign in Pennsylvania, Lee had looked for an opportunity to resume the offensive. However, the detachment of troops to Bragg had reduced his strength to less than 50,000 men—about half as many as Meade—but when he learned that Meade had sent two corps to Grant at Chattanooga, Lee decided to try to repeat his successes of the previous year against Pope. He began to march northward on October 9, 1863. Unlike Pope, Meade did not stop to contest Lee's crossing of the Rappahannock but fell back along the Orange and Alexandria Railroad. On October 14, Hill saw what he thought was an opportunity to net half the Union's III Corps at Broad Run. Without a proper reconnaissance he rushed two of his brigades directly into a Union trap. The Confederates lost heavily. About 1,400 were killed and wounded and another 450 taken prisoner in the action now generally known as Bristoe Station.

Lee continued his pursuit until he ran into the Union troops entrenched in a strong position along the Centerville-Chantilly ridge. With winter approaching and a vulnerable supply line, Lee decided to withdraw. Meade sent his cavalry in pursuit but it was ambushed and driven back. Meade moved forward again, his advance hampered by the need to repair the railroad along the way. By the end of October he was back at the Rappahannock, where Lee had stopped and entrenched. It was a strong position, but an unexpected night attack on Kelly's Ford succeeded in turning Lee's position and forcing him back across the Rapidan.

By the end of November, Meade was receiving intelligence reports that Lee's army now numbered only about 40,000 troops (Lee actually had 48,000) against Meade's own 84,000. Correspondingly, Meade decided to cross over the Rapidan into the fringe of the Wilderness, the scene of Hooker's undoing seven months previously, relying on speed and superior numbers to catch Lee unprepared.

The inevitable delays allowed Lee's troops time to prepare, and by the time the Union troops arrived at Mine Run, they found his Army of Northern Virginia strongly entrenched behind seven miles of earthworks. After reassessing the situation Meade decided to abandon the attack, and withdrew from positions after sunset on December 1. Lee set off in pursuit, but Meade's head start allowed him to recross the Rapidan. Both sides then went into winter camps.

Grant in the East

On March 12, 1864, President Lincoln promoted Ulysses S. Grant to the position of General-in-Chief of the Armies of the United States, taking over the strategic direction of the Union war effort. Major-General Hallack was made Chief of Staff to oversee the administration and logistic details freeing Grant to concentrate on overall Union strategy.

Grant's strategy was fairly straightforward. Sherman, now in command of the Union armies in the Western Theater, would advance against the Confederate Army of Tennessee defending Atlanta, while Grant would attack Lee's Army of Northern Virginia and Richmond. Whichever army achieved its objective first would then join the other for final offensive operations.

To bolster his fighting strength, many "rear area" units within Grant's command were reassigned to combat duties, and Sheridan was brought in to command the 13,000-strong cavalry. Grant was ready by the beginning of May to move south.

The Forty Days

On May 4, 1864, Grant began his advance, taking the same route through the Wilderness as that followed by Hooker and Meade. He hoped that by moving at a rapid pace, he would be clear of the tangled undergrowth before Lee could react. As a diversionary tactic, Major-General Ben Butler was ordered to advance his Army of the James up the Yorktown peninsula to threaten Richmond from the south and east.

Lee reacted quickly, caught Grant in the Wilderness, and over three days of confused fighting inflicted heavy casualties on the Union. By May 7, both sides were digging-in. In spite of the confused nature of the fighting, it was clear that Grant had been as decisively beaten as his predecessors. He had taken 17,666 casualties and had inflicted only about 7,800. Both Grant's flanks had been turned and Lee stood squarely in his front. Unlike his predecessors, Grant did not retreat. Instead he pulled out of his lines and moved down the Brock Road, toward Spotsylvania. Grant knew the North could afford to take the losses and replace them; the South could not.

Realizing that the loss of Spotsylvania would cut him off from Richmond, and then force him to attack a numerically superior force in an entrenched position, Lee raced back to Spotsylvania and was able to beat off the Union attacks on May 8.

The following day, May 9, Grant lost one of his best subordinates, Major-General John Sedgwick, to a Confederate sniper's bullet. Heavy fighting on May 10 and 12 around a salient in the Confederate lines known as the Mule Shoe preceded an all-out attack on May 12 that penetrated the Confederate line, capturing three generals, 30 artillery pieces, and a division of troops. Fierce counterattacks allowed the Confederates to restabilize their lines at the base of the salient, and on May 20, having failed to find any other weaknesses in Lee's lines, Grant began another flanking movement.

Corresponding thrusts met with little success. Butler's Union Army of the James had become bottled up in the Bermuda Peninsula, while Sigel's Union forces in the Shenandoah Valley had met a reverse at the hands of Major-General Breckinridge at the Battle of New Market on May 15, prompting Grant to replace Sigel with Major-General David Hunter.

With Butler's force indisposed, Grant faced a major task. On May 20 he sent Hancock's corps towards Hanover Junction to try to draw Lee out of his entrenchments. Lee would not take the bait however, and marched south to the North Anna River, were he entrenched in another strong blocking position.

At this point, Lee set a trap, which Grant was slow to recognize. The Confederate army was deployed in a thin wedge south of the North Anna River, with the apex of the wedge touching the river at Ox Ford. Three Union corps crossed the river—Wright's and Warren's upstream of Ox Ford and Hancock's downstream. While moving forward, they suddenly realized that Lee's position would enable him to fight a holding action on one flank, while moving the bulk of his army to inflict a heavy defeat on a significant part of the Army of the Potomac. The Union army began rapidly entrenching to protect itself, but was spared from attack when Lee was incapacitated by an intestinal complaint and could not personally direct his forces. His subordinates showed little initiative, allowing Grant to disengage from the potential trap and move to the left.

After a large, but indecisive, cavalry clash, Grant moved toward Cold Harbor, where he planned to link up troops detached from Butler's Army of the James. Again, Lee again anticipated the move and ordered his cavalry to hold Cold Harbor until the infantry could be brought up. On May 31 they engaged Sheridan's cavalry, with the Union troopers taking the position as night fell. After receiving a message that spelt out the extreme tenuousness of his position, Grant and Meade sent back word to Sheridan to hold Cold Harbor "at all hazards."

Lee badly needed to recover the position and push back the Union left flank before Grant could launch an attack on his own right. From his sickbed he ordered a Confederate attack but, unable to properly oversee the operations, the assault was mismanaged, and by mid-morning on June 1, Wright's corps had arrived to relieve Sheridan. The Union position held and Lee abandoned the idea of recapturing Cold Harbor, and again entrenched in strong defensive works.

Between June 1 and 3, Grant ordered a series of ill-advised frontal assaults against Lee's entrenchments and was repulsed each time. The main assault of June 3 cost him some 7,000 men, to the Confederates 1,500. Although the Union forces could more easily replace battle losses, these were unsustainable.

The opposing lines stabilized for ten days while Grant considered his options. He had lost over 50,000 casualties (some 41 percent of his original strength), but his plan appeared to be working. Lee was now tied up and none of his troops could be sent to help Johnston in front of Atlanta, where Sherman was still making steady progress. Southern losses were much lower than those of the Federals, but Lee had still lost about 27,000 men, or 40 percent of his own strength. These were losses the Confederacy would not be able to replace.

On June 12, Grant crossed the James River and attempted a new approach at Richmond from the south through Petersburg. Although delays and tactical failures on the part of his subordinates hampered this last maneuver, Lee was now bottled up inside his Richmond defenses. Grant undertook a ten-month long siege that tied Lee down and removed any chance for him to conduct any major offensive operations against the Union.

Early's Washington Raid

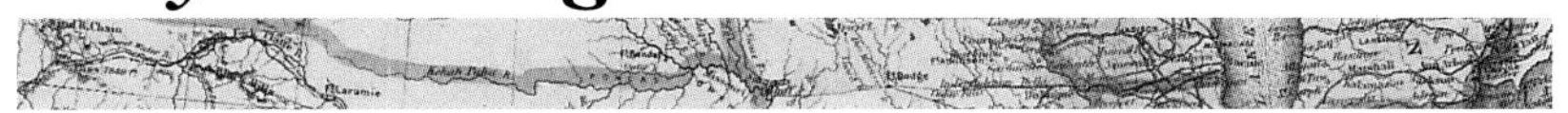

Lee recognized that if he could only divert some of Grant's strength from his front, he might still be able to find a way to attack him, and detached

Lieutenant-General Early with one cavalry and four infantry divisions to undertake an offensive in the Shenandoah Valley. Early moved out on June 7, 1864, and on June 18, defeated Hunter's Union forces at Lynchburg. On June 27, Early reorganized his forces for a thrust north at Staunton; he had with him some 10,000 infantry and 4,000 cavalry.

He crossed the Potomac into Maryland on July 5, prompting Grant to send reinforcements from the Army of the Potomac to Baltimore. They arrived on July 7, and on July 9 they clashed with Early's force at Frederick, Maryland, in an engagement that became known as the Battle of Monocacy, and were forced to fall back to Baltimore.

Utilizing some of his cavalry to protect his rear, Early sent a cavalry brigade to threaten Baltimore. With the remainder of his forces, he marched on Washington, D.C., reaching the outskirts at about midday on July 11. Seeing its defenses had been reinforced, he spent the rest of the day looking in vain for a weak point to launch an assault the following day. That night the Union VI Corps arrived to strengthen the defenses still further, and after heavy skirmishing around Fort Stevens, Early concluded he lacked the strength for a successful assault and withdrew.

The Union pursuit was badly disorganized, allowing Early to take advantage of the situation and renew his offensive operations. He met and defeated Crook's forces at Kernstown on July 23–24, and moved two cavalry brigades to Chambersburg, Pennsylvania, burning the town on July 30 in reprisal for Union depredations.

Early's raid convinced Grant to take drastic steps to prevent the Confederacy from using the Shenandoah Valley for strategic diversions, putting Sheridan in command of newly reorganized and consolidated Union forces in the area.

The Shenandoah Valley Campaign

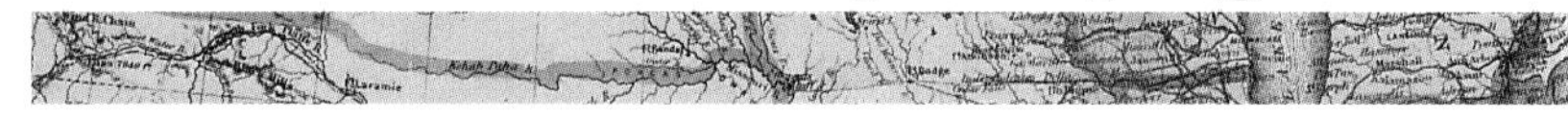

Major-General Sheridan took command of the newly established Middle Military Division on August 7, 1864, and reorganized the various forces under his command, totaling some 48,000 men, to include a cavalry corps of three divisions. Early's Army of the Valley, with four infantry divisions and a division of cavalry, was reinforced by mid-August with another infantry division and a cavalry division. With these additional troops, Early's strength was about 23,000 men—far less than the Union estimates of 40,000. Nevertheless, based on this intelligence Sheridan was ordered to assume the defensive.

During late August and early September, the two forces jockeyed for position. Because of the lack of activity, part of Early's reinforcement was ordered to return to Lee, leaving Early with about 12,000 infantry and 6,500 cavalry. Thus weakened, but suffering from a bout of overconfidence, Early was defeated at Winchester on September 19. He fell back to Fishers Hill, and was again defeated on September 22. The demoralized Confederate troops reached Browns Gap where they met a reinforcement division. Believing he had swept the valley of Early's force, Sheridan began the process of transferring troops to reinforce Grant. His decision proved somewhat hasty when, in a brilliant surprise attack at dawn on October 19, Early's numerically inferior forces struck the Union troops in their camp at Cedar Creek. Despite initial successes, Sheridan arrived on the scene and helped rally his men to counterattack and rout Early's command for the last time.

Sheridan thereafter detached most of his infantry to rejoin Grant and Sherman, but kept his cavalry corps of about 10,000 troopers. Early was left with only two brigades under Wharton (about 2,000 men) and two artillery battalions. Sheridan decided to eliminate this remaining Confederate force and at Waynesboro on March 2, 1865, his cavalry division quashed these remaining troops.

The Atlanta Campaign

As Grant was beginning his drive against Lee, Sherman moved forward against the Confederate Army of Tennessee. Now under the command of General Joseph E. Johnston, who had done much to restore its

Right: A modern map of the city of Atlanta, produced by the Georgia State Highway Department, as part of the Civil War Centennial. The arrows indicate Union and Confederate troop positions and movements during the battles of Peach Tree Creek, July 20, 1864; Atlanta, July 22, 1864, and Ezra Church, July 28, 1864.

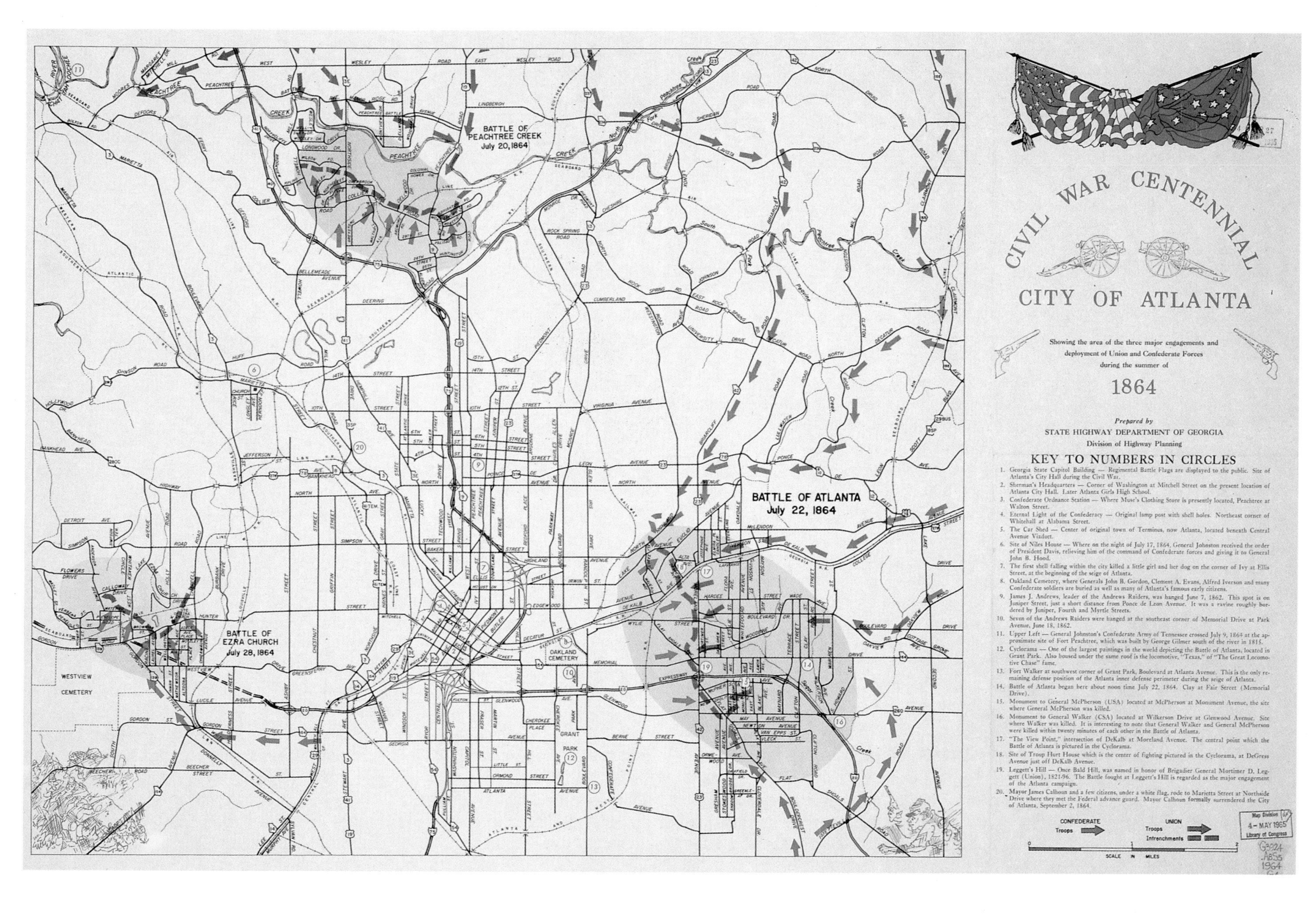
CIVIL WAR CENTENNIAL
CITY OF ATLANTA
Showing the area of the three major engagements and deployment of Union and Confederate Forces during the summer of
1864
Prepared by
STATE HIGHWAY DEPARTMENT OF GEORGIA
Division of Highway Planning
KEY TO NUMBERS IN CIRCLES
1. Georgia State Capitol Building — Regimental Battle Flags are displayed to the public. Site of Atlanta's City Hall during the Civil War.
2. Sherman's Headquarters — Corner of Washington at Mitchell Street on the present location of Atlanta City Hall. Later Atlanta Girls High School.
3. Confederate Ordnance Station — Where Muse's Clothing Store is presently located, Peachtree at Walton Street.
4. Eternal Light of the Confederacy — Original lamp post with shell holes. Northeast corner of Whitehall at Alabama Street.
5. The Car Shed — Center of original town of Terminus, now Atlanta, located beneath Central Avenue Viaduct.
6. Site of Niles House — Where on the night of July 17, 1864, General Johnston received the order of President Davis, relieving him of the command of Confederate forces and giving it to General John B. Hood.
7. The first shell falling within the city killed a little girl and her dog on the corner of Ivy at Ellis Street, at the beginning of the seige of Atlanta.
8. Oakland Cemetery, where Generals John B. Gordon, Clement A. Evans, Alfred Iverson and many Confederate soldiers are buried as well as many of Atlanta's famous early citizens.
9. James J. Andrews, leader of the Andrews Raiders, was hanged June 7, 1862. This spot is on Juniper Street, just a short distance from Ponce de Leon Avenue. It was a ravine roughly bordered by Juniper, Fourth and Myrtle Streets.
10. Seven of the Andrews Raiders were hanged at the southeast corner of Memorial Drive at Park Avenue, June 18, 1862.
11. Upper Left — General Johnston's Confederate Army of Tennessee crossed July 9, 1864 at the approximate site of Fort Peachtree, which was built by George Gilmer south of the river in 1815.
12. Cyclorama — One of the largest paintings in the world depicting the Battle of Atlanta, located in Grant Park. Also housed under the same roof is the locomotive, "Texas," of "The Great Locomotive Chase" fame.
13. Fort Walker at southwest corner of Grant Park, Boulevard at Atlanta Avenue. This is the only remaining defense position of the Atlanta inner defense perimeter during the seige of Atlanta.
14. Battle of Atlanta began here about noon time July 22, 1864. Clay at Fair Street (Memorial Drive).
15. Monument to General McPherson (USA) located at McPherson at Monument Avenue, the site where General McPherson was killed.
16. Monument to General Walker (CSA) located at Wilkerson Drive at Glenwood Avenue. Site where Walker was killed. It is interesting to note that General Walker and General McPherson were killed within twenty minutes of each other in the Battle of Atlanta.
17. "The View Point," intersection of DeKalb at Moreland Avenue. The central point which the Battle of Atlanta is pictured in the Cyclorama.
18. Site of Troup Hurt House which is the center of fighting pictured in the Cyclorama, at DeGress Avenue just off DeKalb Avenue.
19. Leggett's Hill — Once Bald Hill, was named in honor of Brigadier General Mortimer D. Leggett (Union), 1821-96. The Battle fought at Leggett's Hill is regarded as the major engagement of the Atlanta campaign.
20. Mayor James Calhoun and a few citizens, under a white flag, rode to Marietta Street at Northside Drive where they met the Federal advance guard. Mayor Calhoun formally surrendered the City of Atlanta, September 2, 1864.
CONFEDERATE Troops
UNION Troops
Intrenchments
0 1 2
SCALE IN MILES
BATTLE OF PEACHTREE CREEK July 20, 1864
BATTLE OF ATLANTA July 22, 1864
BATTLE OF EZRA CHURCH July 28, 1864
WESTVIEW CEMETERY
OAKLAND CEMETERY
GRANT PARK
Map Division 4-MAY 1965 Library of Congress
G3924 .A6S5 1964

effectiveness, the Army of Tennessee comprised two infantry corps and cavalry under Major-General Joe Wheeler. Although Johnston's army was outnumbered almost two to one, he held excellent defensive terrain and was confident of disrupting Sherman's plans to take Atlanta.

Sherman's forces consisted of three armies: the Army of the Cumberland, the Army of the Tennessee, and the much smaller, corps-sized Army of the Ohio. Later in the campaign, XVII Corps joined Sherman after Johnston had been forced to retreat beyond the Etowah River. Throughout May and into mid-July, Johnston conducted a series of skillfully managed retreats, delaying Sherman's advance and awaiting a mistake that would allow him to move against the Union forces. In mid-May, at Cassville, following actions around Resaca, Johnston thought his chance had come. He had succeeded in deceiving Sherman as to his true line of retreat and prepared to fall upon the Army of the Ohio, but Hood, one of his divisional commanders, noticed a build-up of Union cavalry on his flank, and called off the attack.

The next major encounter was at Kennesaw Mountain where Sherman, impatient at the lack of progress made on his flanks, ordered a series of frontal assaults against Johnston's entrenched troops. He lost about 2,000 casualties to Johnston's 500, but the advance continued. By mid-July, Sherman was across the Chattahoochee River and only six miles north of Atlanta. Jefferson Davis, frustrated with Johnston's strategy, replaced him with a more aggressive commander—John Bell Hood. Hood's first battle in command of the Army of Tennessee was at Peachtree Creek on July 20, in an attempt to hit the Federals while crossing the Creek; poor leadership cost the Confederates the advantage and some 4,800 men to the Union's 1,800. On July 22, at the Battle of Atlanta, another opportunity presented itself to strike McPherson's left flank. Again, delays and bad management cost the Confederates dearly, resulting in another 8,000 casualties to 3,700 Federals. On July 28, at the Battle of Ezra Church, Hood attacked again, this time losing about 5,000 men to only 600 Union casualties. At the end of July, Hood finally decided that offensive action was not to his advantage, and withdrew behind Atlanta's fortifications.

Rather than risk a potentially costly attack on these positions, Sherman decided instead to try to cut Hood's supply lines with the Union cavalry. They utterly failed to do this, and Sherman moved from his base to try and destroy the railroads with his infantry. Hood was unable to prevent the loss of his vital supply line at the Battle of Jonesboro, and ordered the evacuation of Atlanta on September 1. Ordering the destruction of military stores that could not be saved, Atlanta was devastated by a series of powerful explosions and the remnants of the Army of Tennessee slipped away during the night, to regroup beyond contact with Sherman's Federals. The victorious Union army entered the city the following day.

In Washington, D.C., President Lincoln, whose political position had become precarious after the series of failed Union campaigns, received notification of the desperately needed victory on the afternoon of September 2, 1864. It began with the simple statement that, "Atlanta is ours, and fairly won."

Hood's Tennessee Campaign

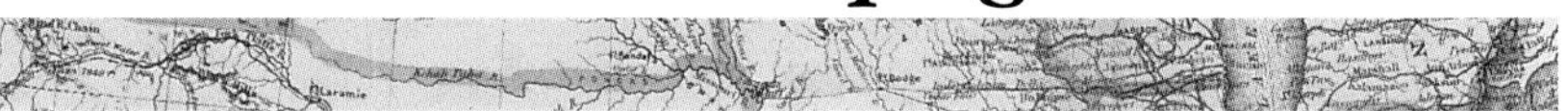

Following the loss of Atlanta, Hood proposed to take his Army of Tennessee west to strike Sherman's lines of communication and tempt him north. When this did not work, Hood decided to move against Nashville. Sherman detached Thomas and elements of the XXIII and IV Corps to Nashville to deal with Hood, while he continued with the plans for his famous "March to the Sea."

Hood crossed the Alabama-Tennessee border on November 21, and on November 27 made contact with 30,000 Union troops at Columbia. He flanked the Columbia position and stole a march on the Union commander, Schofield, whose retreat was too slow. The Army of Tennessee found itself in a position to cut Schofield off from the main pike leading to Nashville, but misunderstandings allowed the whole Union force to escape past the Confederate camp at Spring Hill on the night of November 29.

Schofield moved to the previously prepared defensive works at Franklin, and set about repairing the railroad bridge there. Hood, enraged by the lost opportunity, ordered a series of frontal assaults on Franklin with only two of the three corps of his army and practically no artillery support. Predictably, the assaults were a disaster. Hood lost at least 1,750 men killed, 3,800 wounded, and 702 captured, while the Union suffered 2,326 casualties. Five Confederate generals were killed, one captured, and six wounded. His command structure ravaged, many regiments now no larger than companies, the battered remnants of Hood's Army of Tennessee followed the Union force to Nashville. On

December 15–16, Thomas forced the Confederates back and then routed them. Only a brilliant rearguard action saved the army from complete destruction during its retreat to winter quarters at Tupelo, Mississippi. In January 1865, Hood was relieved of command. The last Confederate offensive campaign of the war had ended.

Sherman's March to the Sea

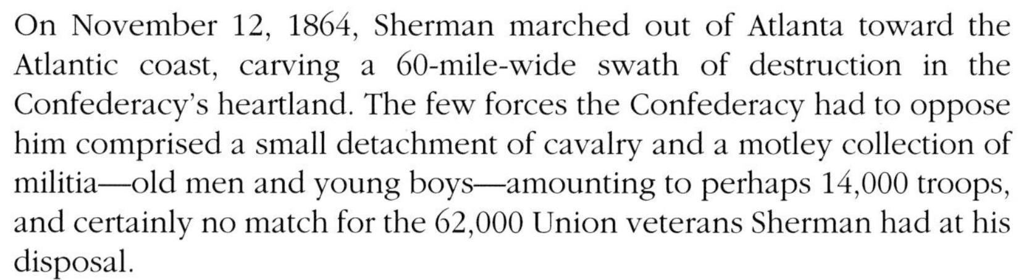

On November 12, 1864, Sherman marched out of Atlanta toward the Atlantic coast, carving a 60-mile-wide swath of destruction in the Confederacy's heartland. The few forces the Confederacy had to oppose him comprised a small detachment of cavalry and a motley collection of militia—old men and young boys—amounting to perhaps 14,000 troops, and certainly no match for the 62,000 Union veterans Sherman had at his disposal.

His army reached Savannah on December 10, shortly after the Confederate garrison of 10,000 troops had evacuated the city via a pontoon bridge. He did not linger, and despite the miserable weather was soon on the march again. He was little troubled by the fragmented Confederate forces in the region and entered Columbia, South Carolina, on February 17, 1865. The city was torched by his men, resentful toward South Carolina as the state they believed responsible for starting the war.

With the Confederacy in crisis, Robert E. Lee was named General-in-Chief of the Confederacy's armed forces and Johnston given command of all remaining forces in North Carolina. The tattered remnants of the Army of Tennessee arrived via a patchwork railroad/overland route from Tupelo, but these were too few and too late, and often in no condition to fight.

An opportunity to do some damage to the might of Sherman's army presented itself on March 19, 1865. The two advancing columns had become widely separated and Johnston concentrated his 21,000 troops near Bentonville to try to crush one before the other could arrive to support. Initially the Confederate attacks went well, but Slocum, commanding the Union column, was able to bring up reinforcements to withstand the repeated assaults. On the 21st Sherman's entire command was in position to launch a counterattack, forcing Johnston to conduct a skillful retreat during the night toward Smithfield.

Petersburg and Appomattox

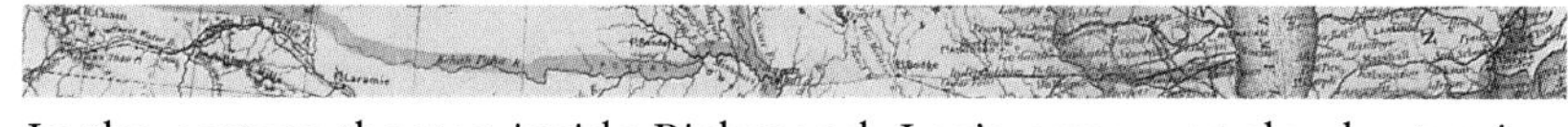

In the eastern theater, inside Richmond, Lee's army was slowly starving after months of protracted siege. Between mid-February and mid-March eight percent of his now dejected army deserted. Grant, meanwhile, took little offensive action but continued to extend his line southward, stretching Lee's already over-extended defenses almost to the breaking point.

On March 25, 1865, Lee tried to break through Grant's lines at Fort Stedman, but despite some initial success, was beaten back with heavy losses. On April 1 Sheridan defeated Pickett's division in the Battle of Five Forks. With Sheridan now in Lee's rear and threatening the Danville Railroad, his last supply line, Lee had no choice but to evacuate Richmond. The Confederate government and its remaining gold reserve were put on a special train and sent south. Richmond fell on April 2.

Lee's last gamble was undertaken against long odds, but he was determined to have one last throw of the dice. He attempted to link up his army with the remaining forces that Johnston had under his command, clinging onto the hope that their combined force could defeat either Grant or Sherman before one could come to the other's aid.

He advanced along the line of the Appomattox River, seeking a point at which he could turn south. Grant kept moving his own army in a parallel course and prevented Lee from changing direction. By the time Lee reached Appomattox Court House, where the rations that were supposed to be waiting for him had not materialized, Grant had succeeded in cutting off any possible retreat. On April 9, 1865, he surrendered.

The End

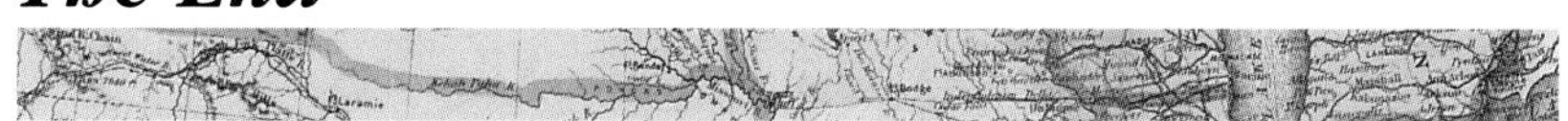

Johnston, upon learning of Lee's surrender, petitioned Sherman for terms and formally surrendered his forces on April 26, 1865, at Durham Station, North Carolina. Other sporadic Confederate resistance in the Alabama heartland and Mobile ended soon after, and the Trans-Mississippi Confederates laid down their arms in May and June. The last Confederate forces to capitulate, the Confederate Cherokees, surrendered to Union forces on June 23, 1865. After four long and bloody years, the American Civil War had finally ended.

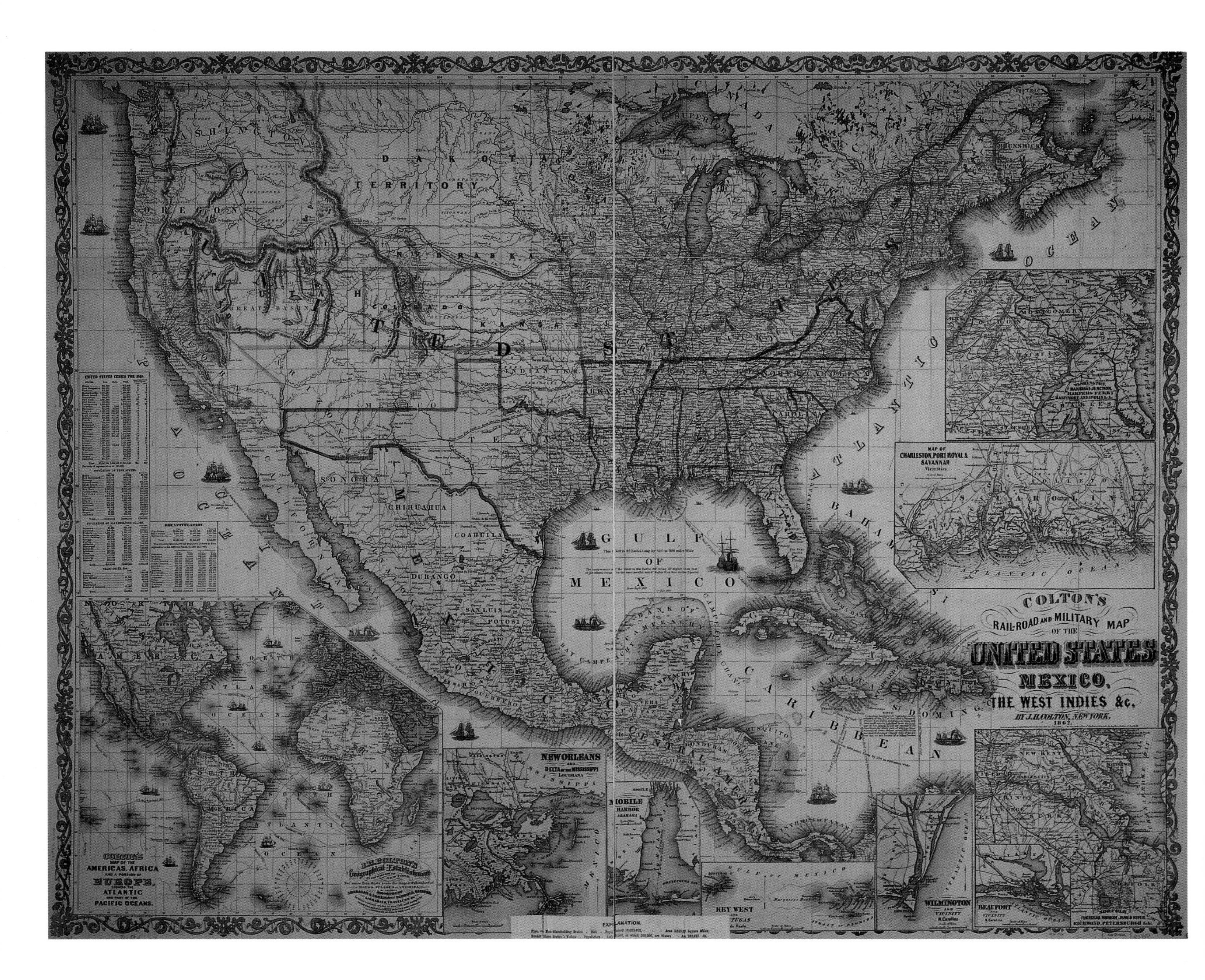
COLTON'S
RAIL-ROAD AND MILITARY MAP
OF THE
UNITED STATES
MEXICO,
THE WEST INDIES &c.
BY J.H. COLTON, NEW YORK.
1862.
DAKOTA
TERRITORY
NEBRASKA
COLORADO
GREAT BASIN
SONORA
CHIHUAHUA
COAHUILA
DURANGO
SAN LUIS POTOSI
GULF OF MEXICO
CARIBBEAN
ATLANTIC OCEAN
MAP OF CHARLESTON, PORT ROYAL & SAVANNAH Vicinities
NEW ORLEANS AND DELTA OF THE MISSISSIPPI LOUISIANA
MOBILE HARBOR ALABAMA
KEY WEST
WILMINGTON AND VICINITY N. Carolina
BEAUFORT AND VICINITY N. Carolina
NORFOLK, FORTRESS MONROE, JAMES RIVER, RICHMOND, PETERSBURGH &c.
NEW KENT
COLTON'S MAP OF THE AMERICAS, AFRICA AND A PORTION OF EUROPE, SHOWING THE ATLANTIC AND PART OF THE PACIFIC OCEANS.
J.H. COLTON'S Geographical Establishment
EXPLANATION.

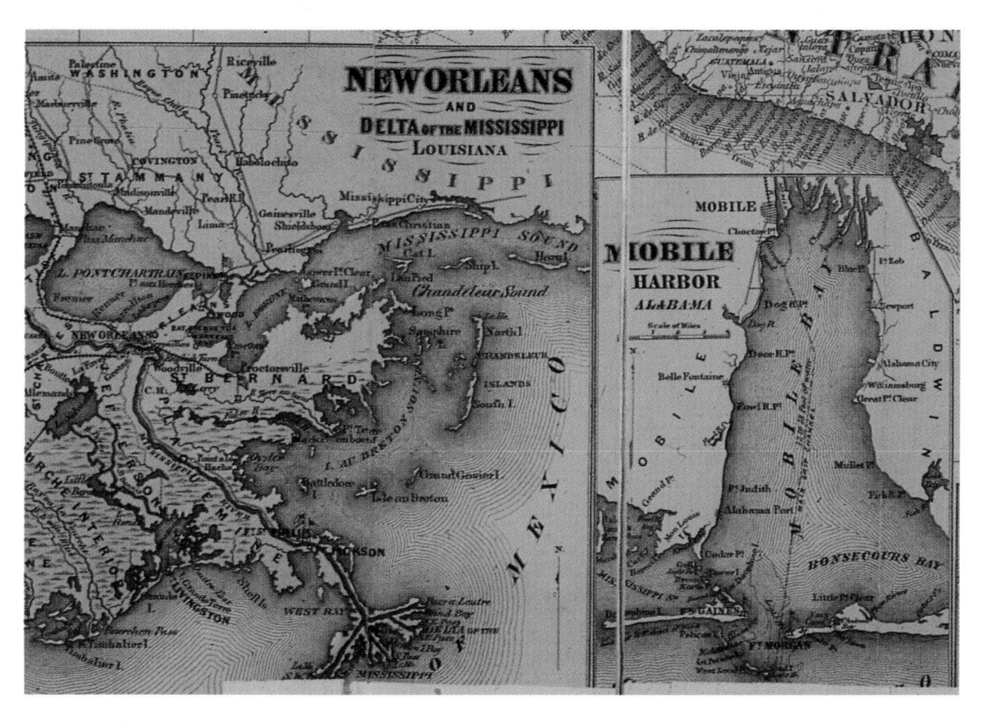

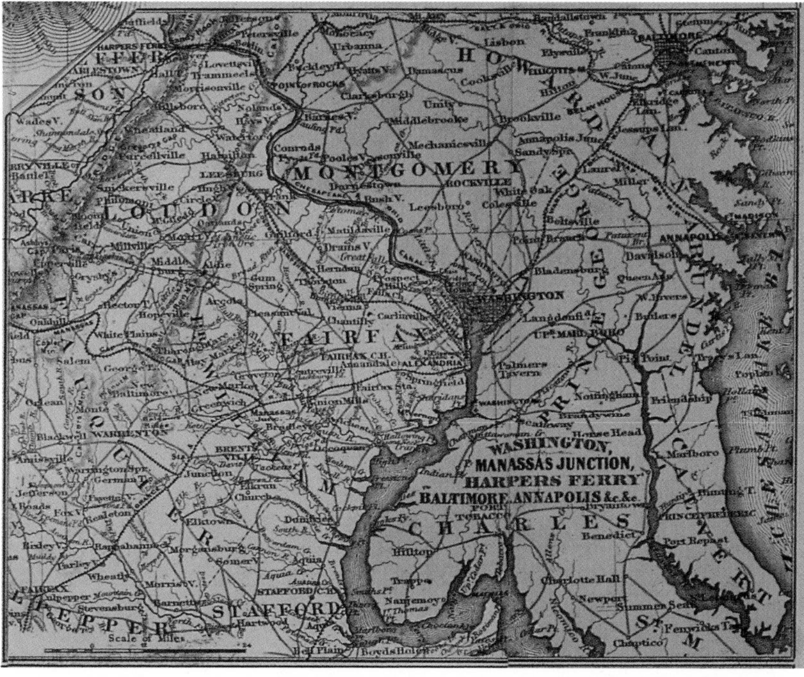

North and Central America, 1862

Left and This Page (details): J. H. Colton's 1862 "Railroad and Military Map" of the United States, Central America, the Caribbean and the West Indies, and the Gulf of Mexico, printed by Laing and Laing in New York. On this page are details of insets on New Orleans and the Mississippi delta (**Above Left**); Mobile (**Above**); Virginia and Maryland centering on the Union capital, Washington, D.C. (**Above Right**); Beaufort, North Carolina (**Right**); and the southern Chesapeake Bay showing the area around the capital of the Confederacy, Richmond, Virginia (**Far Right**).

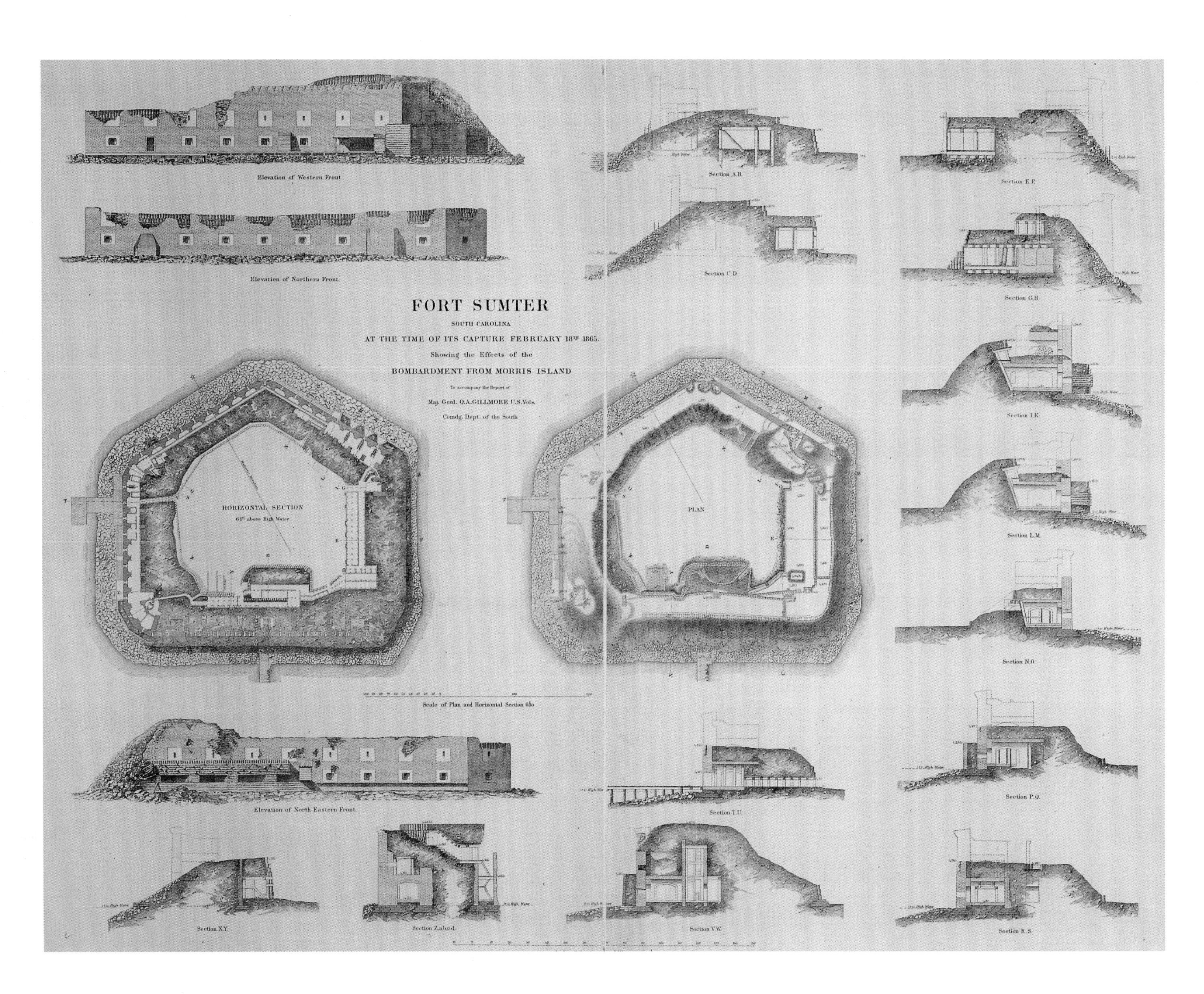
FORT SUMTER
SOUTH CAROLINA
AT THE TIME OF ITS CAPTURE FEBRUARY 18TH 1865.
Showing the Effects of the
BOMBARDMENT FROM MORRIS ISLAND
Maj. Genl. Q.A.GILLMORE U.S.Vols.
Comdg. Dept. of the South
Elevation of Western Front
Elevation of Northern Front.
Elevation of North Eastern Front.
HORIZONTAL SECTION
6 Ft above High Water
PLAN
Scale of Plan and Horizontal Section
Section A.B.
Section C.D.
Section E.F.
Section G.H.
Section I.K.
Section L.M.
Section N.O.
Section P.Q.
Section R.S.
Section T.U.
Section V.W.
Section X.Y.
Section Z.a.b.c.d.

Fort Sumter, South Carolina, 1861

Left: Illustration produced in 1865 to accompany the report of Major-General Q. A. Gillmore, commander of the Department of the South, after the capture of Fort Sumter in South Carolina. This detail shows the northern edge of the fort, and a section through the emplacements. It was, of course, the bombardment of the fort on April 12, 1861, that started the military action of Civil War.

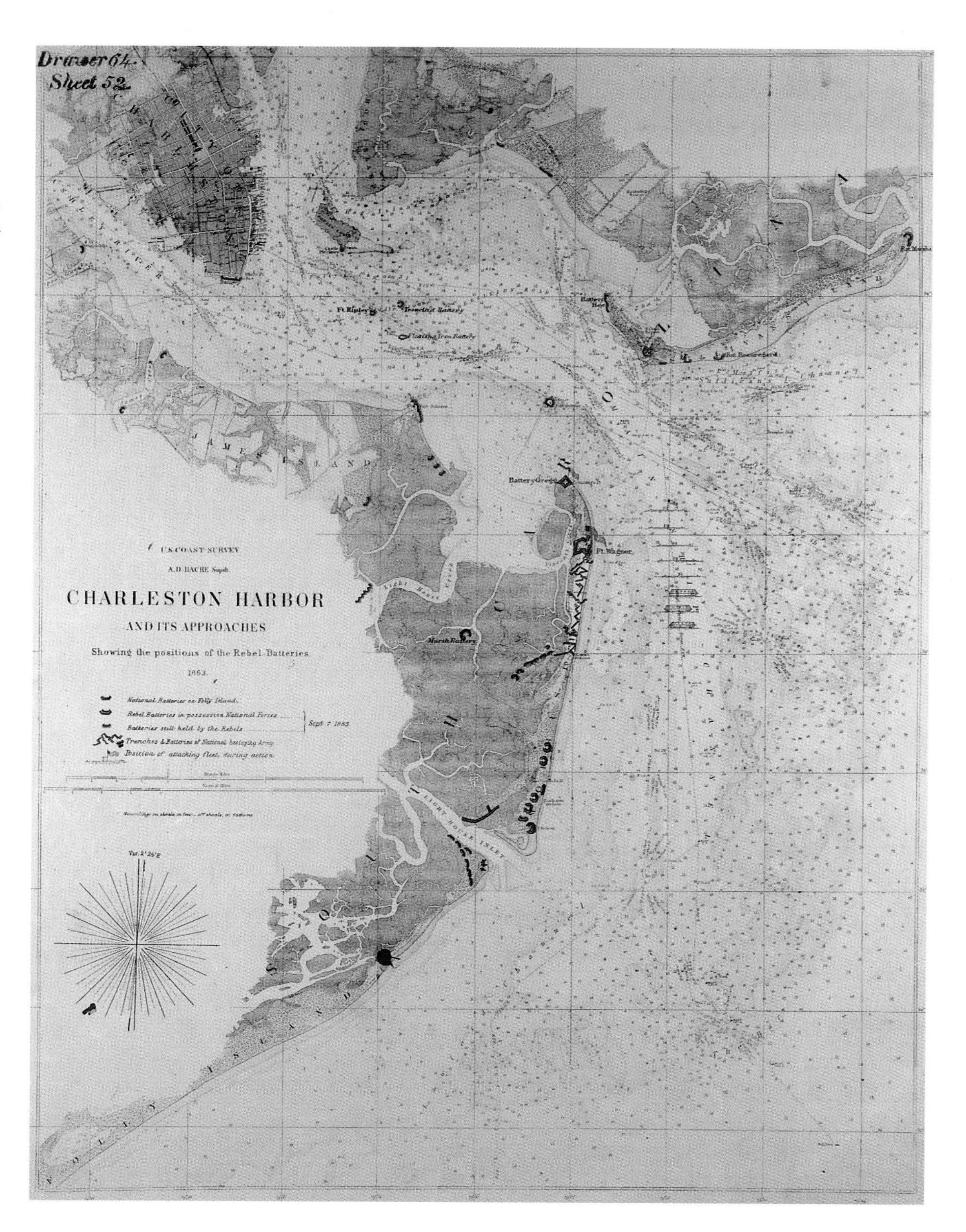

Charleston Harbor, South Carolina, 1863

Right: Map of Charleston Harbor and its approaches, including Fort Sumter, showing the positions of the Union army and naval forces, captured Confederate batteries, and those still held by the Rebels, as on September 7, 1863. This was based on an (uncolored) U.S. coastal survey map produced earlier in the year.

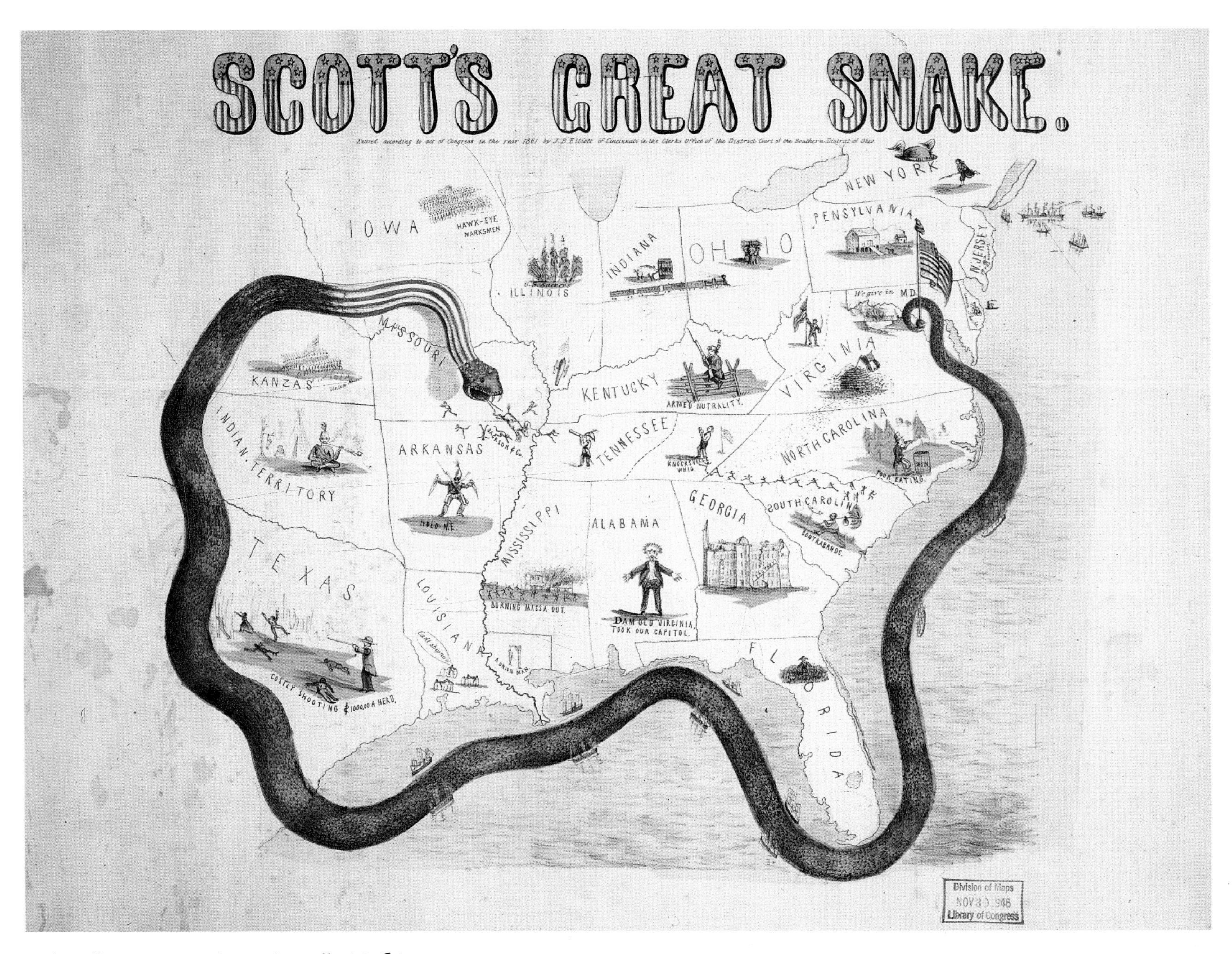

The "Anaconda Plan," 1861

Above: Cartoon map produced in 1861 by the commercial publisher J. B. Elliot in Cincinnati, Ohio. It illustrates General Winfield Scott's plan to blockade Southern ports and to mount a major offensive down the Mississippi. Scott's plan was roundly ridiculed by the Press, who dubbed it the "Anaconda Plan," although it proved generally successful. Elliot's map is a prime example of the pioneering use of the map as a tool of propaganda during the Civil War.

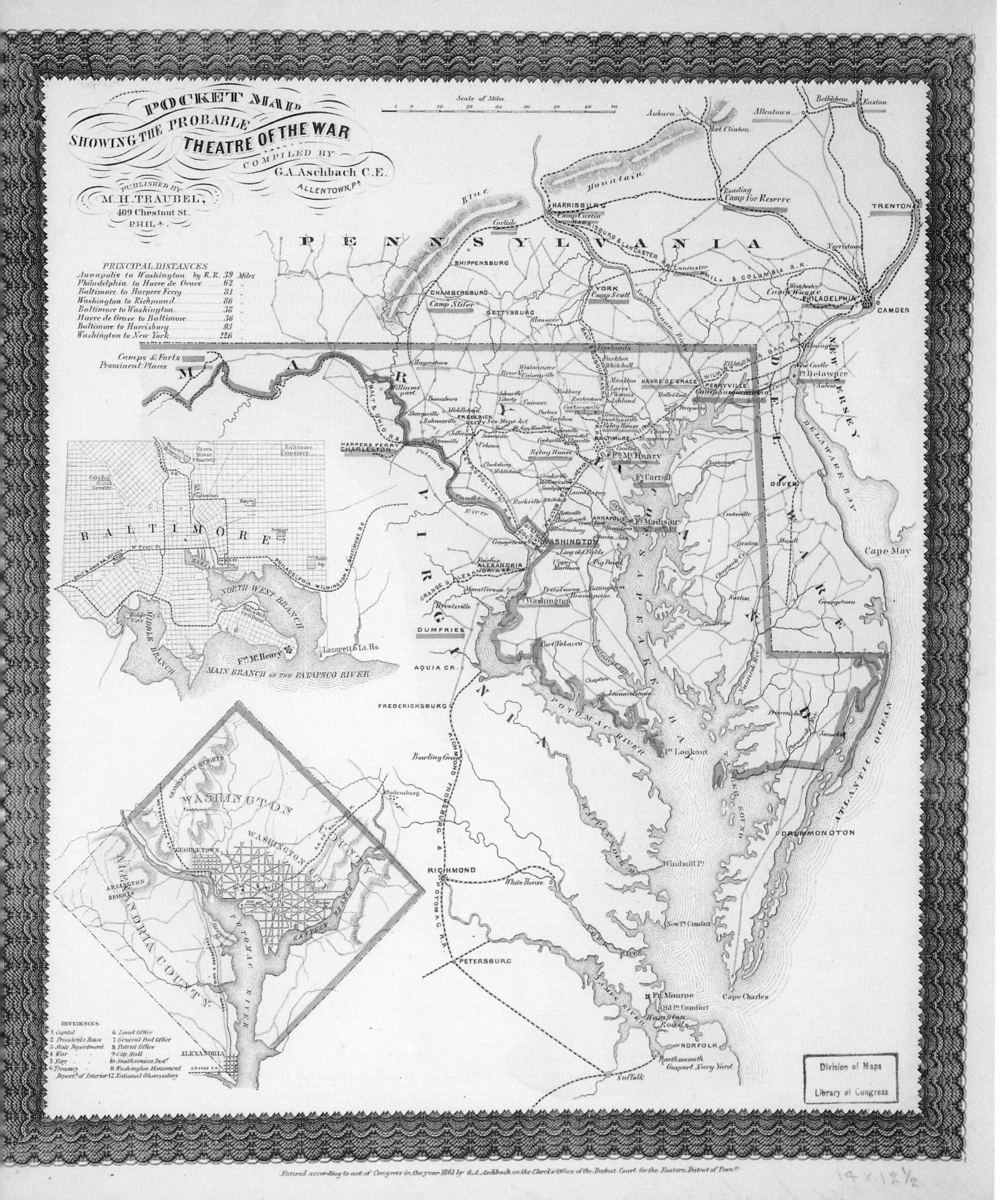

Maryland, 1861

Left: Commercial publishers produced countless maps during the course of the war. The majority of them were based in the North, in New York, Philadelphia, Washington, and Boston, although Southern mapmakers were also quick to capitalize on this profitable business. One of the earliest maps, shown here, was the "Pocket Map of the Probable Theatre of the War" produced by the civil engineer G. A. Asbach for M. H. Traubel of Philadelphia. Note how the compiler has underlined camps and forts in red to assist the map user.

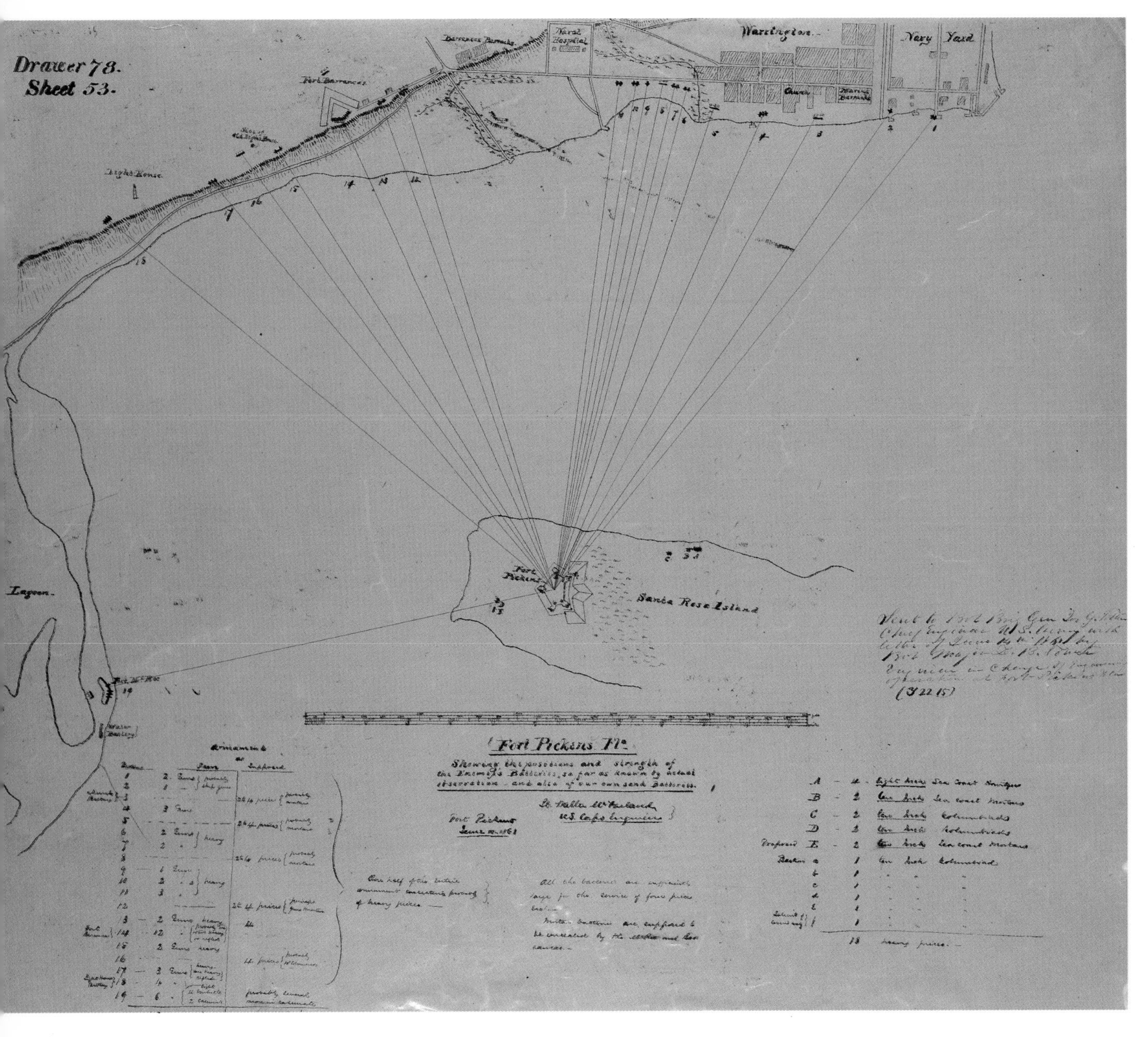

Fort Pickens, Florida, 1861

Left: Map of Fort Pickens on Santa Rosa Island in Pensacola Bay, Florida, showing the Confederate shore batteries and Union batteries on the island. The map was compiled by Lieutenant Walter McFarland of the U.S. Corps of Engineers and shows the limits of fire from the fort to the shore and also has notes on the supposed and observed armament of the Confederate forces.

Virginia, 1861

Right: A panorama of the seat of war in Virginia, Maryland, Delaware and the District of Columbia. Engraved by J. Schedler in 1861, it was printed by W. Schaus and shows forts, towns, railroads, main roads, and relief by shading.

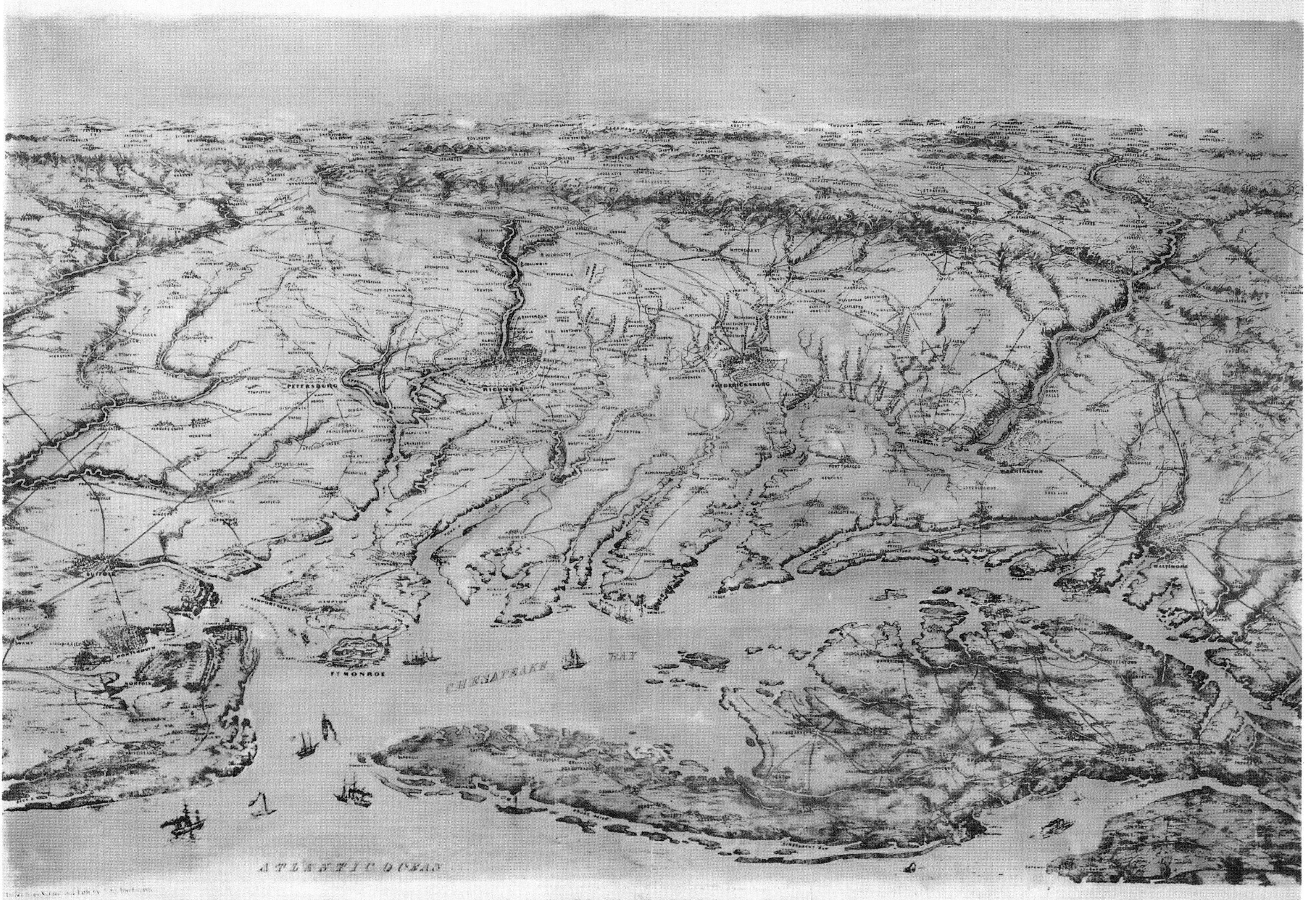
Panorama of the Seat of War.
CHESAPEAKE BAY
ATLANTIC OCEAN
PETERSBURG
RICHMOND
FREDERICKSBURG
WASHINGTON
BALTIMORE
FT MONROE
NORFOLK
BIRDS EYE VIEW
OF VIRGINIA, MARYLAND DELAWARE AND THE DISTRICT OF COLUMBIA

Battle of Wilson's Creek, Missouri, August 10, 1861

Right: An 1865 engraving of the battlefield at Wilson's Creek, near Belmont, Missouri, compiled by the Chief Engineer of the Department, showing Confederate dispositions in red, and those of the Union in blue. Note also how the mapper has named some of the residents and his use of hachures (short lines) to show relief.

Battle of Rich Mountain, West Virginia, July 10–12, 1861

Far Right: Plan of the battle of Rich Mountain, drawn by Lt. O. M. Poe of the U.S. Topographical Engineers. The sketch depicts the operations of Federal forces under McClellan, and indicates the "crest of Rich Mountain," "Hart's House," the positions of Federal troops, skirmishers, and reserves, the "trail by which Federal troops approached," and the "place where the dead were buried."

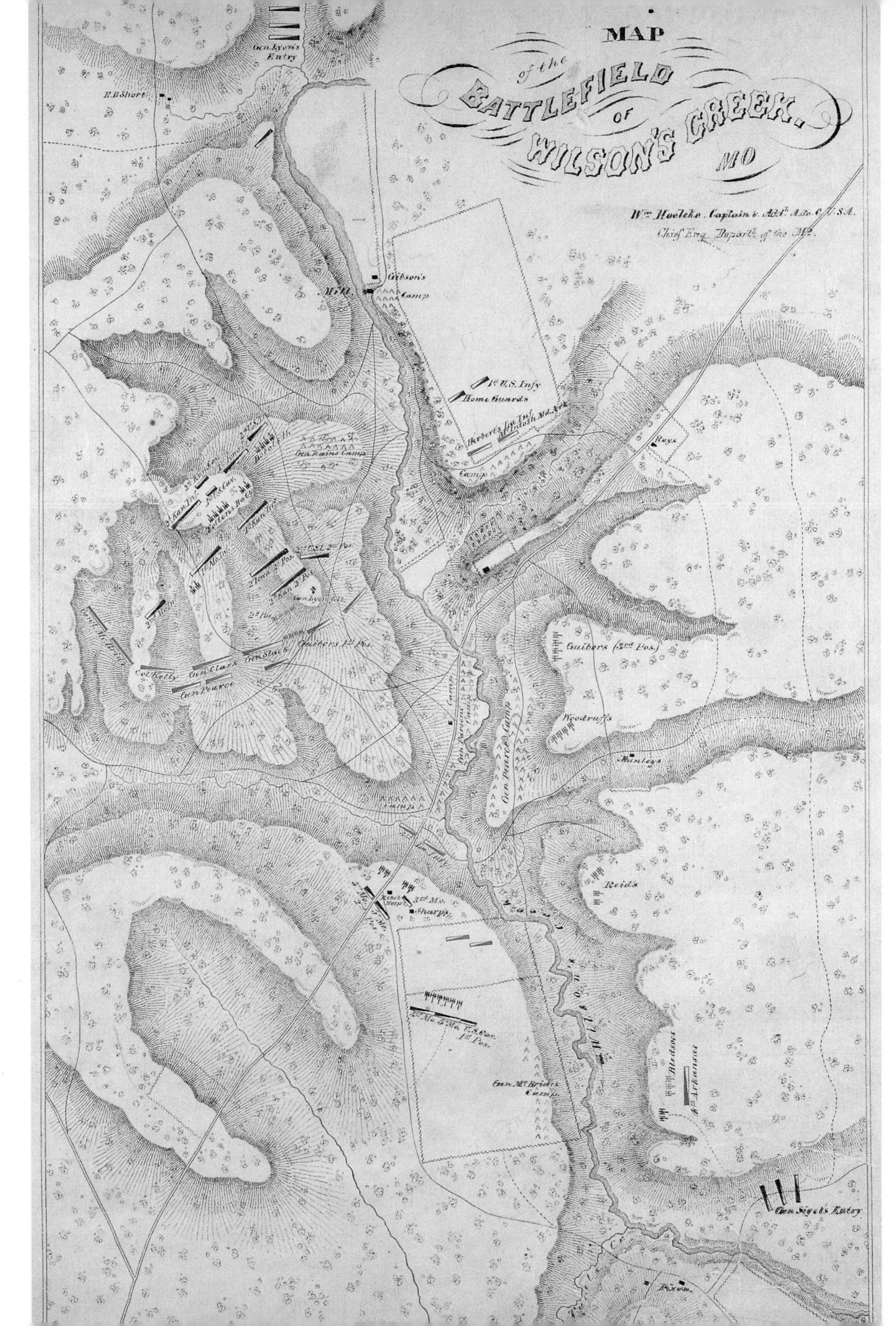

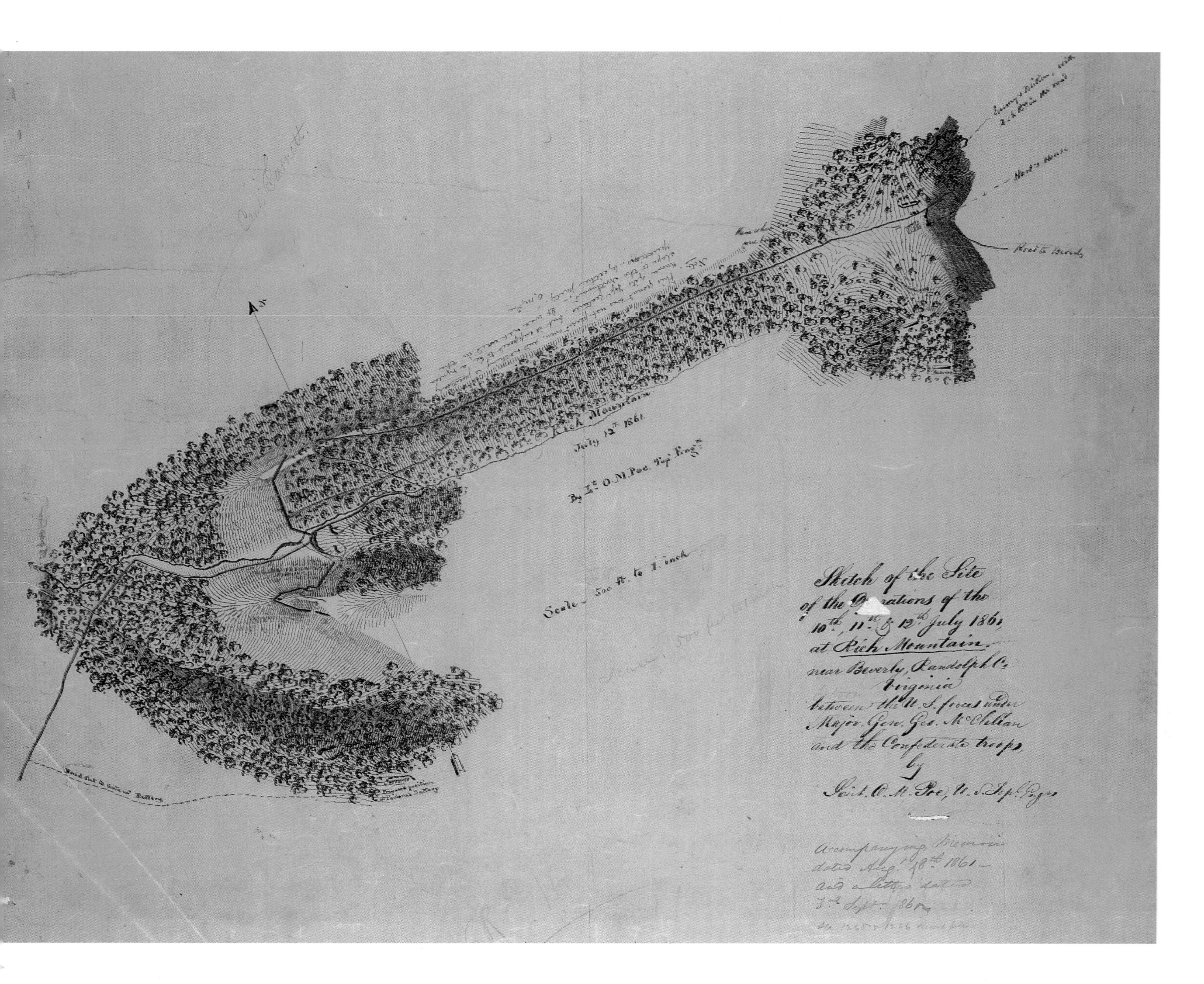
Sketch of the Site
of the Operations of the
10th, 11th & 12th July 1861,
at Rich Mountain
near Beverly, Randolph Co.
Virginia
between the U. S. forces under
Major. Gen. Geo. McClellan
and the Confederate troops,
by
Lieut. O. M. Poe, U. S. Topl. Engrs
Accompanying Memoir
dated Aug. 18th 1861 –
and a letter dated
3rd Sept. 1861
Rich Mountain
July 12th 1861
By Lt. O. M. Poe, Top. Engrs
Scale – 500 ft. to 1. inch
Road to Beverly
Hart's House

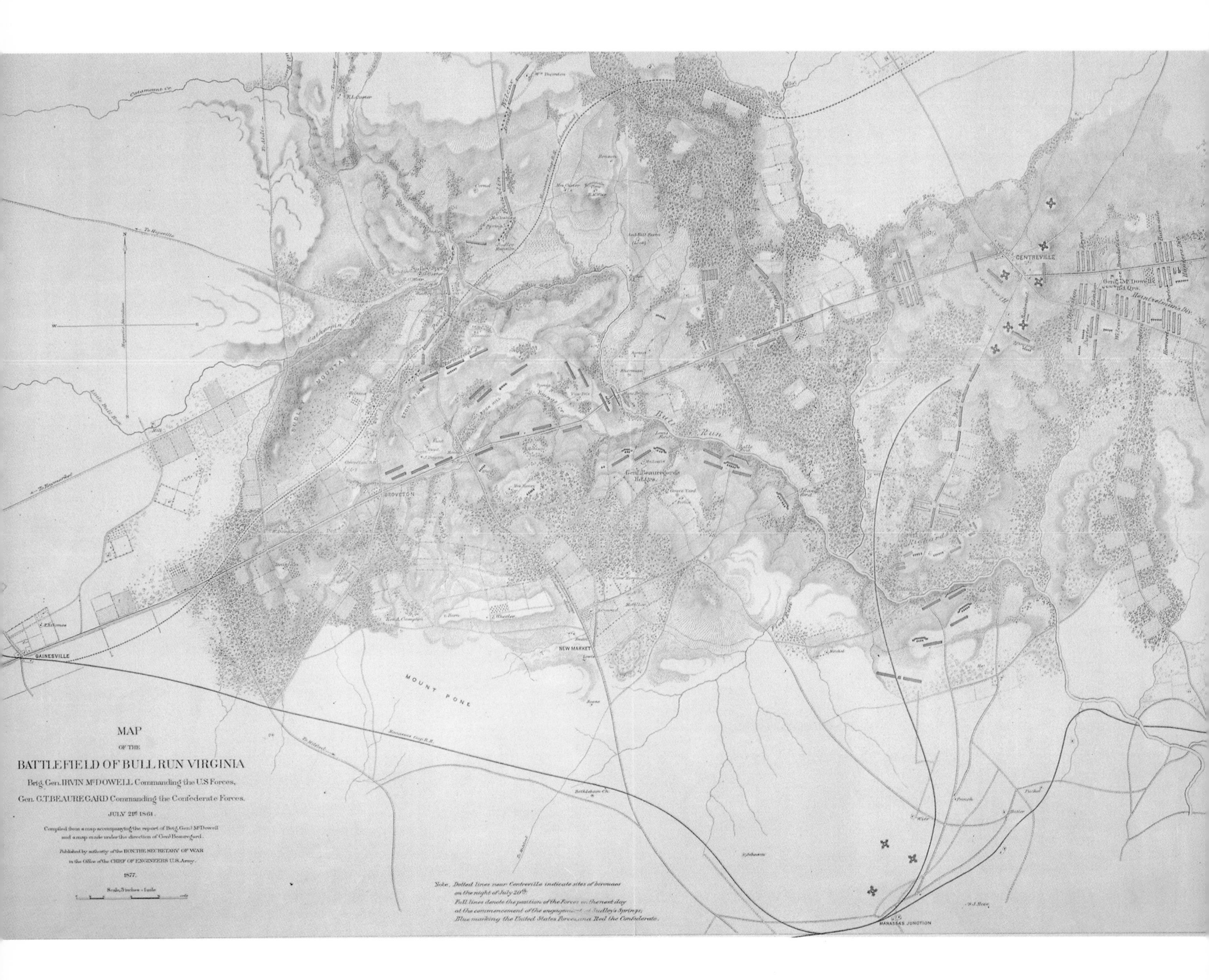

MAP
OF THE
BATTLEFIELD OF BULL RUN VIRGINIA
Brig. Gen. IRVIN McDOWELL Commanding the U.S Forces,
Gen. G.T.BEAUREGARD Commanding the Confederate Forces.
JULY 21st 1861.
Compiled from a map accompanying the report of Brig. Genl. McDowell
and a map made under the direction of Genl. Beauregard.
Published by authority of the HON. THE SECRETARY OF WAR
in the Office of the CHIEF OF ENGINEERS U.S. Army.
1877.
Note. Dotted lines near Centreville indicate sites of bivouacs
on the night of July 20th.
Full lines denote the position of the Forces on the next day
at the commencement of the engagement at Sudley's Springs;
Blue marking the United States Forces, and Red the Confederate.
CENTREVILLE
GAINESVILLE
GROVETON
NEW MARKET
MOUNT PONE
MANASSAS JUNCTION
STONY RIDGE
Bull Run
Genl. Beauregard's Hd.Qrs.
Genl. McDowell's Hd.Qrs.
Heintzelman's Div.

1st Battle of Bull Run (Manassas), Virginia, July 21, 1861

Left, Right (details), Pages 40 and 41: Various maps depicting the Battle of Bull Run, near Manassas, which resulted in a victory for the Confederacy. The most reliable and detailed of them is the one by U.S. Army Corps of Engineers (**Left and details Right**), compiled from reports given by both General McDowell and General Beauregard, and published in 1877 under the authority of the office of the Secretary of State for War. Next (**Page 40**) is an unidentified Confederate sketch of the battlefield (which was variously known as the Battle of Young's Branch, 1st Manassas or Bull's Run), with a keyed list of numbers showing where Confederate troops fell or lost their horses. Finally (**Page 41**) a map based on the observations of one Solomon Bamberger and published by the Richmond publisher West and Johnson; it features extensive annotation. These maps raise an interesting topic for students of the Civil War, as they serve to illustrate how perceptions of the various battles could differ.

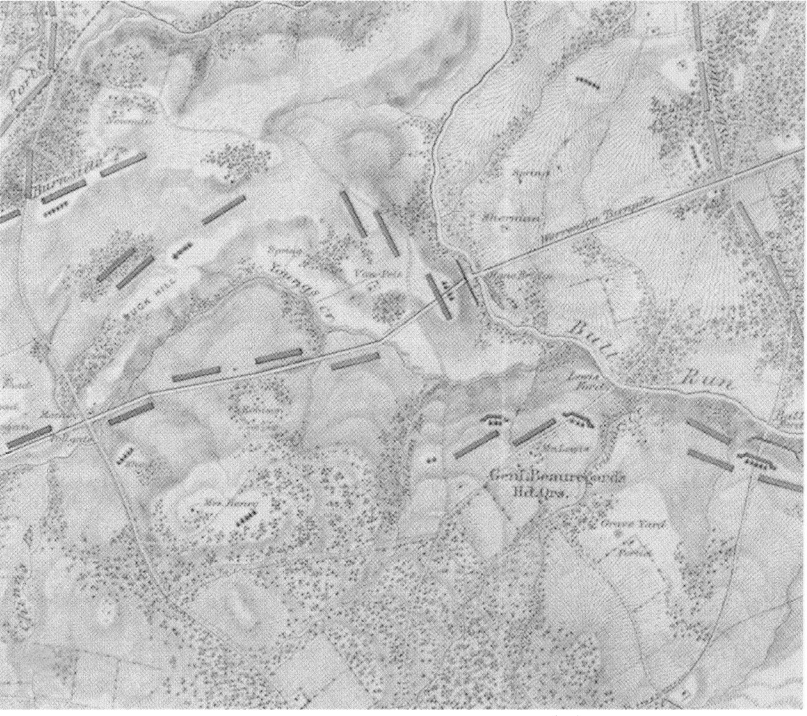

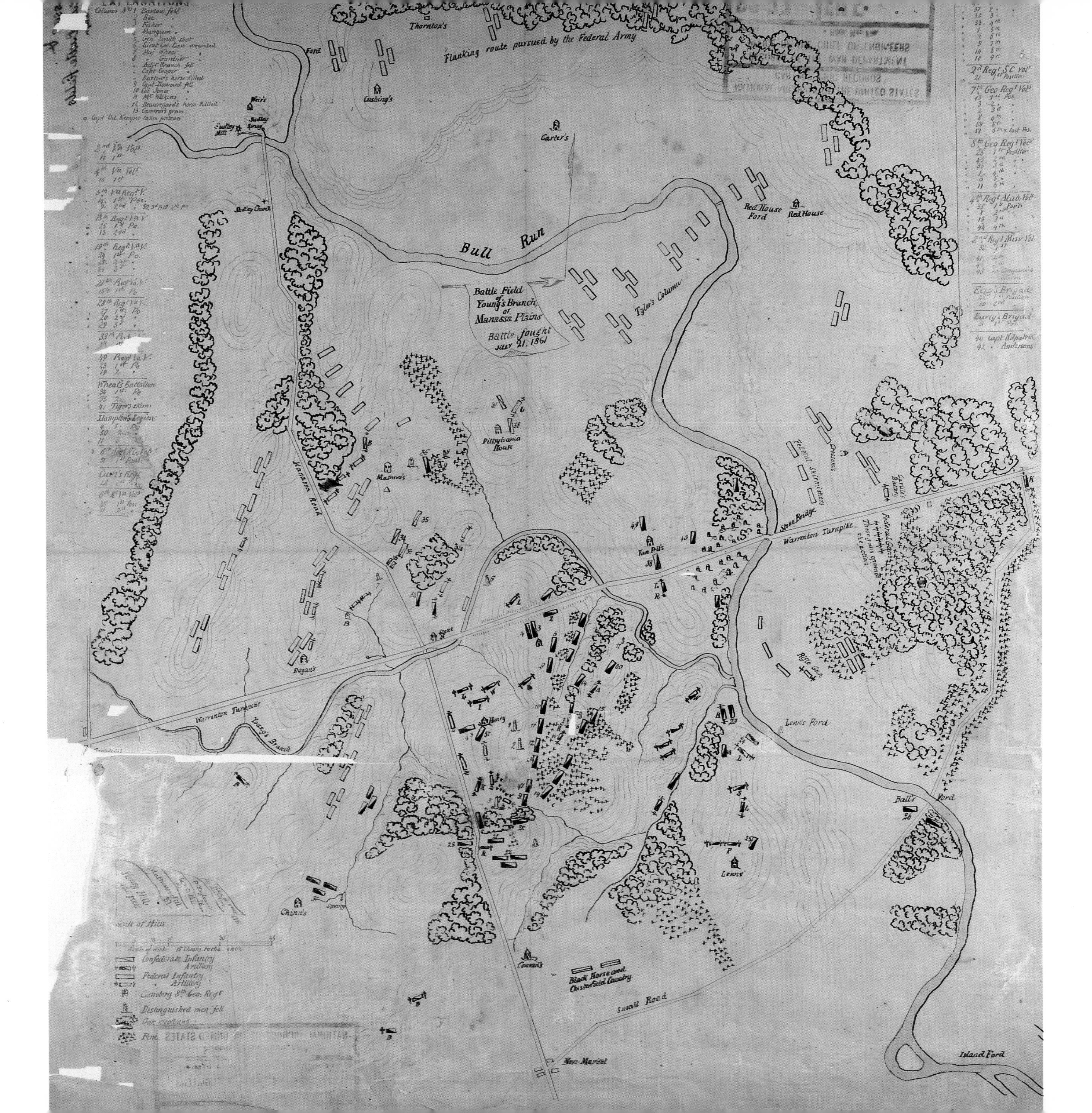
Flanking route pursued by the Federal Army
Thornton's
Ford
Cushing's
Carter's
Sudley Church
Bull Run
Battle Field of Young's Branch or Manassas Plains
Battle fought July 21, 1861
Tyler's Column
Red House Ford
Red House
Pittsylvania House
Mathews's
Stone Bridge
Warrenton Turnpike
Henry
Dogan's
Young's Branch
Lewis Ford
Lewis
Ball's Ford
Chinn's
Black Horse and Chesterfield Cavalry
Sudley Road
New Market
Island Ford
Federal Skirmishers
Scale of Hills
Confederate Infantry
Artillery
Federal Infantry
Artillery

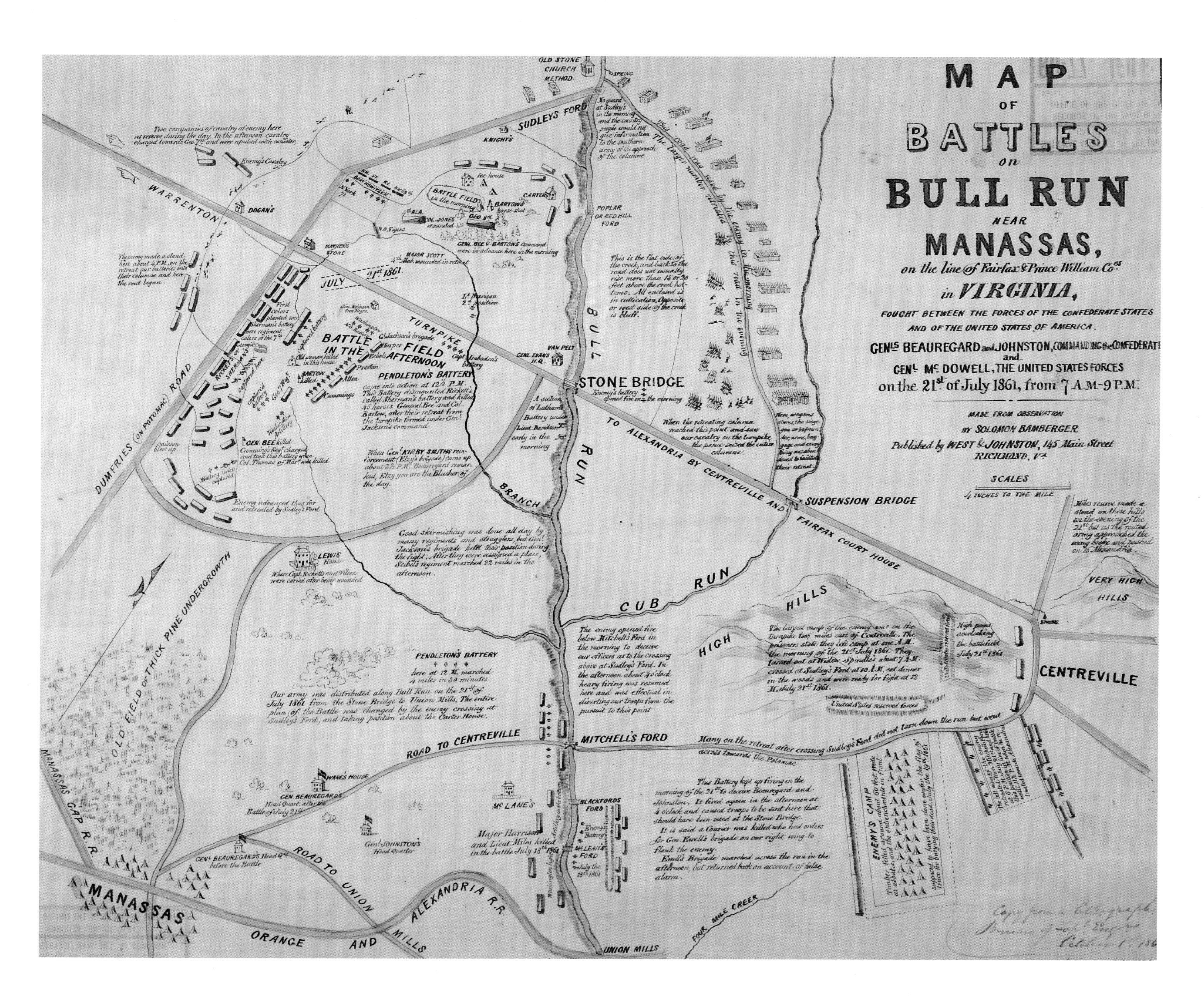
MAP
OF
BATTLES
on
BULL RUN
NEAR
MANASSAS,
on the line of Fairfax & Prince William Cos.
in VIRGINIA,
FOUGHT BETWEEN THE FORCES OF THE CONFEDERATE STATES
AND OF THE UNITED STATES OF AMERICA.
GENLS BEAUREGARD and JOHNSTON, COMMANDING the CONFEDERATES
and
GENL. MC DOWELL, THE UNITED STATES FORCES
on the 21st of July 1861, from 7 A.M.-9 P.M.
MADE FROM OBSERVATION
BY SOLOMON BAMBERGER
Published by WEST & JOHNSTON, 145 Main Street
RICHMOND, Va.
SCALES
4 INCHES TO THE MILE
SUDLEYS FORD
STONE BRIDGE
SUSPENSION BRIDGE
MITCHELL'S FORD
UNION MILLS
CENTREVILLE
MANASSAS
BULL RUN
CUB RUN
HIGH HILLS
VERY HIGH HILLS
BATTLE IN THE FIELD AFTERNOON
PENDLETON'S BATTERY
WARRENTON TURNPIKE
TO ALEXANDRIA BY CENTREVILLE AND FAIRFAX COURT HOUSE
DUMFRIES (ON POTOMAC) ROAD
ROAD TO CENTREVILLE
ROAD TO UNION MILLS
ORANGE AND ALEXANDRIA R.R.
MANASSAS GAP R.R.
OLD FIELD OF THICK PINE UNDERGROWTH
FOUR MILE CREEK
BRANCH
JULY 21st 1861
OLD STONE CHURCH METHOD.
POPLAR OR RED HILL FORD
BLACKFORDS FORD
McLEANS FORD
KNIGHTS
DOGAN'S
LEWIS House
McLANE'S
ENEMY'S CAMP
Our army was distributed along Bull Run on the 21st of July 1861 from the Stone Bridge to Union Mills. The entire plan of the Battle was changed by the enemy crossing at Sudley's Ford, and taking position about the Carter House.
Good skirmishing was done all day by many regiments and stragglers, but Genl. Jackson's brigade held their position during the fight. After they were assigned a place, Sebel's regiment marched 22 miles in the afternoon.
Many on the retreat after crossing Sudley's Ford did not turn down the run but went across towards the Potomac

Rappahannock River, Virginia, winter 1862–63

Right: Confederate map on tracing paper with colored and lead pencils by Jedediah Hotchkiss, one of the outstanding topographical engineers of war, whose collection of maps and papers were purchased by the Library of Congress in 1948. This depiction of the winter 1862–63 headquarters of Generals Jackson, A.P. Hill, and Early on the Rappahannock River near Fredericksburg clearly shows his skill.

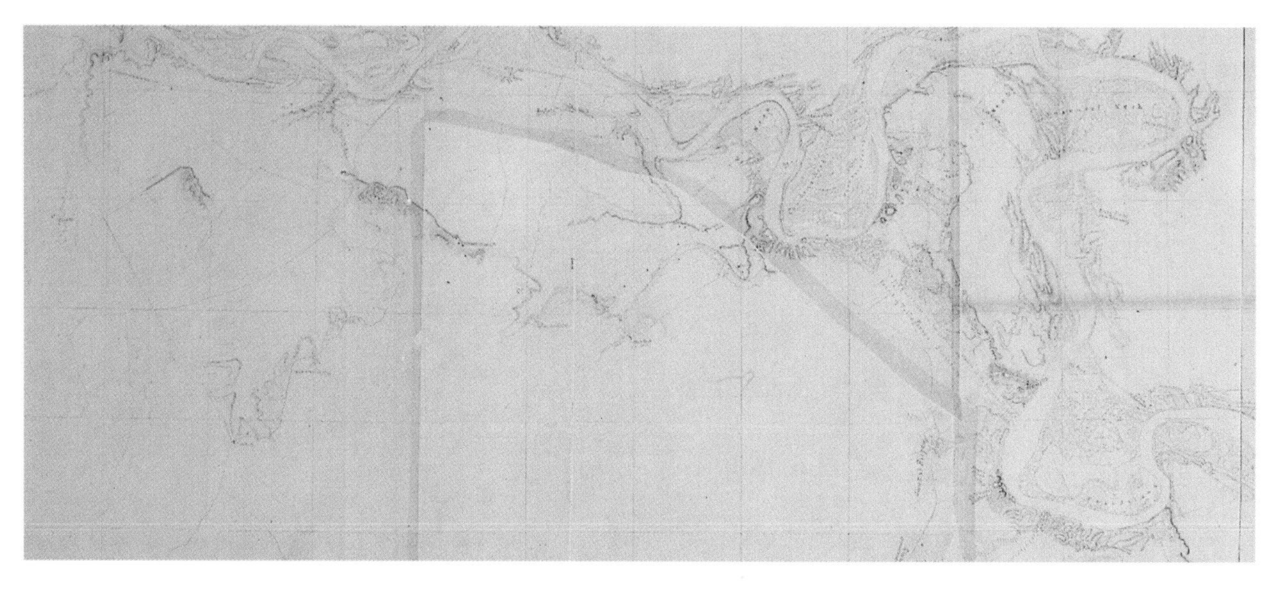

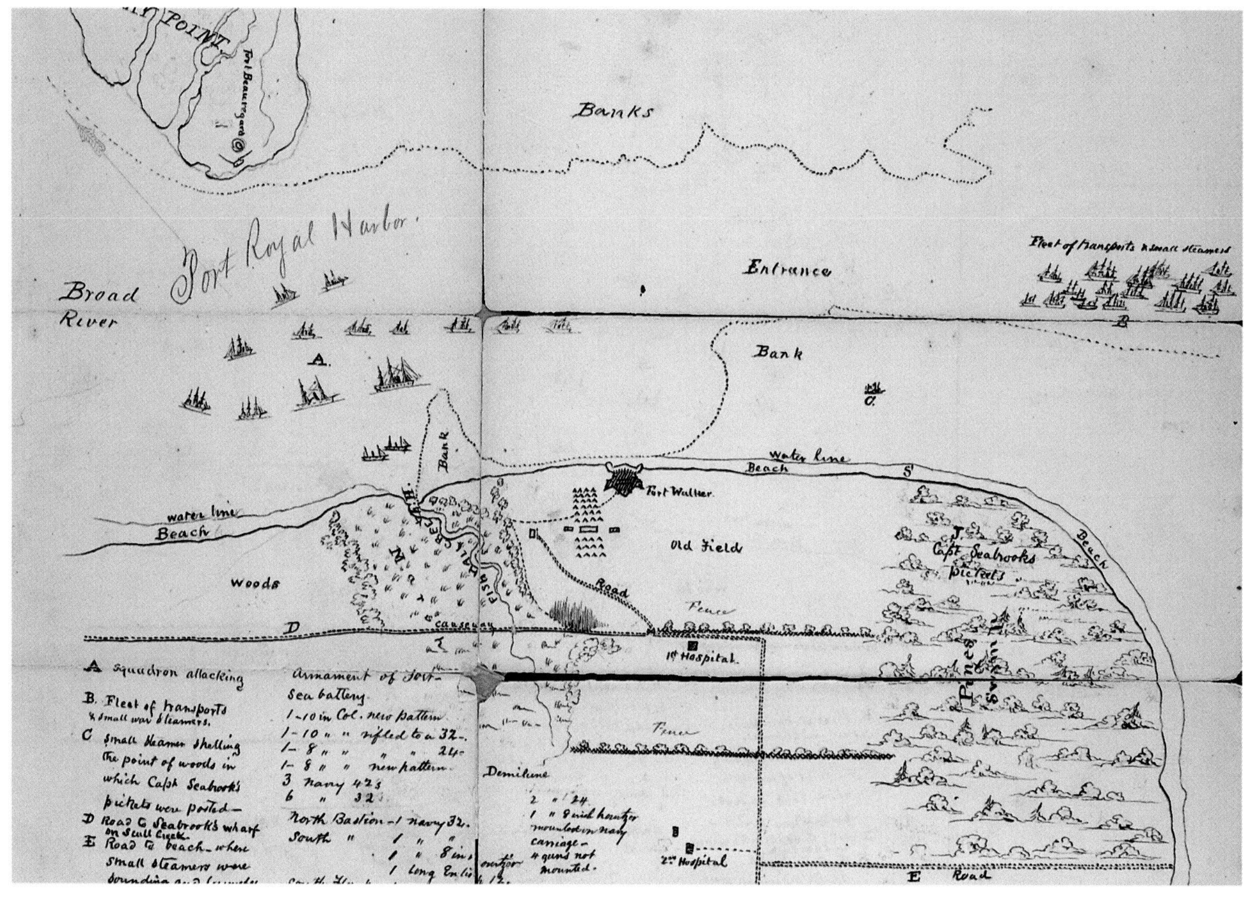

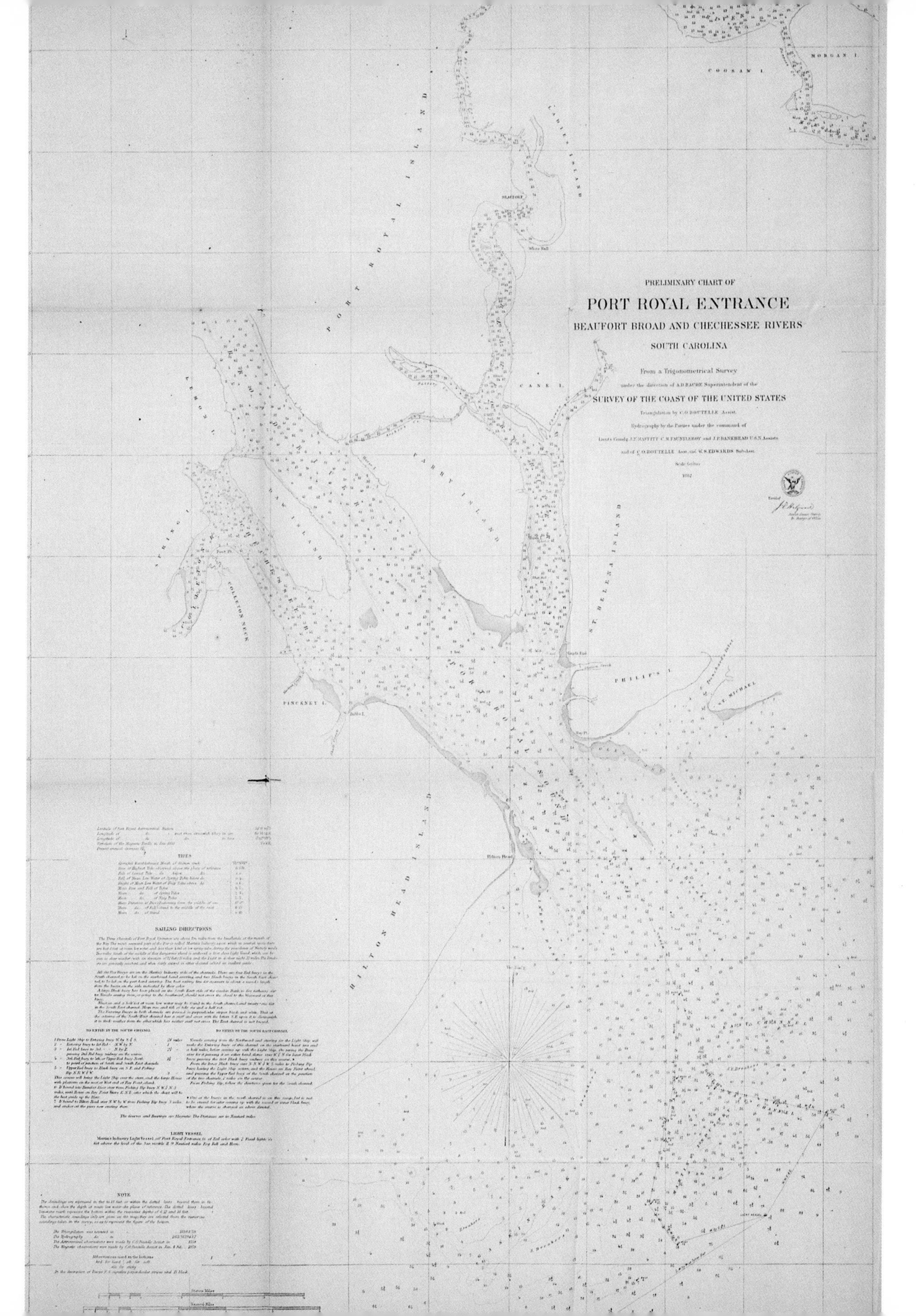

Port Royal Harbor, Virginia, 1862

Left and Far Left: Confederate mapping resources were rather less sophisticated than those of the Union, and from the outbreak of war the rebel armies suffered from a real lack of maps. Today, contemporary Confederate maps are rare. This (**Far Left**) drawing of the mouth of the Broad River and the fortifications surrounding Port Royal Harbor, although artistically executed, demonstrates this point. Compare this map with the accompanying chart (**Left**) produced from hydrographical survey conducted by the U.S. Coast Survey Office in 1862. On assuming command of the Army of North Virginia in June 1862, Robert E. Lee made strident attempts to improve the mapping situation by establishing a Topographical Department under Captain Albert Campbell.

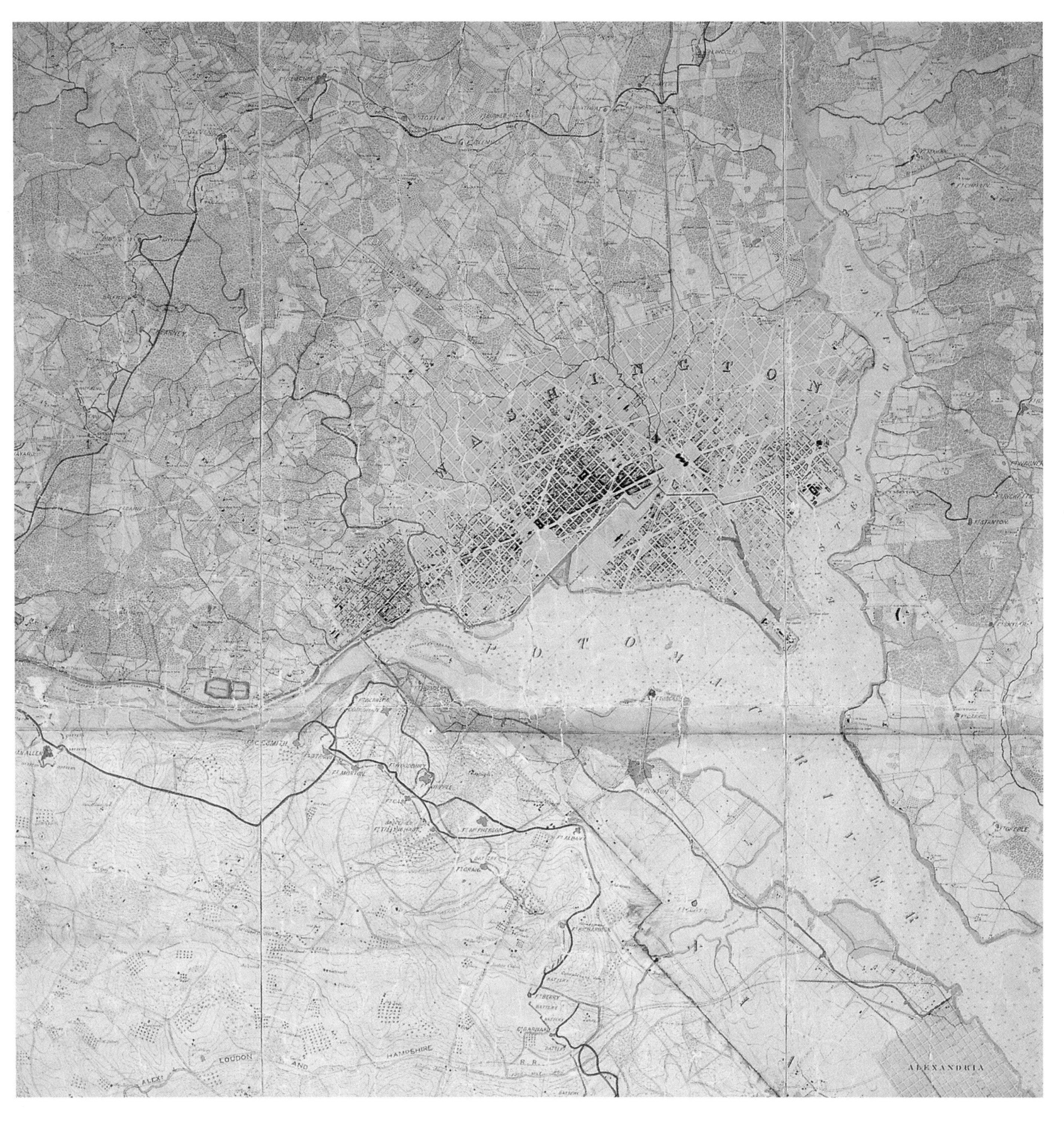

Washington, D.C., 1861–62

Left and Right: Two maps of Washington, D.C. showing the city defenses. The first (a portion of which is shown **Left**) was produced by the U.S Army Corps of Engineers and shows the entire inter-linking network of fortifications around the city, and was compiled to accompany General John Barnard's official report on the defenses of the city. The army mapmakers took as their starting point a commercial map based on a prewar survey by Albert Boschke and first printed in 1861, and added details such as forts, batteries and rifle pits, and the roads linking them.

The second (**Right**), a commercial topographical map of the District of Columbia, was compiled by civil engineer E. G. Arnold for G. Woolworth Colton. An intriguing handwritten note by one W. C. Dodge appears on the original. It states: "This map was suppressed by the Govt. because of the information it would give the rebels. I got this copy in 1862 and have had it ever since."

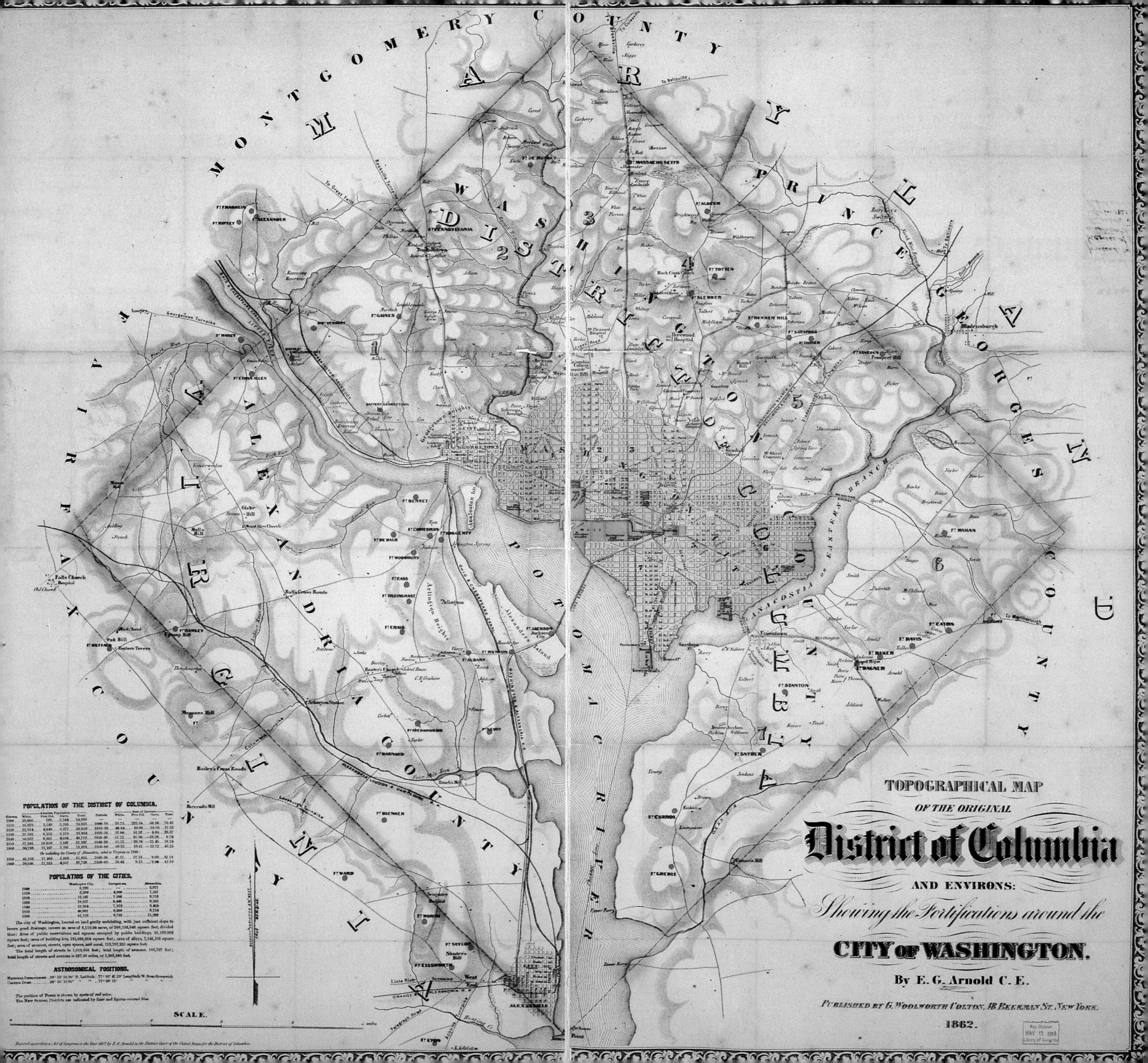

TOPOGRAPHICAL MAP
OF THE ORIGINAL
District of Columbia
AND ENVIRONS:
Showing the Fortifications around the
CITY OF WASHINGTON.
By E. G. Arnold C. E.
PUBLISHED BY G. WOOLWORTH COLTON, 18 BEEKMAN ST. NEW YORK.
1862.
MONTGOMERY COUNTY
PRINCE GEORGES COUNTY
FAIRFAX COUNTY
ALEXANDRIA COUNTY
MARYLAND
VIRGINIA
WASHINGTON
DISTRICT
WASHINGTON COUNTY
POTOMAC RIVER
ANACOSTIA OR EASTERN BRANCH
GEORGETOWN
ALEXANDRIA
Arlington Heights
Arlington
Analostan Island
Alexanders Island
Bladensburgh
Falls Church
Balls Cross Roads
Baileys Cross Roads
Meridian Hill
Columbia College
Rock Creek Church
Soldiers Home
Prospect Hill
Uniontown
Insane Asylum
Greenleafs Point
POPULATION OF THE DISTRICT OF COLUMBIA.
POPULATION OF THE CITIES.
ASTRONOMICAL POSITIONS.
SCALE.

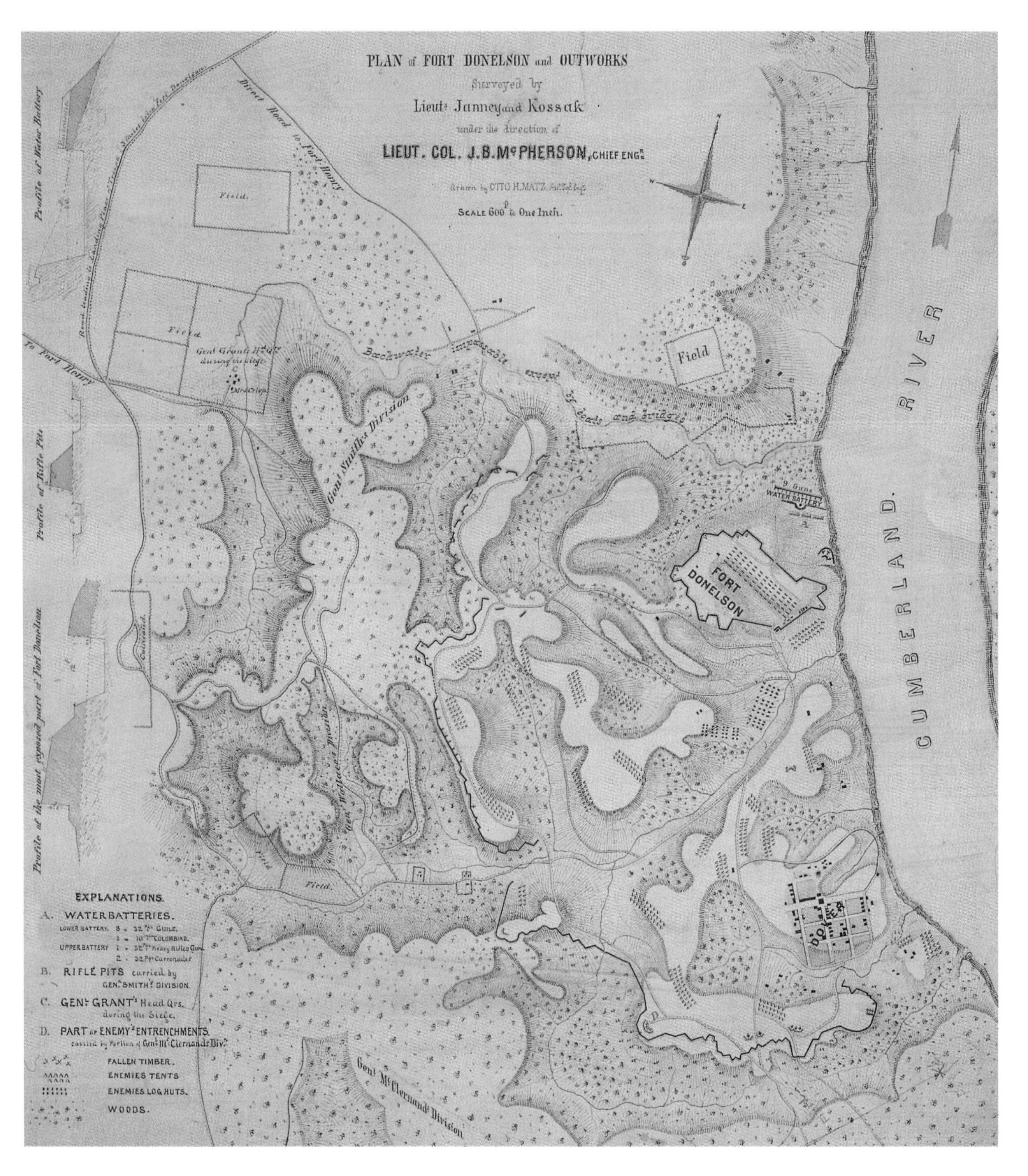

Siege of Fort Donelson, Tennessee, February 16, 1862

Left and Right: A sketch map (**Right**) of Fort Donelson and the defensive works surrounding it. The compilers, Lieutenants W. L. B. Jenney and W. Kossack, have included details such as fallen timber, campsites, barracks, and headquarters positions. Fort Donelson fell on February 16, 1862, to forces under General Ulysses S. Grant after a four-day siege neighboring Fort Henry fell soon after. The loss of these strategically situated forts represented a huge blow to Confederate forces, as both the Cumberland and Tennessee rivers were now in Union control.

The second of the maps (**Left**) was drawn by Otto H. Matz from a different perspective, based on Jenney and Kossack's survey and also probably using their sketch map as a guide. Both have used hachures to indicate relief, although Matz has also added color.

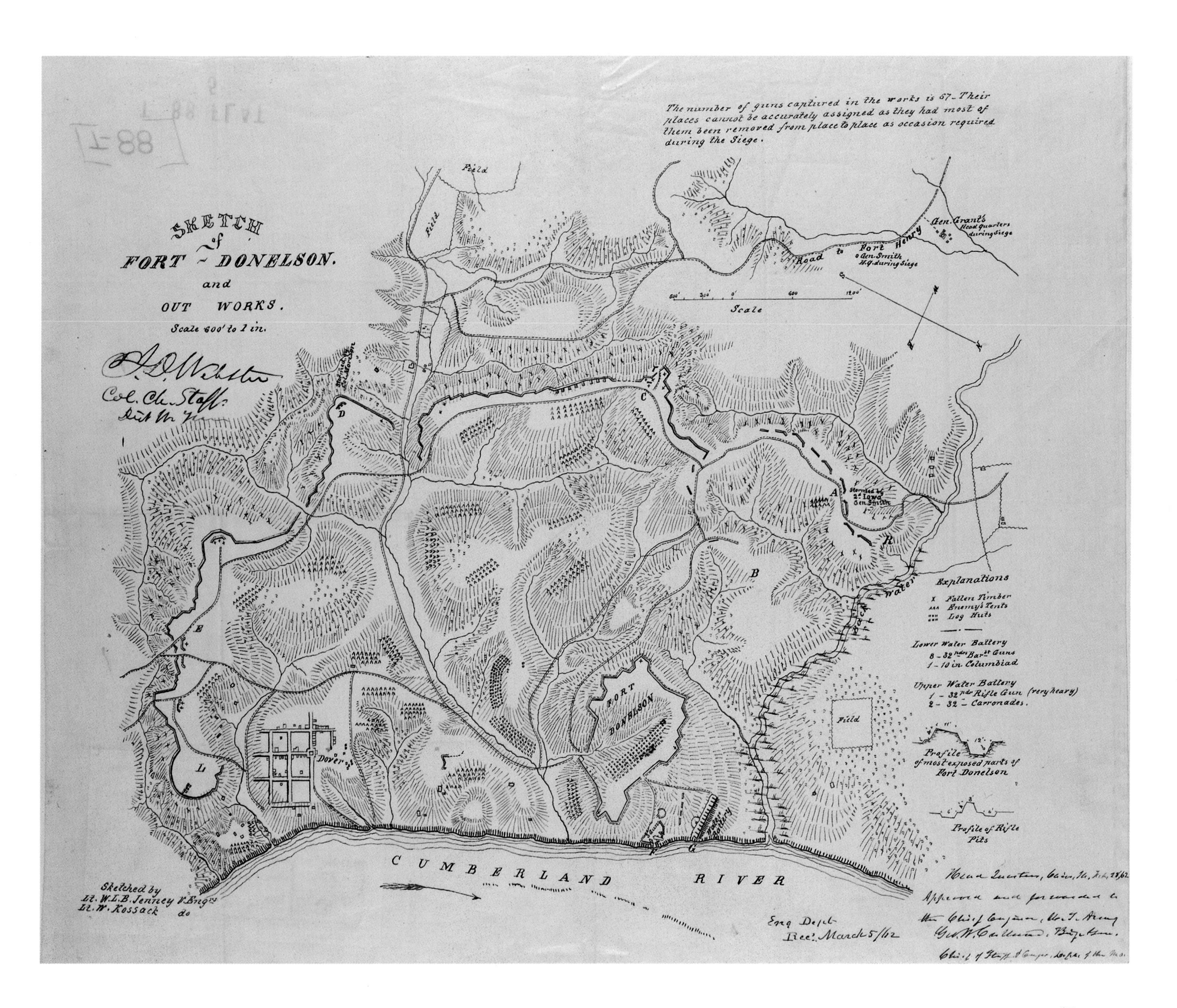
SKETCH of FORT DONELSON and OUT WORKS.
Scale 600' to 1 in.
The number of guns captured in the works is 67. Their places cannot be accurately assigned as they had most of them been removed from place to place as occasion required during the Siege.
Gen. Grant's Head Quarters during Siege
Road to Fort Henry
Gen. Smith H.Q. during Siege
Scale
Field
Stormed by 2d Iowa Gen. Smith
FORT DONELSON
Dover
Explanations
Fallen Timber
Enemy's Tents
Log Huts
Lower Water Battery
8 - 32 pdrs Bar.d Guns
1 - 10 in. Columbiad
Upper Water Battery
1 - 32 pdr Rifle Gun (very heavy)
2 - 32 - Carronades.
Profile of most exposed parts of Fort Donelson
Profile of Rifle Pits
CUMBERLAND RIVER
Sketched by Lt. W. L. B. Jenney V. Engrs
Lt. W. Kossack do
Eng Dept Recd March 5/62

Fort Monroe, Virginia, March 22, 1862

Right: A well-executed perspective drawing of Fort Monroe, Virginia, by Jacob Wells with important places keyed to a list below the map. Fort Monroe, occupying a strategic position at lower Chesapeake Bay, was regarded as "the key to the south."

The key identifies:

1 Old Point Comfort
2 Fortress Monroe
3 Water Battery
4 Hampton Roads
5 Rip Raps
6 Chesapeake Bay
7 Sewall's Point
8 Craney Island
9 Elizabeth River
10 Norfolk
11 Dismal Swamp
12 Portsmouth
13 Atlantic Ocean
14 Cape Hatteras, N.C.
15 Nansemond River
16 James River
17 Newport News
18 Hampton
19 Mill Creek
20 Land approach to Fortress

15
16
17
1
2
19
20

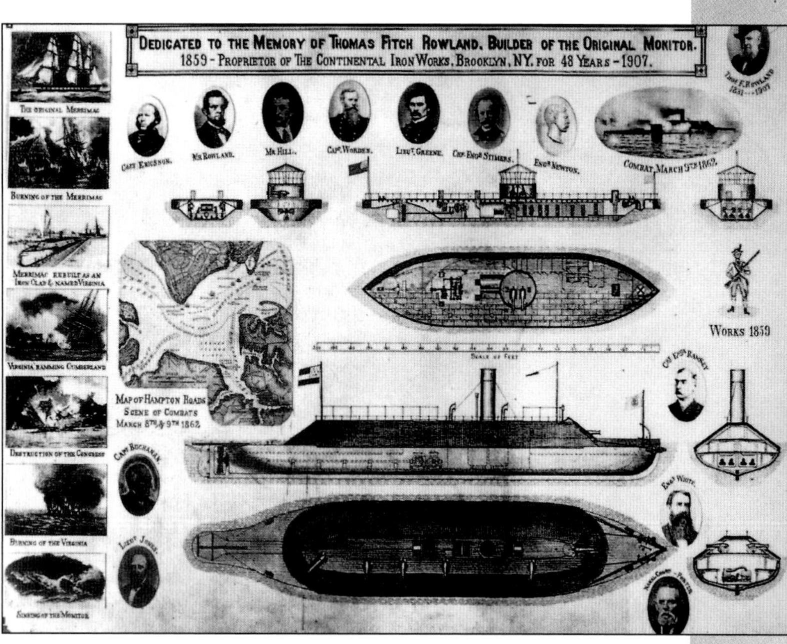

Monitor, *March 9, 1862*

Above: The battle between the Federal *Monitor*, designed by John Ericsson, and the Confederate *Virginia* (originally the Federal *Merrimac*) in Hampton Roads, Virginia. The battle—the first between such armored giants—was inconclusive. *Virginia* would stay in her boltphole on the Elizabeth River until scuttled ahead of the advancing Federals on May 10.

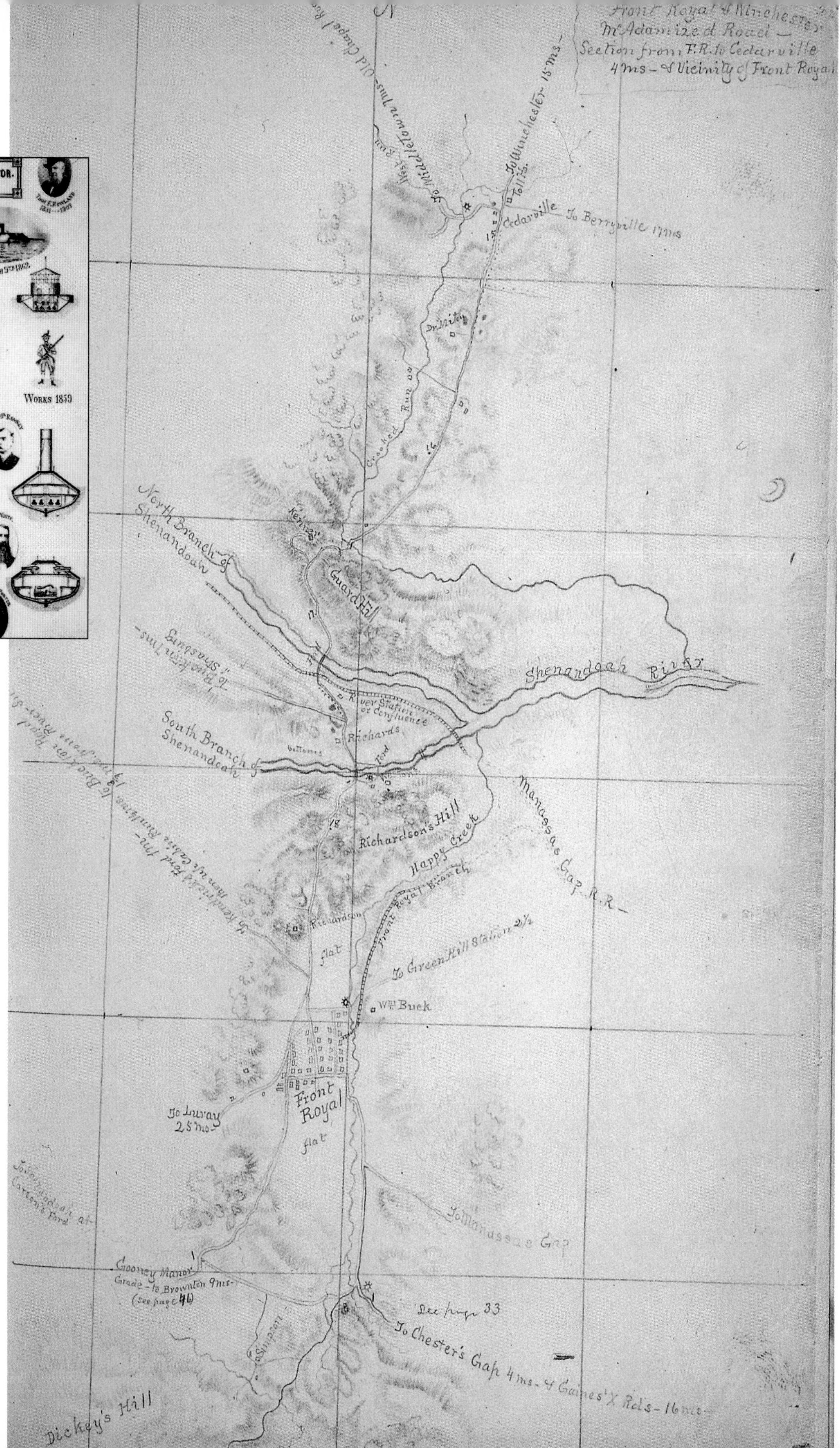

Front Royal & Winchester, West Virginia, 1862

Right: Sketch map of "Front Royal & Winchester McAdamized Road" in West Virginia from the sketch book of Jedediah Hotchkiss, compiled when he was attached to the Army of North Virginia. Hotchkiss drew most of the sketch maps from the saddle and, as he notes on the cover, they were "often used in conferences with Generals Jackson, Ewell, and Early."

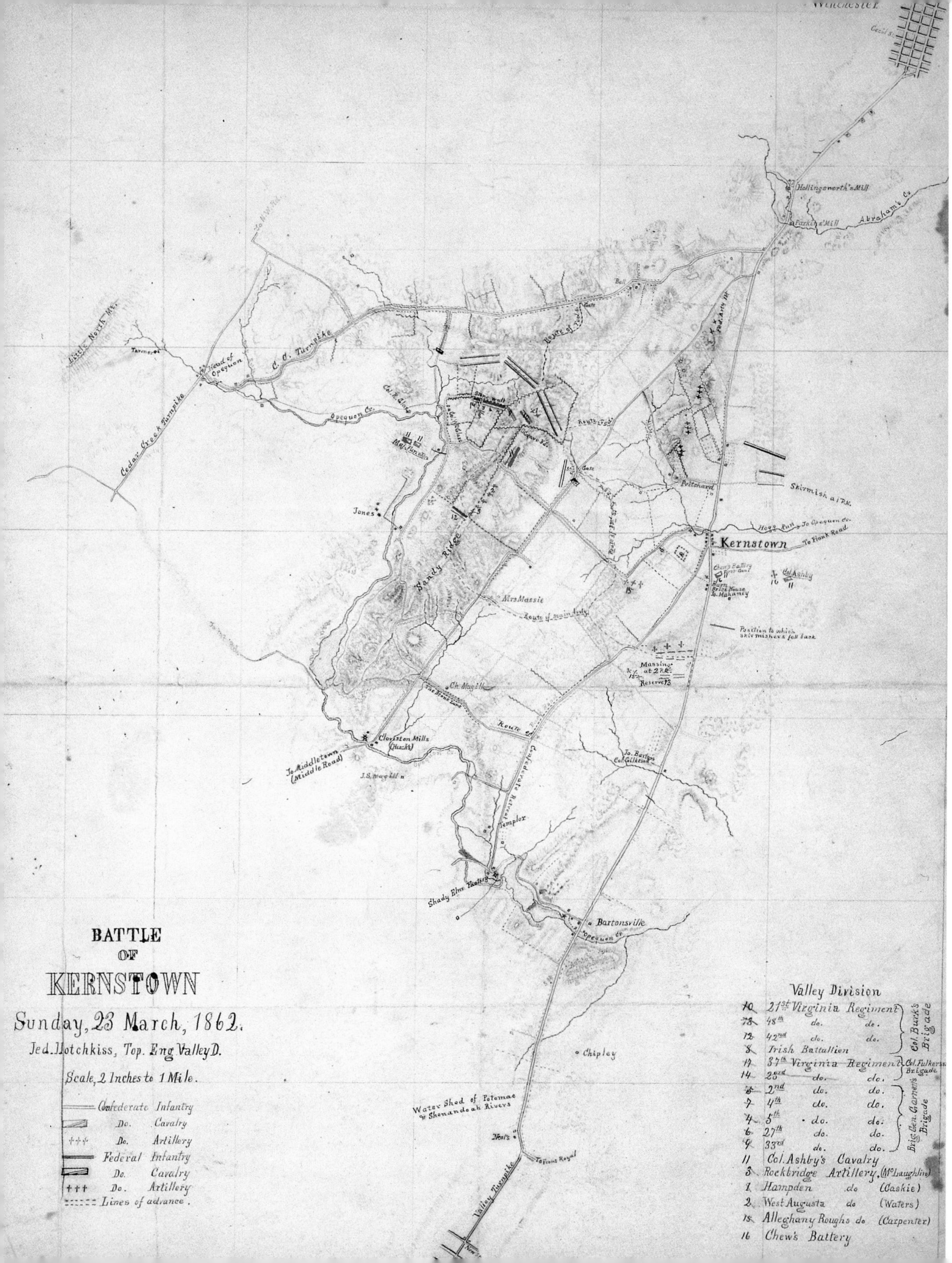

Battle of Kernstown, Virginia, March 23, 1862

Left: Jedediah Hotchkiss's map of the battlefield at Kernstown, Virginia, which includes a list of regiments and brigades in the Valley Division. Fought on a Sunday, this battle was the preliminary to the Shenandoah Valley campaign, and despite being forced to retreat, the outnumbered Confederate forces under General Jackson successfully forced Lincoln to divert troops to counter the threat of an attack on Washington.

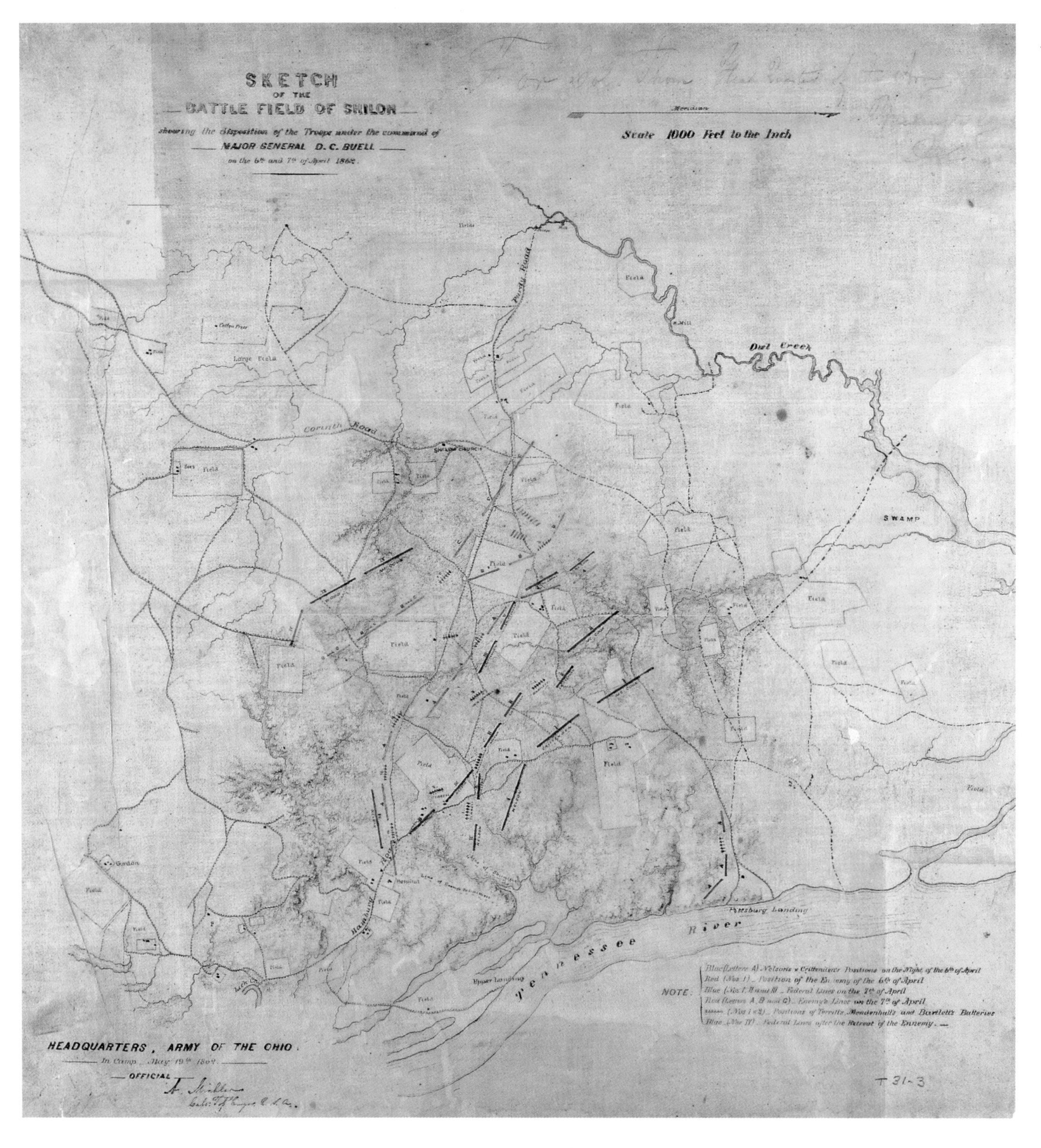

Battle of Shiloh, Tennessee, April 6, 1862

Left and Right: Two maps depicting the the Battle of Shiloh, or Pittsburg Landing, Tennessee April 6, 1862. Again, it is interesting to note how the different camps have chosen to depict the battle, fought between General Johnston's Confederates and General Grant's Union forces.

The first (**Left**) is a manuscript map with Union positions in blue and Confederate in red. Letters and numbers are keyed to a legend denoting successive positions of forces. The second (**Right**) is a Confederate map, is very much less detailed and contains no information on relief.

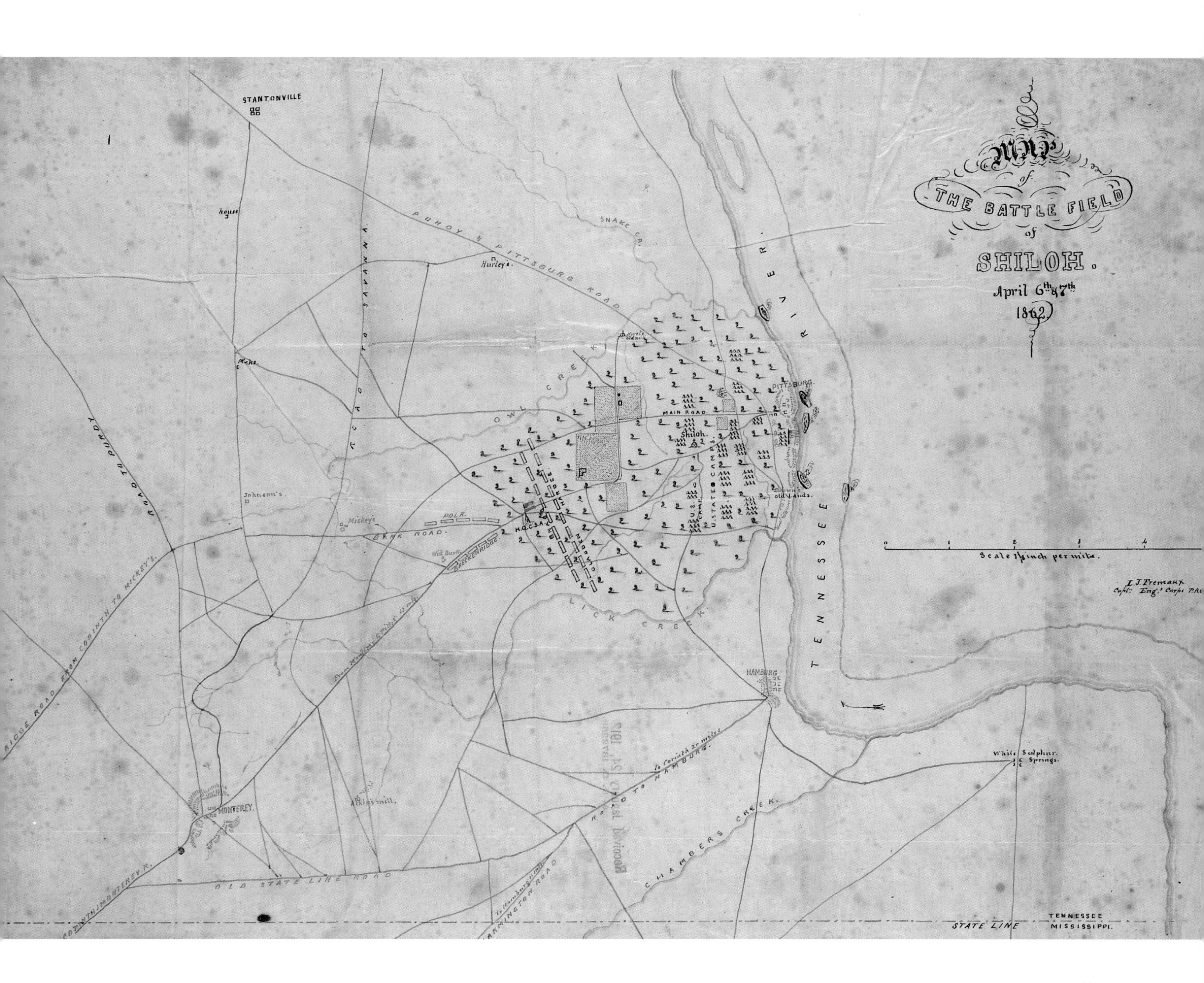
MAP of THE BATTLE FIELD of SHILOH.
April 6th & 7th 1862.
STANTONVILLE
PURDY & PITTSBURG ROAD
SNAKE CR.
OWL CREEK
MAIN ROAD
Shiloh.
PITTSBURG
TENNESSEE RIVER
LICK CREEK
HAMBURG
BARK ROAD
POLK.
BRECKENRIDGE
H.Q.C.S.A.
MONTEREY.
OLD STATE LINE ROAD
CHAMBERS CREEK
ROAD TO HAMBURG
ROAD TO SAVANNA
ROAD TO PURDY
RIDGE ROAD FROM CORINTH TO MICKEY'S
CORINTH & MONTEREY R.
FARMINGTON ROAD
White Sulphur Springs.
Scale 1 inch per mile.
L. J. Fremaux
Capt. Eng. Corps
STATE LINE
TENNESSEE
MISSISSIPPI.

Confederate and Federal Boundaries, May 1862–July 1863

Right: Published by the Office of the U.S. Coast Survey in May 1862, this map details boundaries between the Confederacy and Union states during 1861–62. It was based on a sketch map produced in April 1862, and was the first of four editions of the map (all with slight changes to detail) published between May 1862 and July 1863.

The key identifies:
Blue—States loyal in June 1861.
Green—Limits occupied by U.S. forces March 1, 1862.
Red—Limits occupied by U.S. forces May 15, 1862.

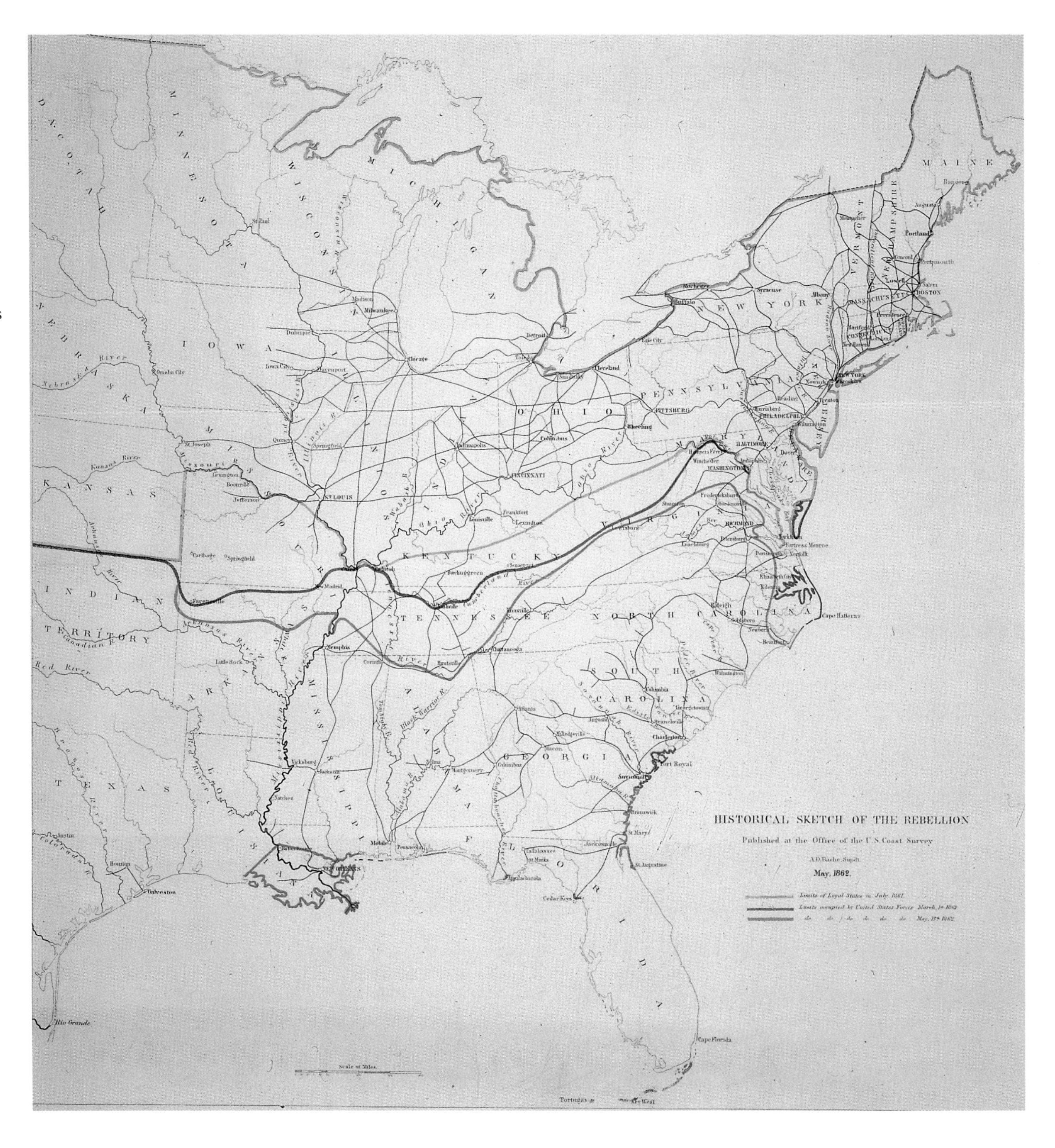

Siege of Yorktown, Virginia, April–May 1862

Far Right: Official plan of the siege of Yorktown, during April and May 1862. General McClellan's Army of the Potomac laid siege to the Confederate stronghold on April 5, and despite reinforcement, General Joseph Johnston evacuated his Confederate troops on May 2, 1862.

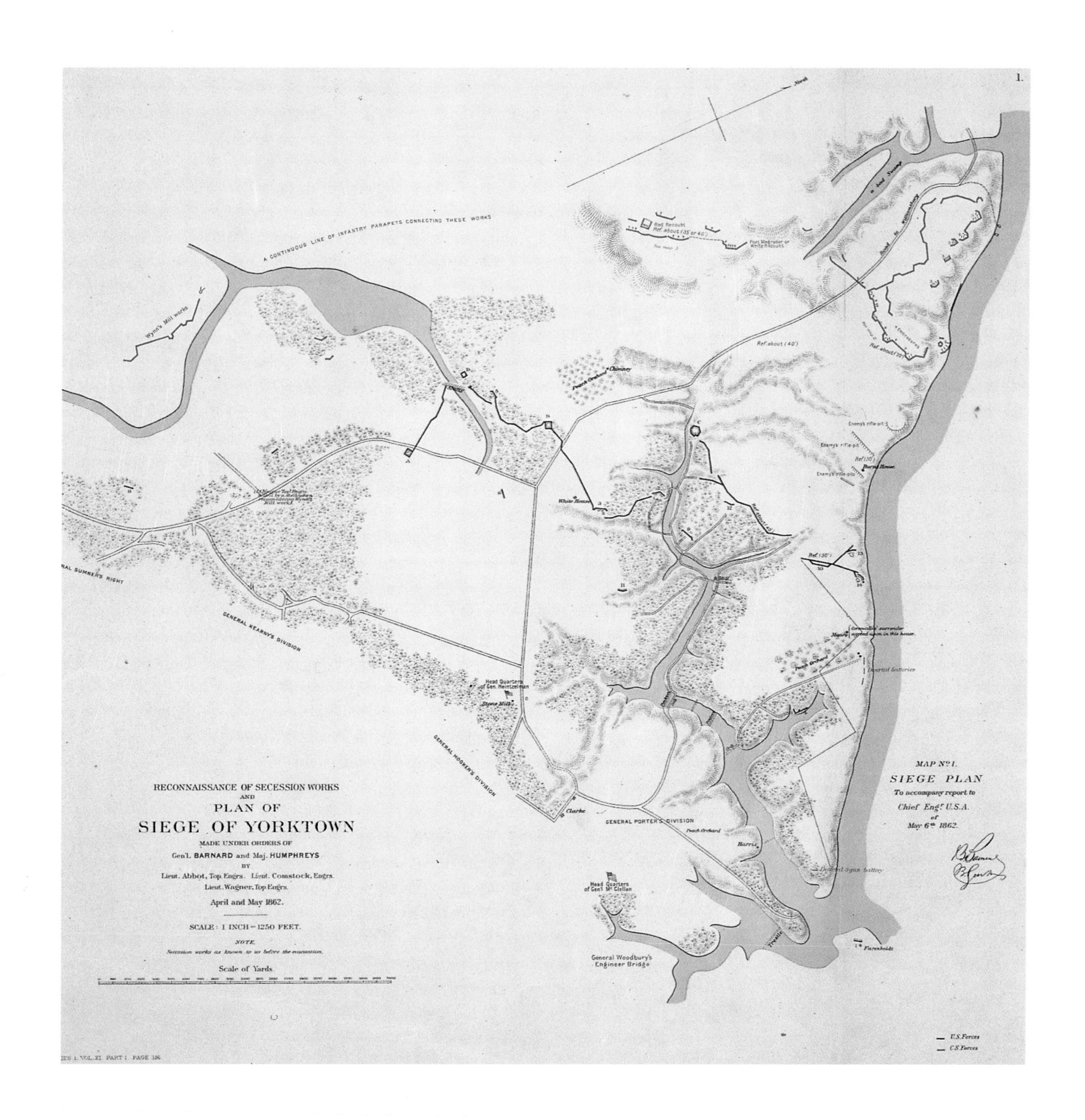
RECONNAISSANCE OF SECESSION WORKS
AND
PLAN OF
SIEGE OF YORKTOWN
MADE UNDER ORDERS OF
Gen'l. BARNARD and Maj. HUMPHREYS
BY
Lieut. Abbot, Top. Engrs. Lieut. Comstock, Engrs.
Lieut. Wagner, Top. Engrs.
April and May 1862.
SCALE: 1 INCH = 1250 FEET.
NOTE.
Secession works as known to us before the evacuation.
Scale of Yards
MAP No. 1.
SIEGE PLAN
To accompany report to
Chief Engr. U.S.A.
of
May 6th 1862.
A CONTINUOUS LINE OF INFANTRY PARAPETS CONNECTING THESE WORKS
Wynn's Mill works
Red Redoubt
Fort Magruder or White Redoubt
White House
Peach Orchard
Chimney
Enemy's rifle-pit
Enemy's rifle-pits
Burns House
Head Quarters of Gen. Heintzelman
Stone Mill
GENERAL KEARNY'S DIVISION
GENERAL HOOKER'S DIVISION
GENERAL PORTER'S DIVISION
Clarke
Head Quarters of Gen'l. McClellan
General Woodbury's Engineer Bridge
Farenholdt
U.S. Forces
C.S. Forces
1.

Williamsburg, Virginia, 1862

Right: Williamsburg, as surveyed and compiled by Captain J. Hope for the Army of the Potomac, with geographical features shown in color. The upper right-hand part of the map is separated by a scratched line, and a note reads: "This part is wrong-an error in scale having been made by Capt. Hope. H.L Abbor, Capt., Engs."

Richmond, Virginia, June 12, 1862

Far Right: Sketch map of the area to the southeast of Richmond, compiled by Lieutenant J. W. Smith on June 12, 1862, prior to the "Seven Days" Campaign. Clearly produced in the field by a professional soldier, rather than a cartographer, this map demonstrates to good effect the type of map common in the field. The Battle at White Oak Swamp was the last in the series of six battles and allowed McClellan to consolidate his positions southeast of Richmond.

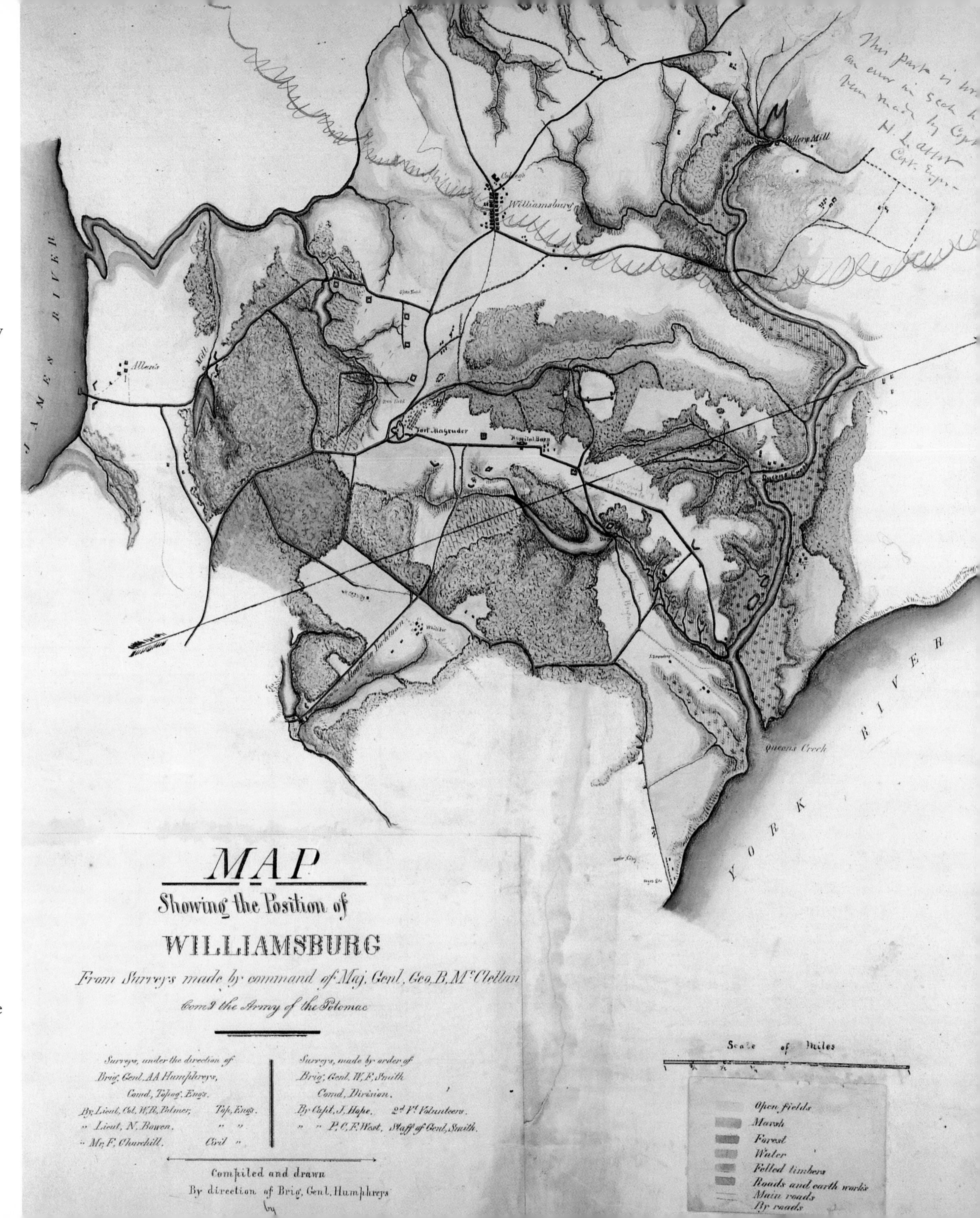

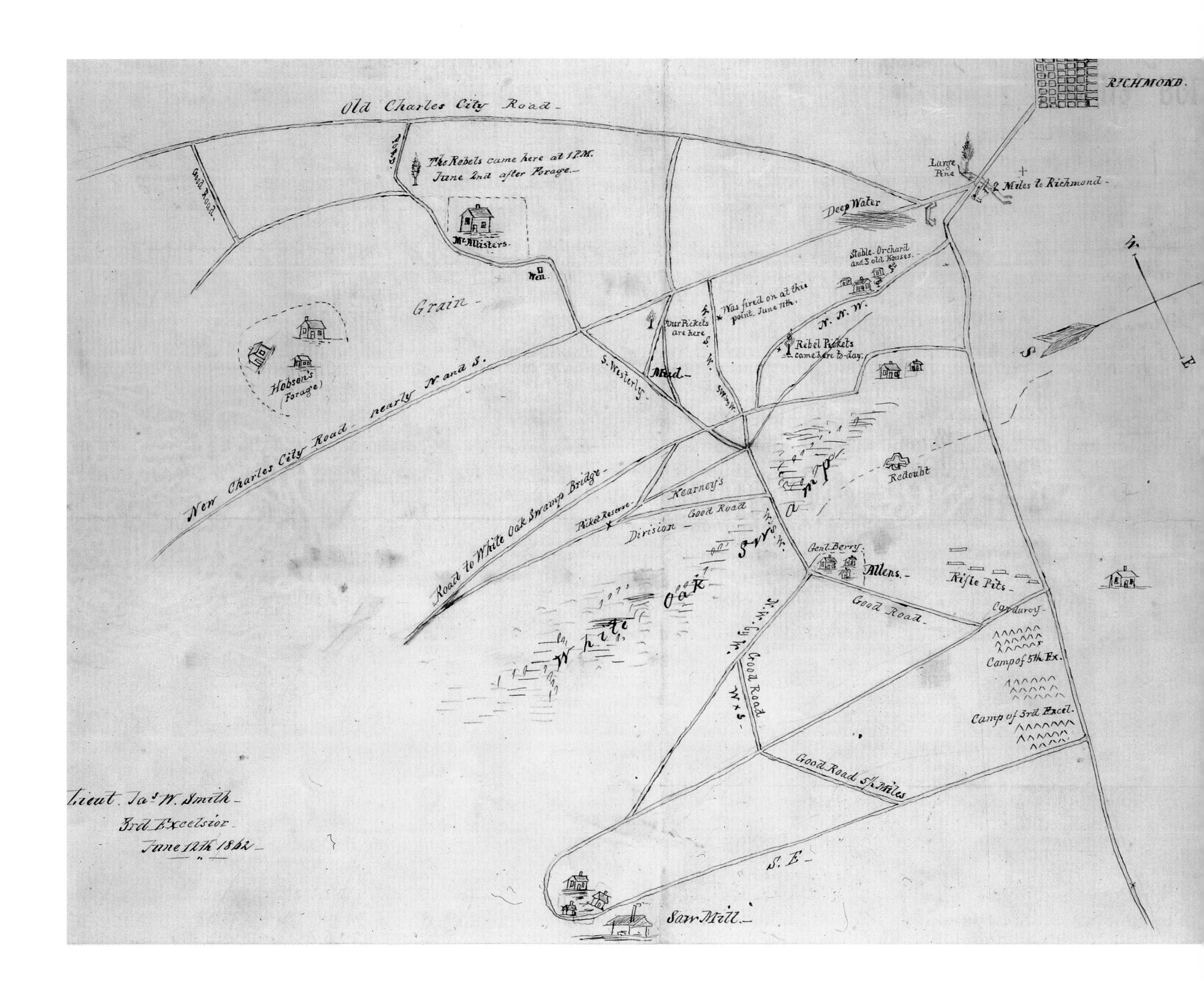
Old Charles City Road
RICHMOND.
The Rebels came here at 1 P.M. June 2nd after Forage
Good Road
McAllisters
Well
Large Pine
2 Miles to Richmond
Deep Water
Stable. Orchard and 3 old Houses.
Grain
Our Pickets are here
Was fired on at this point June 11th.
N. N. W.
Rebel Pickets came here to-day.
Hobson's (Forage)
New Charles City Road nearly N. and S.
S. Westerly
Mud
Redoubt
Road to White Oak Swamp Bridge
Kearney's
Picket Reserve
Good Road
Division
Genl. Berry
Allens
Rifle Pits
White Oak Swamp
Good Road
Corduroy
Camp of 5th Ex.
Good Road
Camp of 3rd Excel.
Good Road 5½ Miles
Lieut. Jas W. Smith
3rd Excelsior
June 12th 1862
S. E.
Saw Mill

BIRDS EYE VIEW
OF THE
SEAT OF WAR AROUND RICHMOND

SHOWING THE BATTLE ON CHICKAHOMINY RIVER JUNE 1862

John Bachmann, Publisher.

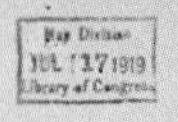

Battle of the Chickahominy River, Virginia, June 29, 1862

Left and This Page (details): This panoramic scene is John Bachmann's splendid depiction of the Battle of the Chickahominy River, and is worthy of inclusion in this volume on its artistic merits alone. Perspective drawings, as can be seen from a number of such illustrations in this book, were very popular at the time. The battles around Richmond on the Chickahominy River were part of the "Seven Days" Campaign.

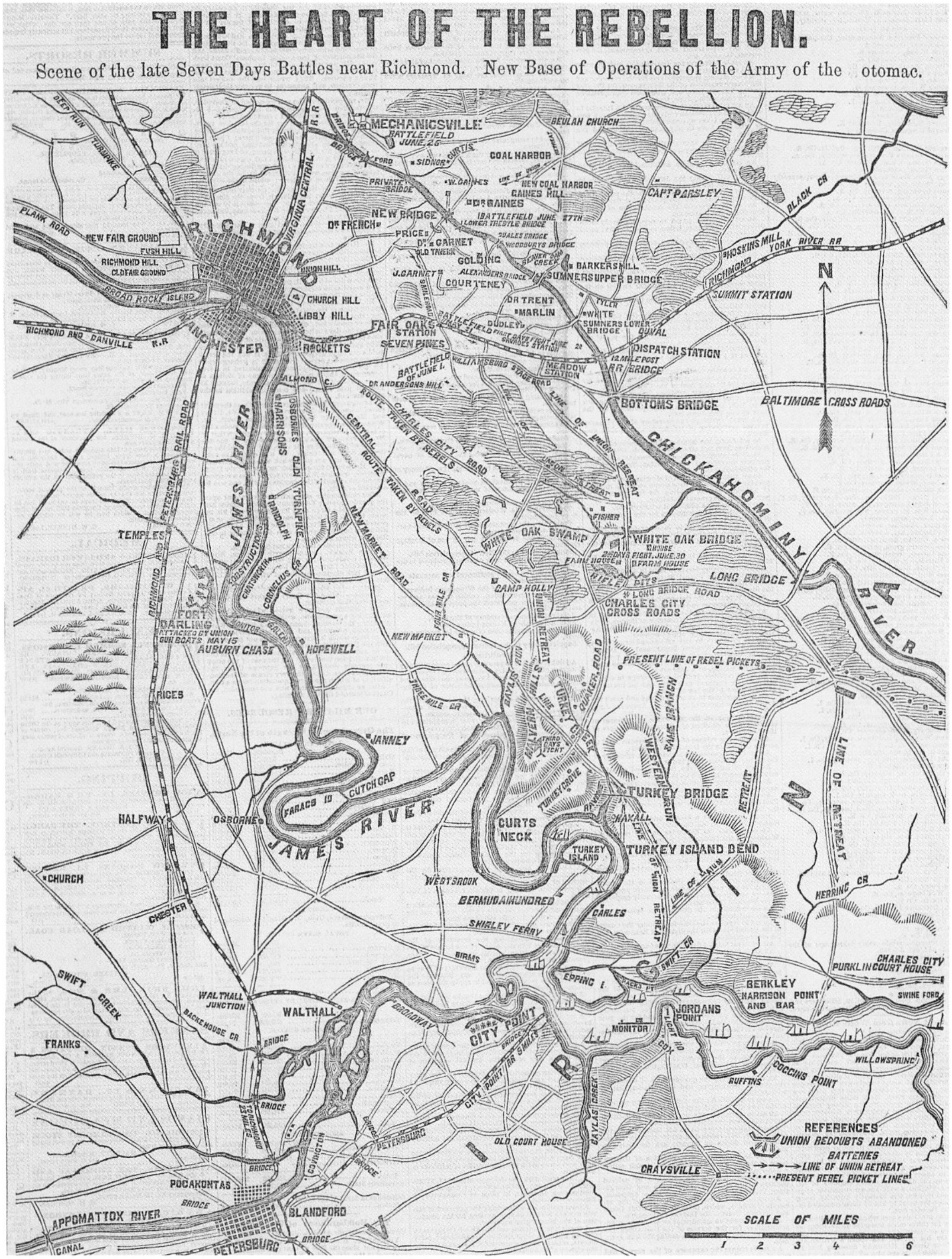

THE HEART OF THE REBELLION.

Scene of the late Seven Days Battles near Richmond. New Base of Operations of the Army of the otomac.

Richmond, Virginia, July 1862

Left: *The Philadelphia Inquirer* published this map on July 19, 1862, to illustrate the new base on operations of the Army of the Potomac in the aftermath of the "Seven Days" Campaign, an effort by Union forces to strike a crippling blow at Richmond, Virginia. The map has been produced using the familiar woodcut technique popular with newspapers. The outline of the map was traced onto a block of wood and then sectioned into several parts. A team of carvers took a section each and when complete these were bolted back together, with place names cast in metal type set into place. An electrotype metal copy of the woodcut was made and the illustration made ready for printing. The whole process took approximately two weeks to complete.

Vicksburg, Mississippi, July 15–16, 1862

Right: Artistic bird's eye view of Vicksburg and vicinity, drawn by L. A. Wrotnowski, and showing the positions of Confederate defenses, gun boats, and ram ships in the Yazoo River, the position of Farragut's fleet in the Mississippi River, and the passage of the Confederate ironclad ram ship *Arkansas* through part of the fleet on July 15.

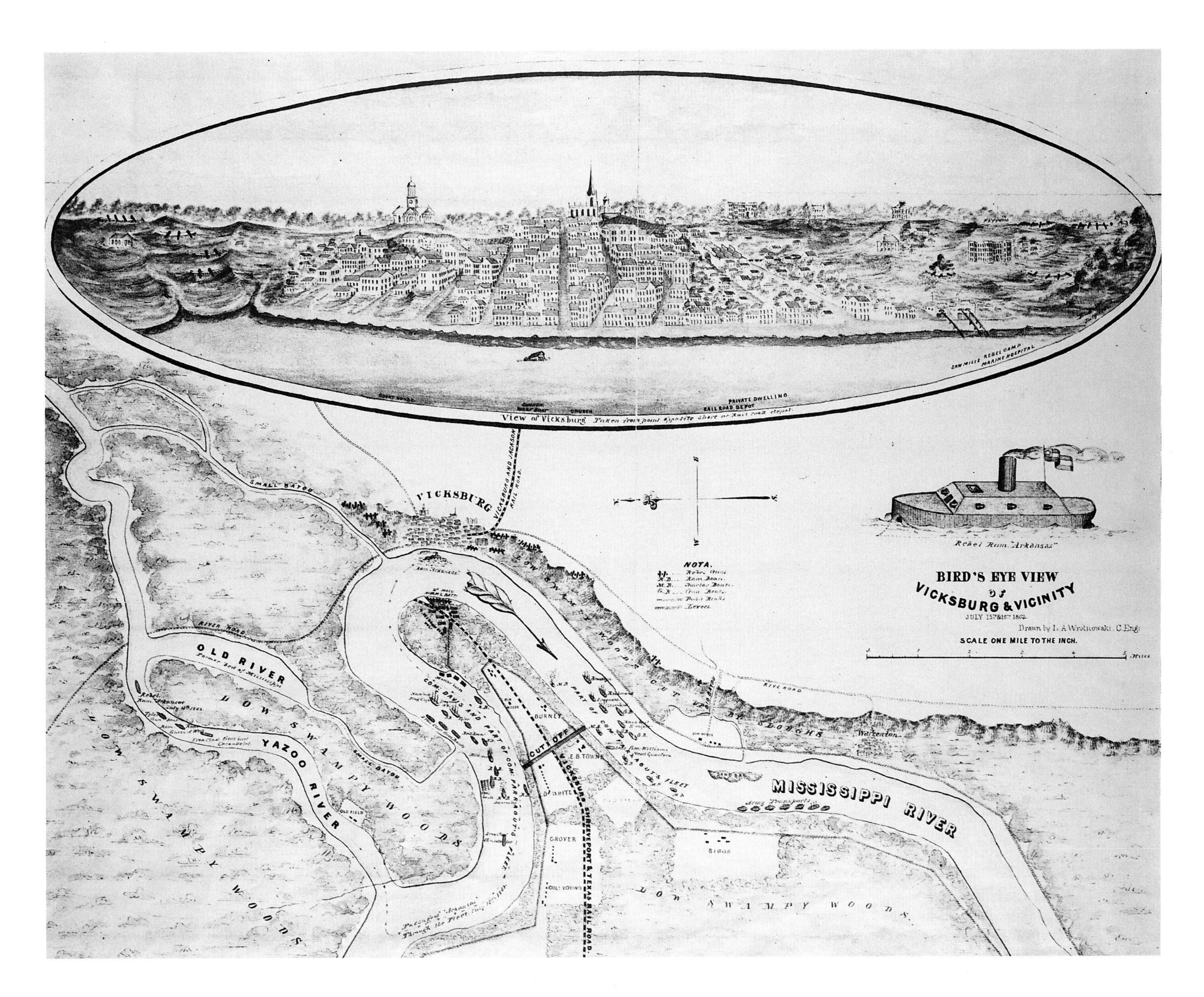
View of Vicksburg Taken from point opposite shore on Rail road depot.
COURT HOUSE
CHURCH
RAILROAD DEPOT
PRIVATE DWELLING
SAW MILLS REBEL CAMP MARINE HOSPITAL
Rebel Ram "Arkansas"
NOTA.
R.B. ... Ram Boats.
M.B. ... Mortar Boats.
Public Roads
Levees.
BIRD'S EYE VIEW
of
VICKSBURG & VICINITY
JULY 15th & 16th 1862.
Drawn by L. A Wrotnowski. C. Eng.
SCALE ONE MILE TO THE INCH.
Miles
VICKSBURG
VICKSBURG AND JACKSON RAIL ROAD.
SMALL BAYOU
RIVER ROAD
OLD RIVER
LOW SWAMPY WOODS
YAZOO RIVER
SMALL BAYOU
OLD FIELD
LOW SWAMPY WOODS
CUT OFF
BURNEY
GROVER
COL. YOUNG
MISSISSIPPI RIVER
Army Transports
RIVER ROAD
BIG BAYOU
SLOUGHS
Warrenton
VICKSBURG SHREVEPORT & TEXAS RAIL ROAD.
LOW SWAMPY WOODS.

Military Map of America, August 1862

Above and Right (details): Britain had a strong interest in the events of the Civil War and British publishers produced a large number of maps pertaining to the conflict. The most celebrated of them was Bacon and Co. of London, which sold a series of six maps known collectively as the "Shilling War Maps," one of which is reproduced here. Published in August 1862, this portrays in color the "Free or non-Slaveholding States," the "Border Slave States," and the "Seceded or Confederate States." Bacon also sold the maps of New York publisher J. H. Colton and Co.

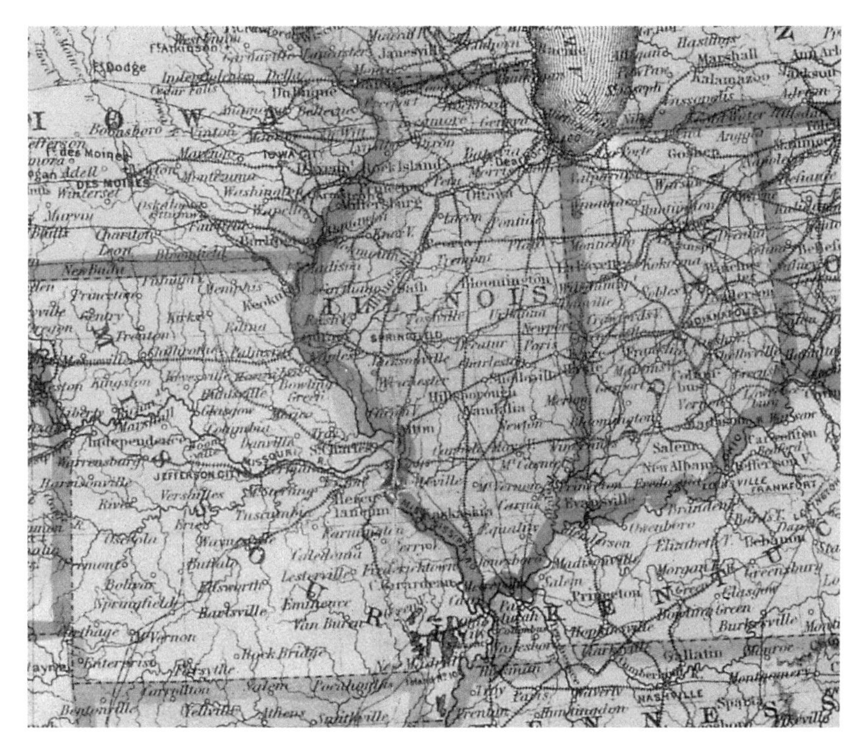

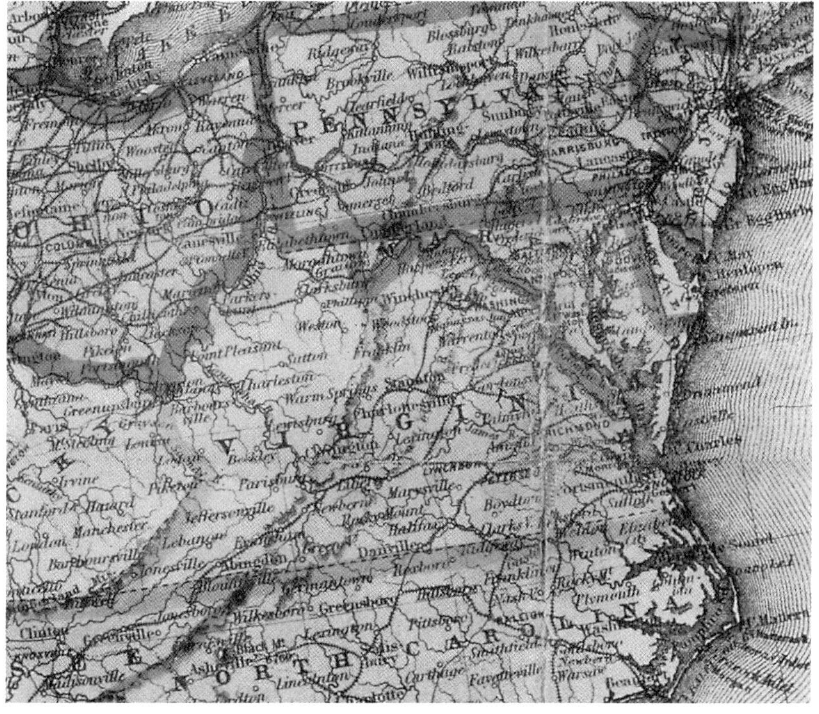

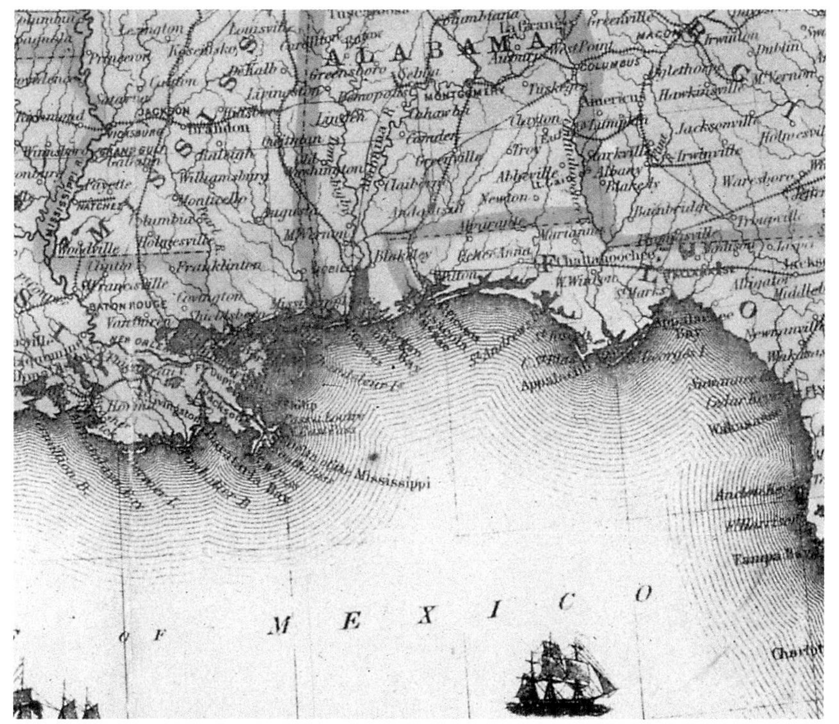

BACON'S
MILITARY MAP OF THE
UNITED STATES
Shewing the
FORTS & FORTIFICATIONS.
Published by BACON & C°. 48 Paternoster Row.
LONDON. 1862
EXPLANATION.
Free or Non-Slaveholding States.
Population 18,000,000, Area 1,828,637. Square Miles
Border Slave States.
Pop.n 3,000,000, 500,000. are Slaves. Area 261,427. d°
Seceded or Confederate States.
Pop.n 10,000,000, 3,500,000, are Slaves. Area 833144. d°

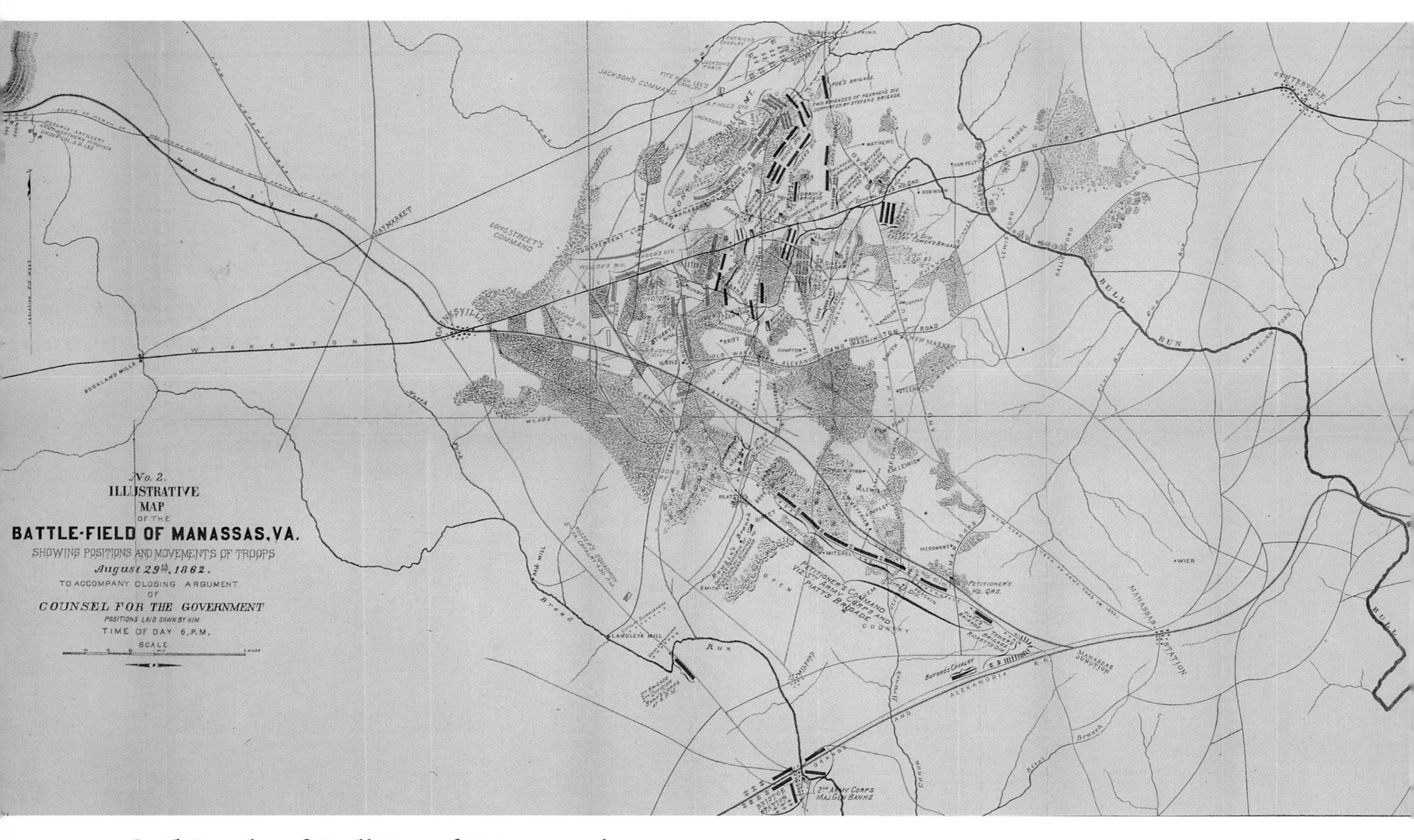

2nd Battle of Bull Run (Manassas), Virginia, August 29, 1862

Above and Right (detail): Battlefield of Manassas, Virginia, showing the positions and movements of troops on August 29. This map was compiled from the evidence of eyewitnesses, one of four produced in 1879. The battle ended in defeat for the Union.

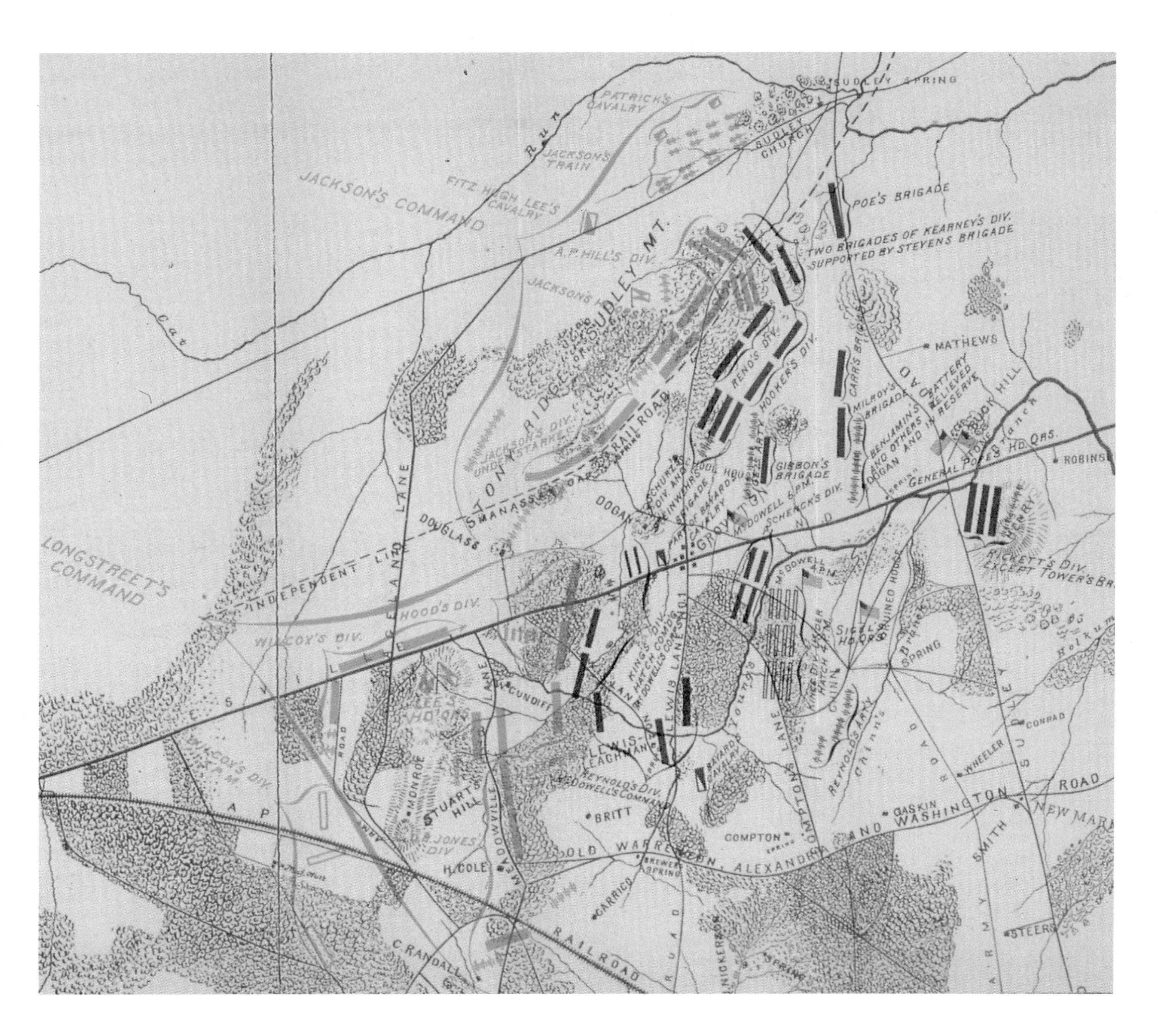

SUDLEY SPRING
PATRICK'S CAVALRY
SUDLEY CHURCH
JACKSON'S TRAIN
JACKSON'S COMMAND
FITZ HUGH LEE'S CAVALRY
POE'S BRIGADE
TWO BRIGADES OF KEARNEY'S DIV. SUPPORTED BY STEVENS BRIGADE
A.P. HILL'S DIV.
SUDLEY MT.
MATHEWS
RENO'S DIV.
HOOKER'S DIV.
CARR'S BRIG.
MILROY'S BRIGADE
BATTERY RELIEVED
BENJAMIN'S AND OTHERS DOGAN AND IN RESERVE
BUCK HILL
GENERAL POPE'S HD. QRS.
ROBINSON
RAILROAD
GIBBON'S BRIGADE
JACKSON'S DIV. UNDER STARKE
MANASSAS GAP
DOGAN
SCHENCK'S DIV.
McDOWELL 6 P.M.
GROVETON
DOUGLASS
LONGSTREET'S COMMAND
INDEPENDENT LINE
HENRY
RICKETT'S DIV. EXCEPT TOWER'S BR
McDOWELL 4 P.M.
HOOD'S DIV.
WILCOX'S DIV.
SIGEL'S HD. QRS.
RUINED HOUSE
SPRING
LEE'S HD. QRS.
CUNDIFF
KING'S DIV. HATCH COMD'G
LEWIS LANE
CHINN
REYNOLD'S ARTY
WILCOX'S DIV. 5 P.M.
LEWIS
STUART'S HILL
MONROE
BAYARD CAVALRY
REYNOLD'S DIV. McDOWELL'S COMMAND
CONRAD
WHEELER
ROAD
BRITT
GASKIN
COMPTON
NEW MARKET
ALEXANDRIA AND WASHINGTON
OLD WARRENTON
JONES' DIV.
H. COLE
BREWER SPRING
CARRICO
SMITH
STEERS
C. RANDALL
RAILROAD
NICKERSON

MAP OF THE
Battlefield of Antietam,
Prepared by
LIEUT. WM. H. WILLCOX, TOP. OFF. & A.A.D.C.
BRIG. GEN. DOUBLEDAY'S STAFF.
FROM ACTUAL SURVEYS.
UNION FORCES.
REBEL FORCES.
Scale of Miles
POTOMAC
Chesapeake & Ohio Canal
DOUBLEDAY
HOOKER
MATHEWS & THOMSON
GIBBONS
MEADE DOUBLEDAY
Cornfield
SEDGWICK
SEYMOUR
GIBBON
DOUBLEDAY
MANSFIELD
STONEWALL JACKSON
Rocky Ledges
COUCH
FRENCH
RICHARDSON
Signal Sta.
Signal Station
Signal St.
Keedysville
or Centre V.
Mill
GEN. McCLELLAN
MORRELL
PORTER
Porterstown
Confederate Line of Battle on the evening of September 17th 1862
SHARPSBURG
GEN. LEE
SYKES
WARREN
ANTIETAM CR.
COOK
WILLCOX
BURNSIDE
N.
Hagerstown
Williamsport
Martinsburg
Sharpsburg
Charlestown
Winchester
Berlin

Battle of Antietam, Maryland, September 17, 1862

Far Left and This Page (details): The third edition of a superbly detailed and colored map of Antietam (Sharpsburg), with troop positions (Union forces in red, Confederates in blue) plotted by William H. Willcox, a lieutenant of the 95th New York who served as a topographical engineer on General Abner Doubleday's staff. The attempt by General Robert E. Lee to invade the North via Maryland was abandoned in the aftermath of his defeat by McClellan at Antietam on September 17, 1862.

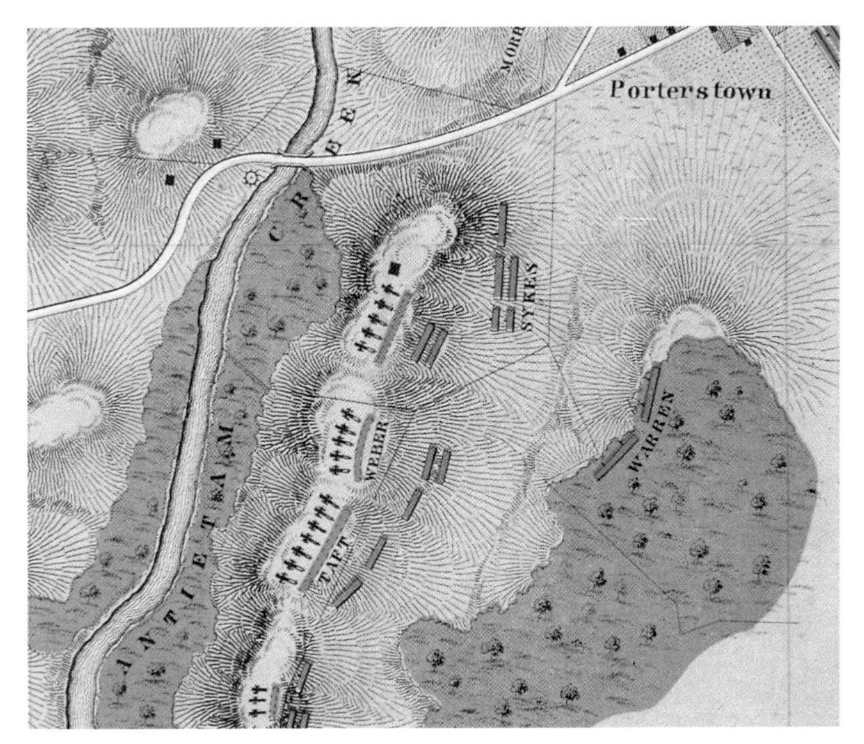

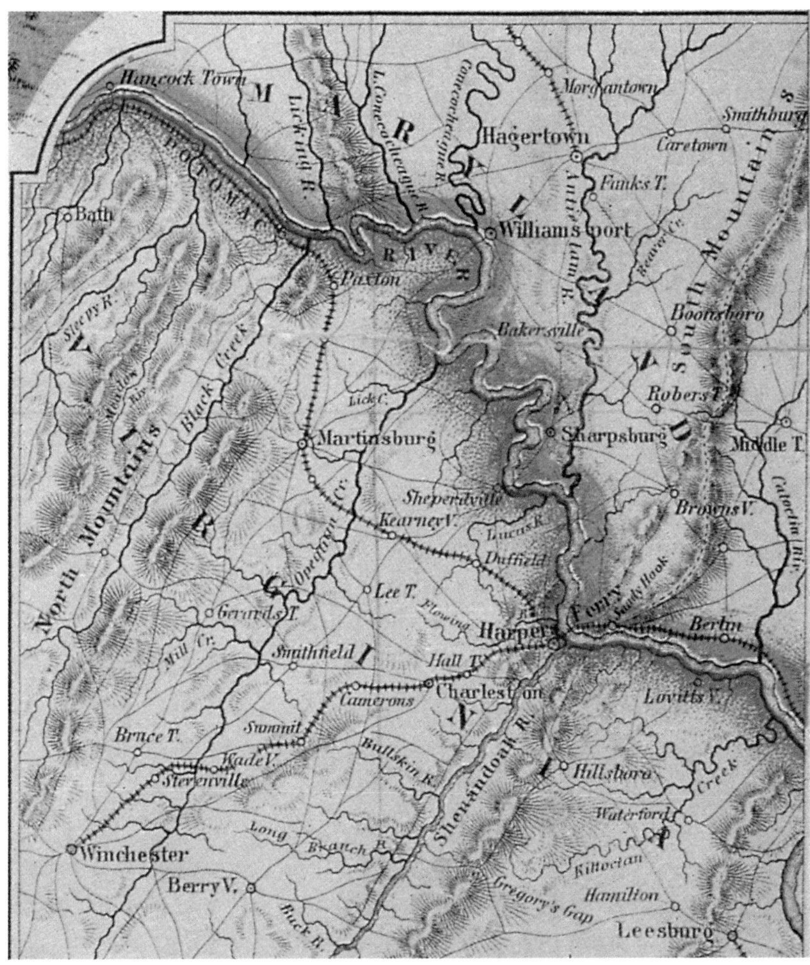

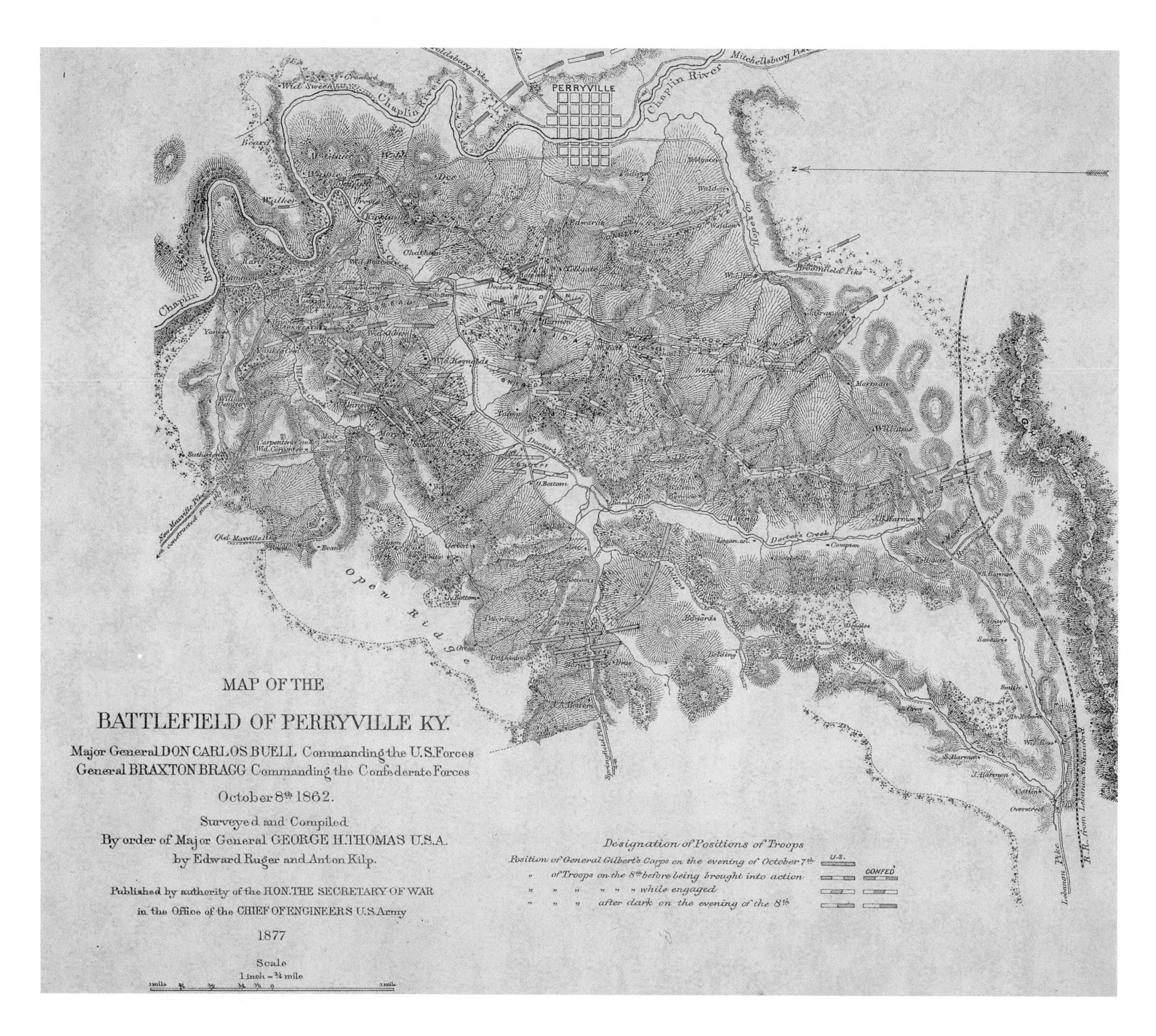
MAP OF THE
BATTLEFIELD OF PERRYVILLE KY.
Major General DON CARLOS BUELL Commanding the U.S. Forces
General BRAXTON BRAGG Commanding the Confederate Forces
October 8th 1862.
Surveyed and Compiled
By order of Major General GEORGE H. THOMAS U.S.A.
by Edward Ruger and Anton Kilp.
Published by authority of the HON. THE SECRETARY OF WAR
in the Office of the CHIEF OF ENGINEERS U.S. Army
1877
Scale
1 inch = 3/4 mile
Designation of Positions of Troops
Position of General Gilbert's Corps on the evening of October 7th
of Troops on the 8th before being brought into action
while engaged
after dark on the evening of the 8th
U.S.
CONFED.
PERRYVILLE
Chaplin River
Mitchellsburg Pike
Open Ridge
Doctor's Creek
Springfield Pike
Lebanon Pike
Bradfordsville Pike
New Maxville Pike
Old Maxville Road

Battle of Perryville, Kentucky, October 8, 1862

Left: Map of the Battlefield of Perryville, Kentucky, surveyed and compiled by Edward Ruger and Anton Kilp (and including information passed to them by officers of both armies) for Major-General George H. Thomas and published in 1877. The map gives the positions of the opposing forces before, during, and after the battle, also the roads, the railroad from Lebanon to Stanford, drainage, vegetation, relief (by hachures), houses, and the names of some of the residents. This was the most significant of the battles fought in Kentucky, and compelled General Bragg to retreat to the southeast.

Virginia, December 1, 1862

Right: "Map of the Seat of the War in Virginia," published by B. Duncan, Columbia, South Carolina. This is one of the few maps that was published in the South for sale to the public. It shows the main battles and important physical features of the area.

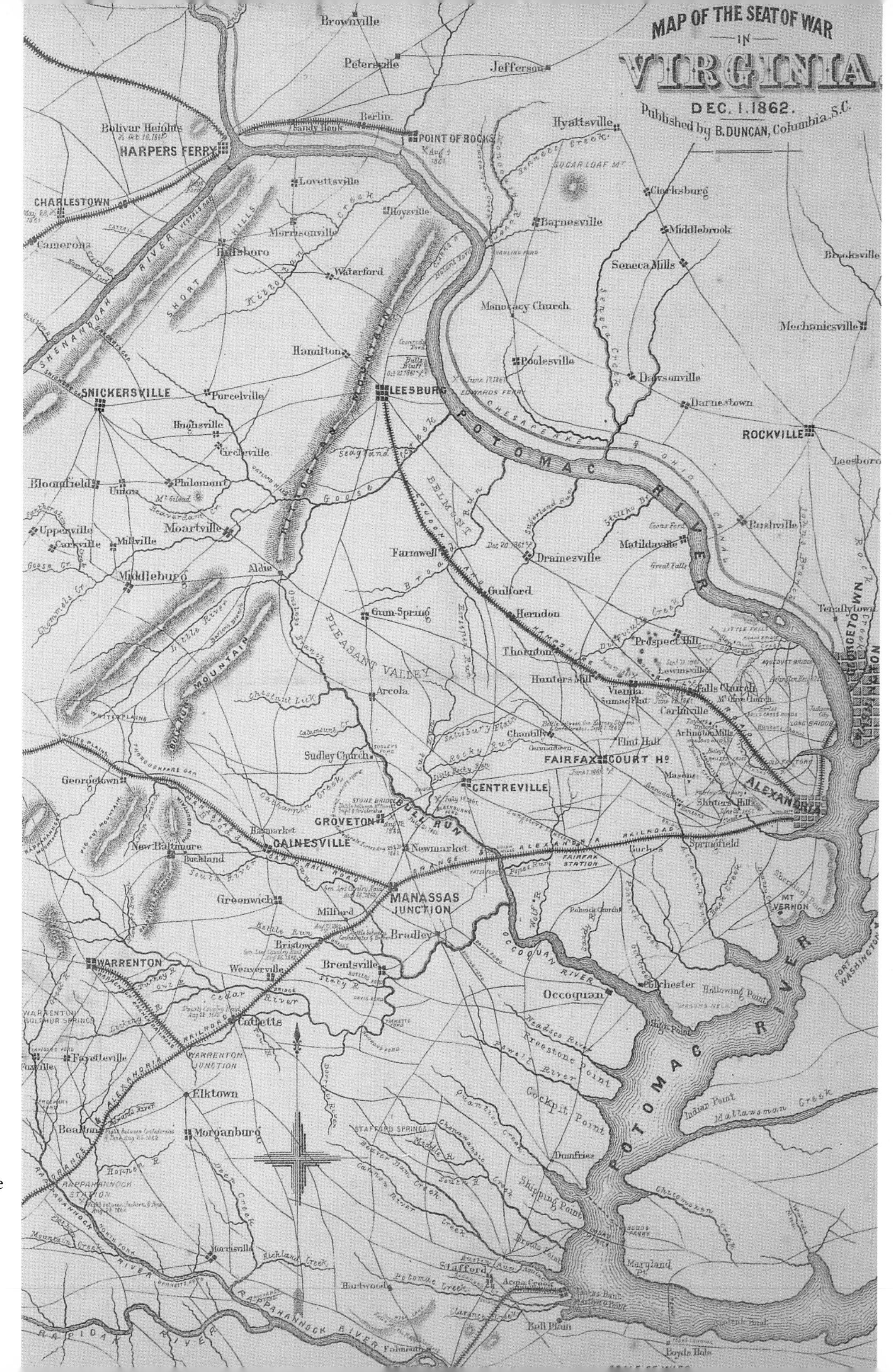

Battle of Pea Ridge, Arkansas, October 22, 1862

Right: The Battlefield at Pea Ridge, Maysville, Arkansas, depicted here on a manuscript map with Federal lines in red and Confederate in blue. Union forces successfully pushed Confederate forces out of the area and into the valley of the Arkansas.

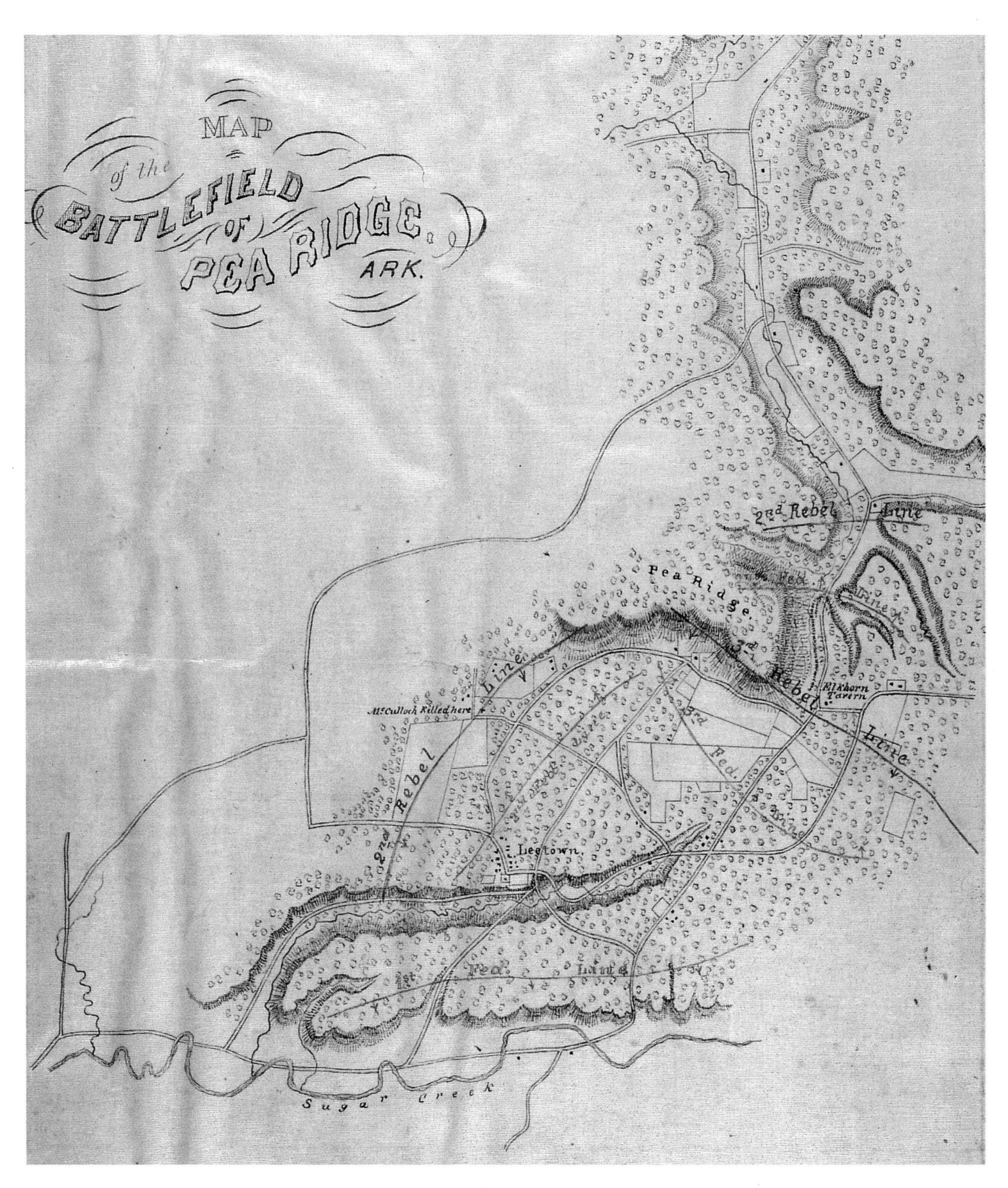

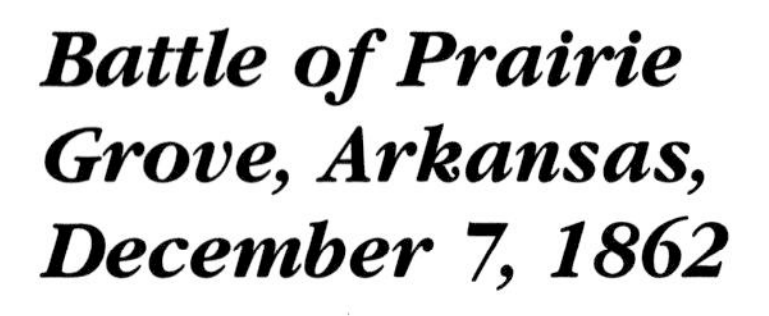

Battle of Prairie Grove, Arkansas, December 7, 1862

Far Right: In the Trans-Mississippi Theater, Confederate forces under General Thomas Hindman surprised a Union force under Generals Blunt and Herron at Prairie Grove, Arkansas, on December 7, 1862. This manuscript map of the battle, showing Federal positions in blue and Confederate in red (successive Federal positions are numbered), was drawn by one T. W. Williams of the 15th Illinois Infantry.

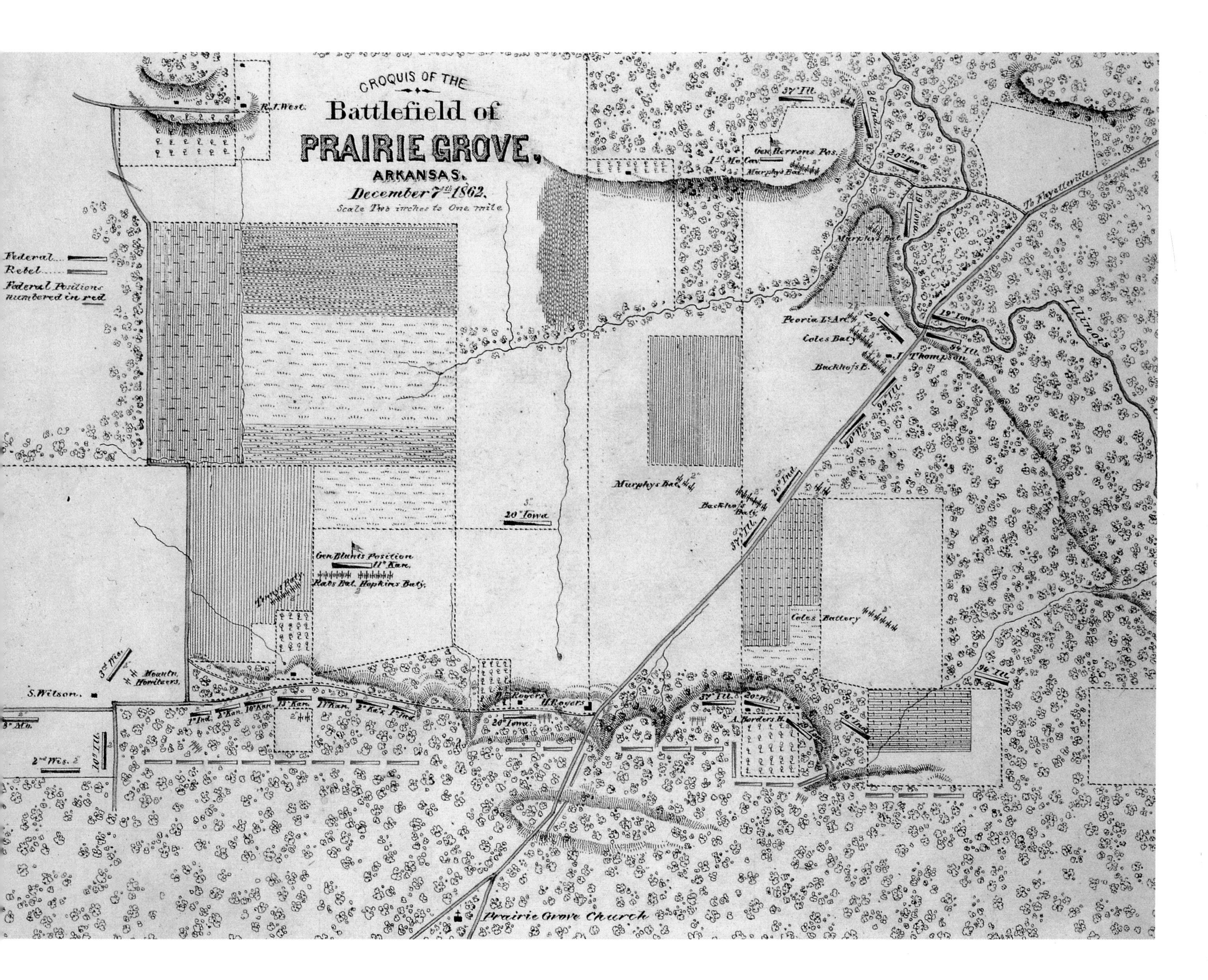

CROQUIS OF THE
Battlefield of
PRAIRIE GROVE,
ARKANSAS.
December 7th 1862.
Scale Two inches to One mile
Federal
Rebel
Federal Positions numbered in red
R. J. West.
37th Ill.
26th Ind.
Gen. Herrons Pos.
1st Mo. Cav.
Murphys Bat.
20th Iowa
19th Iowa
To Fayetteville
Illinois
Peoria Lt. Art.
20th Wis.
Coles Baty
19th Iowa
94th Ill.
J. Thompson
Backhofs B.
94th Ill.
20th Wis.
26th Ind.
Murphys Bat.
Backhofs Baty.
37th Ill.
20th Iowa
Gen. Blunts Position
11th Kan.
Rabs Bat. Hopkins Baty.
Coles Battery
3rd Wis.
Mountn. Howitzers
S. Wilson.
1st Ind.
3rd Kan.
10th Kan.
13th Kan.
11th Kan.
2nd Kas.
1st Ind.
W. Rogers
H. Rogers
20th Iowa
37th Ill.
20th Wis.
A. Borders H.
26th Ind.
94th Ill.
3rd Mo.
2nd Wis.
11th Ill.
Prairie Grove Church

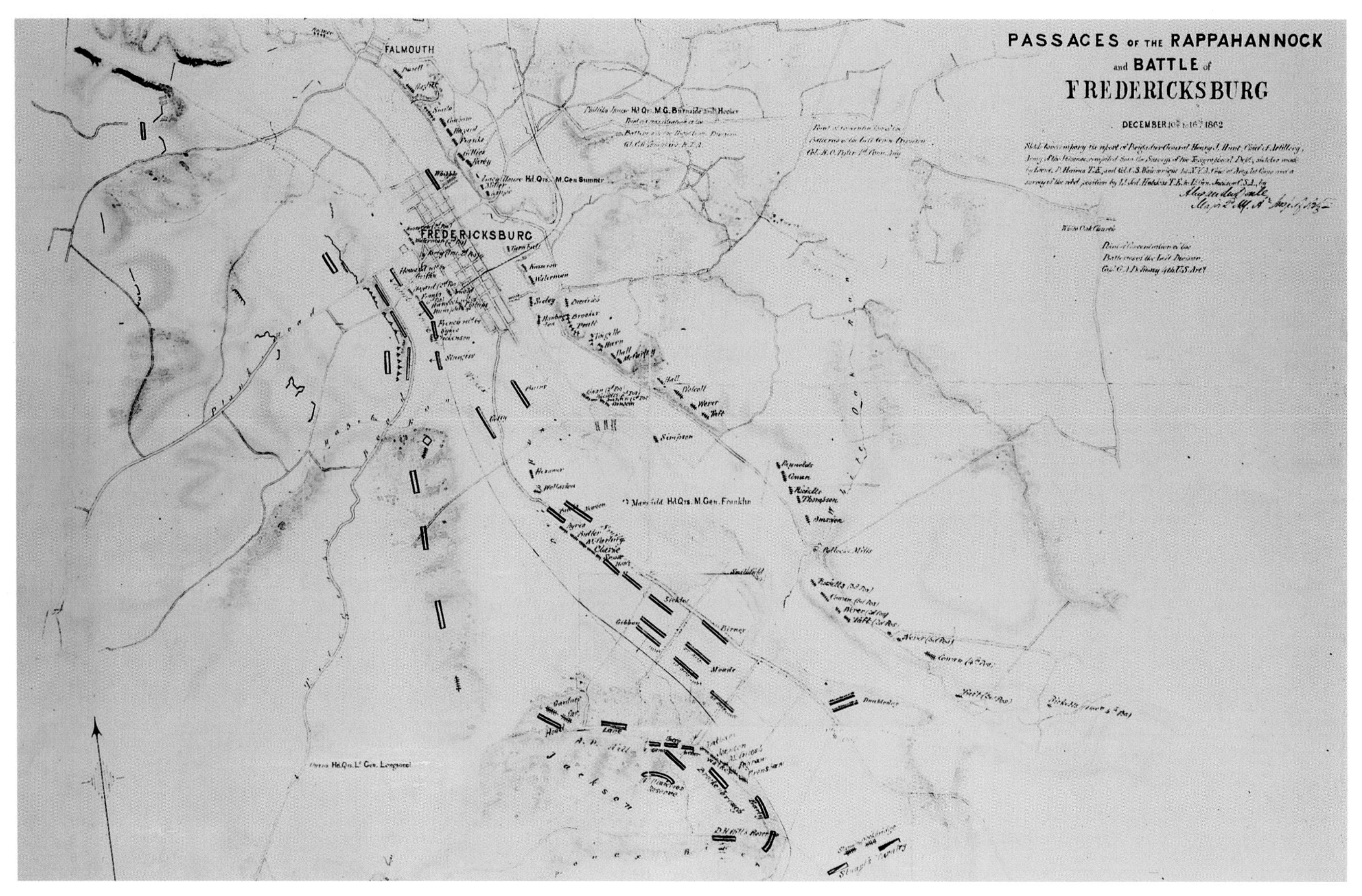

Battle of Fredericksburg, Virginia, December 10–16, 1862

Above: Manuscript map of the Battle of Fredericksburg which was compiled by Union topographers using information from a variety of sources, including a Jedediah Hotchkiss map captured from General Jackson. Fredericksburg was occupied by General Burnside on December 11; his 106,000 troops then attacked Jackson's 72,000 troops north of the city and to the south across the Rappahannock River. Confederate positions are shown in brown and Federal in red and blue. Designations of commands are given and headquarters of commanding generals are located.

Camp Parapet, Louisiana, 1863

Right: Manuscript map of Camp Parapet on the Mississippi, forming part of the defenses of New Orleans, surveyed by M. Maurice Hauke and B. Von Reizenstein in November 1863. New Orleans fell to a Union fleet under Flag Officer David Farragut on April 25, 1862. Drainage channels are shown in blue, buildings in red with surrounding plots in green and brown, roads and streets in brown, and the line of fortifications in blue, green, and brown.

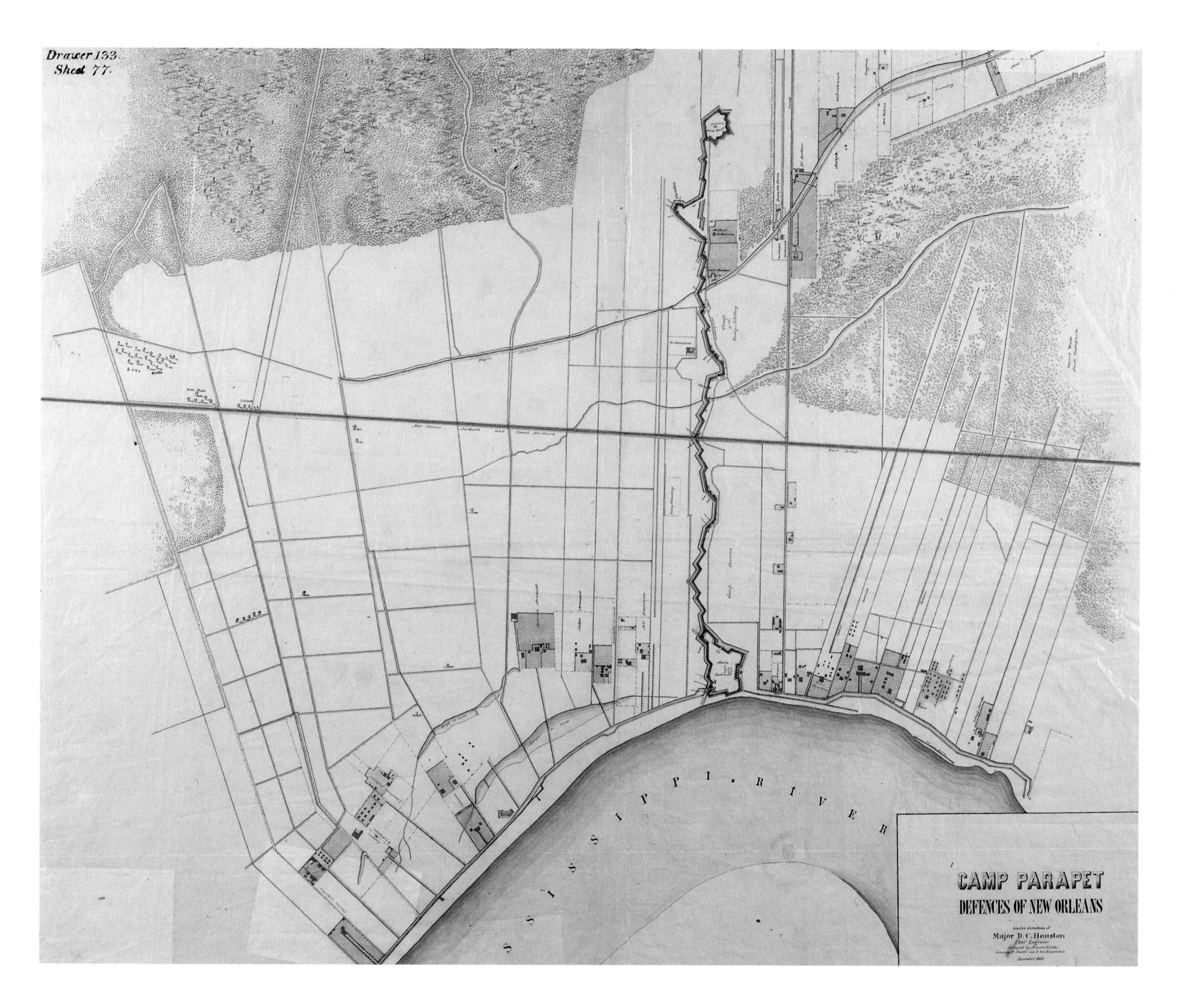
Drawer 133.
Sheet 77.
MISSISSIPPI RIVER
CAMP PARAPET
DEFENCES OF NEW ORLEANS
under direction of
Major D. C. Houston
Chief Engineer

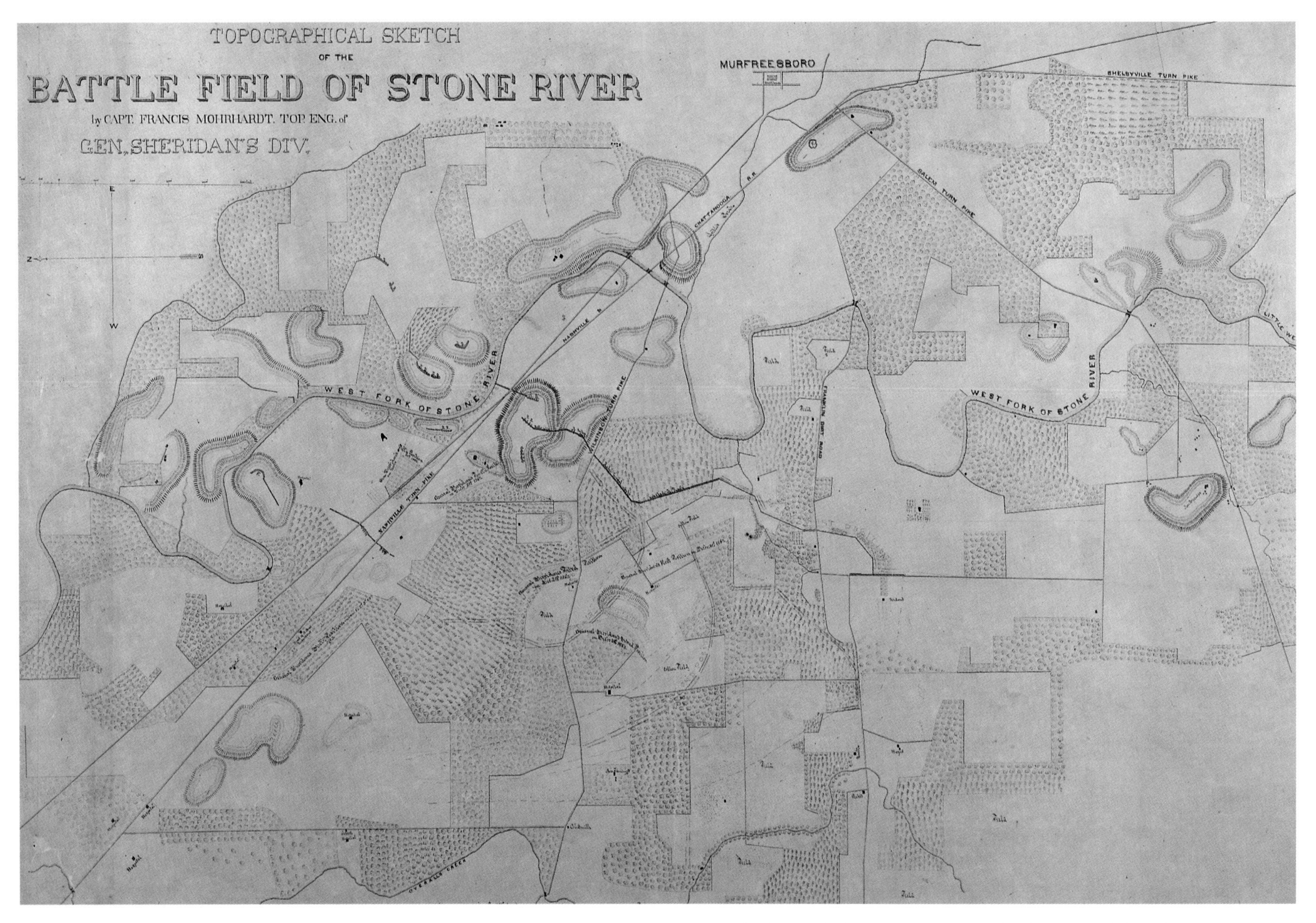

Battle of Stones River, Tennessee, December 29, 1862–January 3, 1863

Above, Right (detail) and Pages 76 and 77: The Battle of Stones River, near Murfreesboro, Tennessee, was fought between December 29, 1862, and January 3, 1863. This (**Above and Right**) is a topographical sketch of the battlefield compiled by an engineer attached to General Sheridan's Division. Note how Union positions are marked in ink, while faint penciled lines show "enemy" positions. The second map (**Pages 76 and 77**) shows the position of Union troops on December 31, 1862. XIV Army Corps positions are in orange, red, and gray. It was surveyed under the direction of Captain Michler by Major J. E. Weiss.

NASHVILLE &
CHATTANO
STONE RIVER
WILKINSON TURN PIKE
FRANKLIN DIRT ROAD
Field
Field
Field
Hospital
Hospital

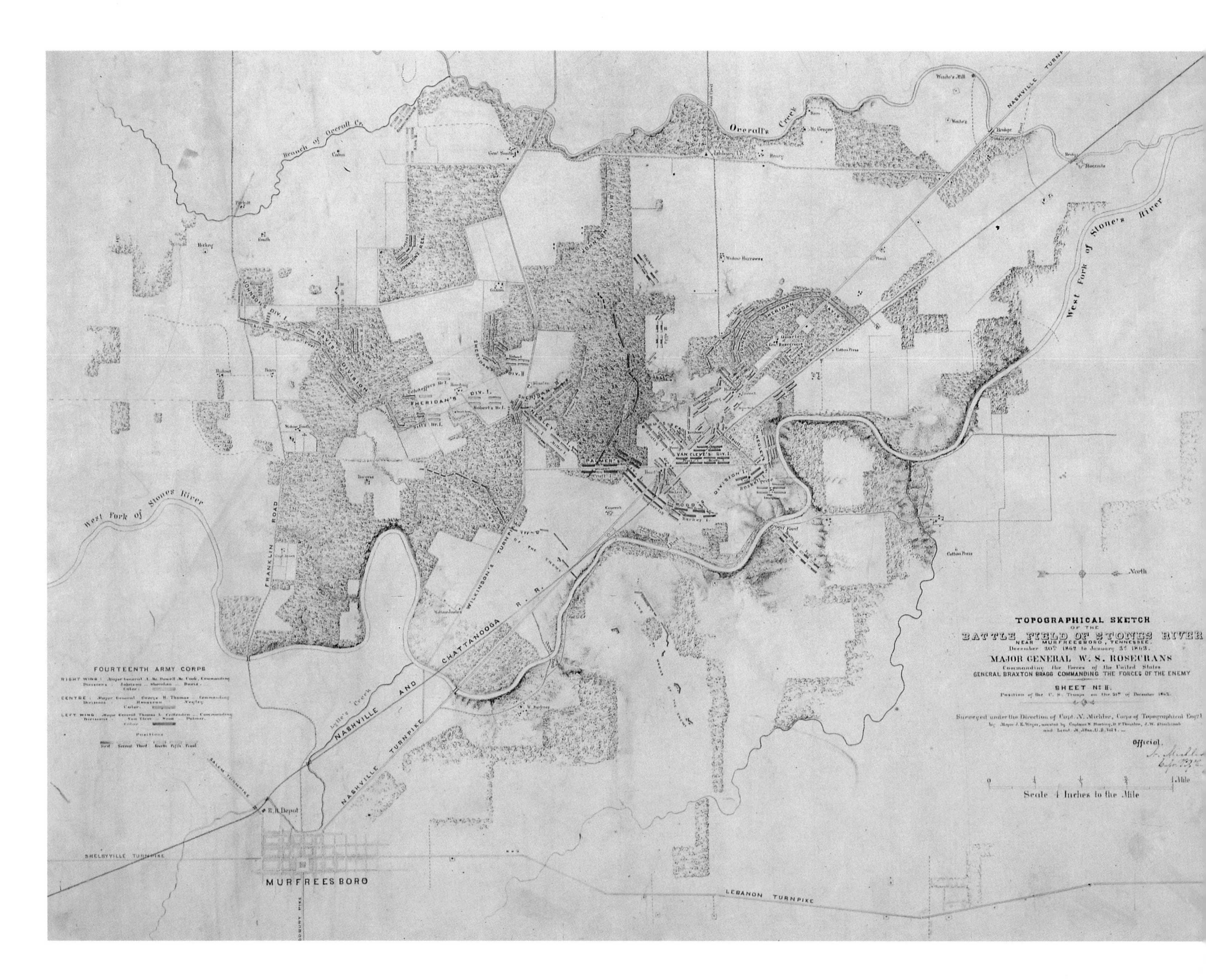

TOPOGRAPHICAL SKETCH
OF THE
BATTLE FIELD OF STONES RIVER
NEAR MURFREESBORO, TENNESSEE.
MAJOR GENERAL W. S. ROSECRANS
GENERAL BRAXTON BRAGG COMMANDING THE FORCES OF THE ENEMY
SHEET No II.
Official.
Scale 4 Inches to the Mile
North
FOURTEENTH ARMY CORPS
RIGHT WING :
CENTRE :
LEFT WING
Positions
Overall's Creek
Branch of Overall Cr.
West Fork of Stones River
NASHVILLE TURNPIKE
NASHVILLE AND CHATTANOOGA R. R.
WILKINSON'S TURNPIKE
FRANKLIN ROAD
SALEM TURNPIKE
SHELBYVILLE TURNPIKE
LEBANON TURNPIKE
MURFREESBORO
R.R. Depot
DAVIS DIVISION
SHERIDAN'S DIV. I.
VAN CLEVE'S DIV. I.
WOOD'S
PALMER'S
SHERIDAN
Cotton Press

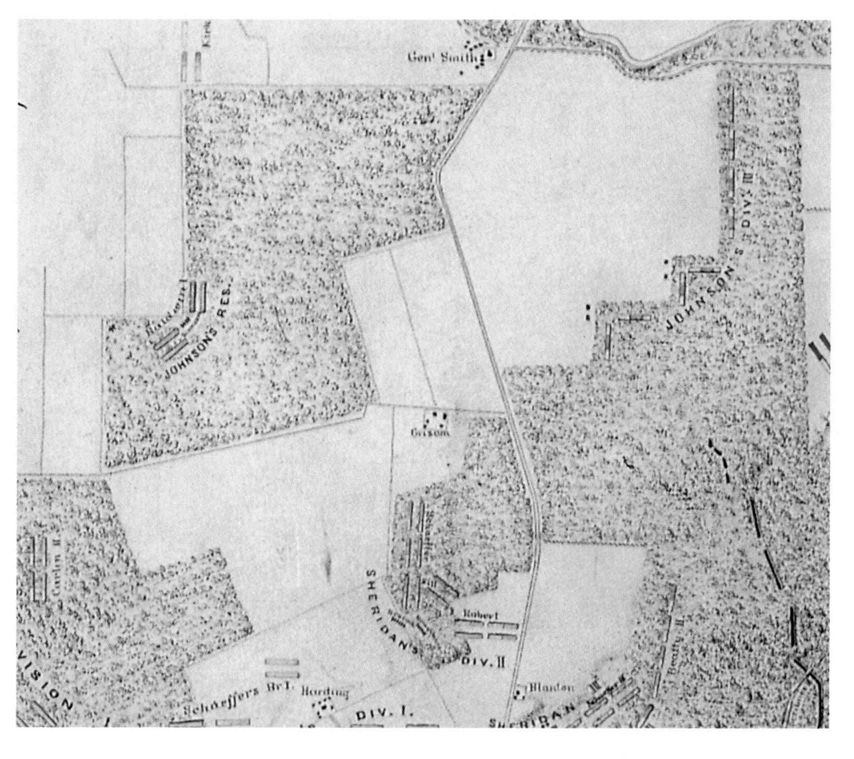

JOHNSON'S RES.
JOHNSON'S DIV. II
SHERIDAN'S DIV. II
Robert
Grisom
DIV. I.

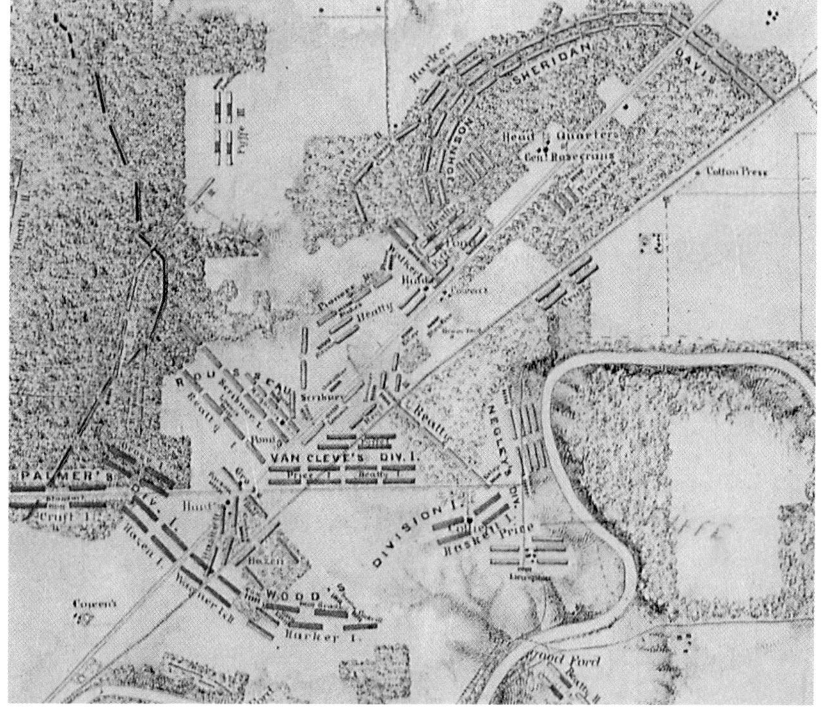

SHERIDAN
DAVIS
JOHNSON
Head Quarters
Cotton Press
VAN CLEVE'S DIV. I.
NEGLEY'S DIV.
DIVISION I.
PALMER'S
WOOD'S
Hazen
Price
Harker I.

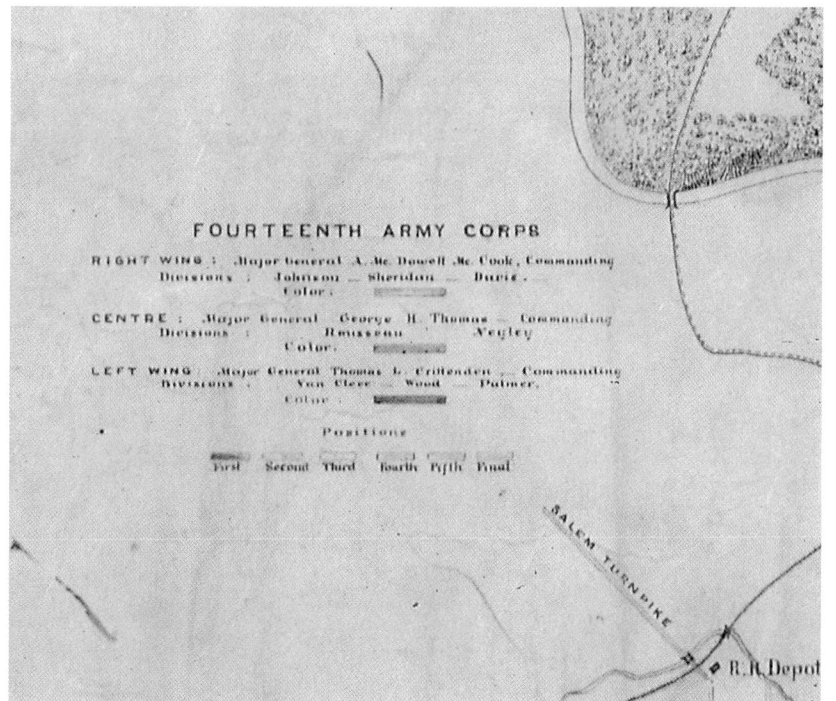

FOURTEENTH ARMY CORPS
RIGHT WING : Major General A. Mc. Dowell Mc. Cook, Commanding
Divisions : Johnson — Sheridan — Davis.
Color :
CENTRE : Major General George H. Thomas — Commanding
Divisions : Rousseau Negley
Color.
LEFT WING : Major General Thomas L. Crittenden — Commanding
Divisions : Van Cleve — Wood — Palmer.
Color :
Positions
First Second Third Fourth Fifth Final
SALEM TURNPIKE
R. R. Depot

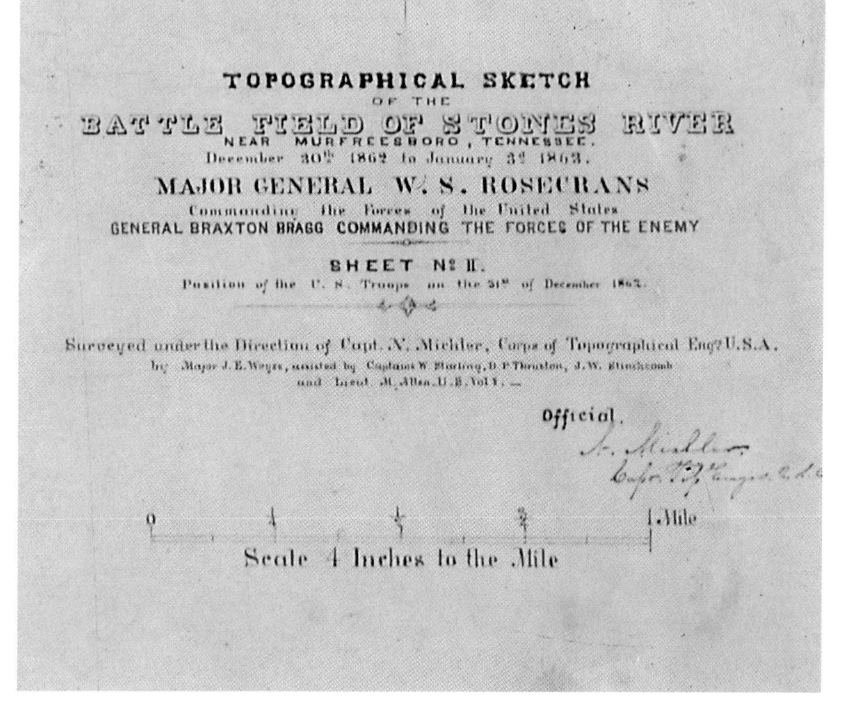

TOPOGRAPHICAL SKETCH
OF THE
BATTLE FIELD OF STONES RIVER
NEAR MURFREESBORO, TENNESSEE.
December 30th 1862 to January 3d 1863.
MAJOR GENERAL W. S. ROSECRANS
Commanding the Forces of the United States
GENERAL BRAXTON BRAGG COMMANDING THE FORCES OF THE ENEMY
SHEET No II.
Position of the U. S. Troops on the 31st of December 1862.
Surveyed under the Direction of Capt. N. Michler, Corps of Topographical Engrs U.S.A.
Official.
Scale 4 Inches to the Mile
0 1/4 1/2 3/4 1 Mile

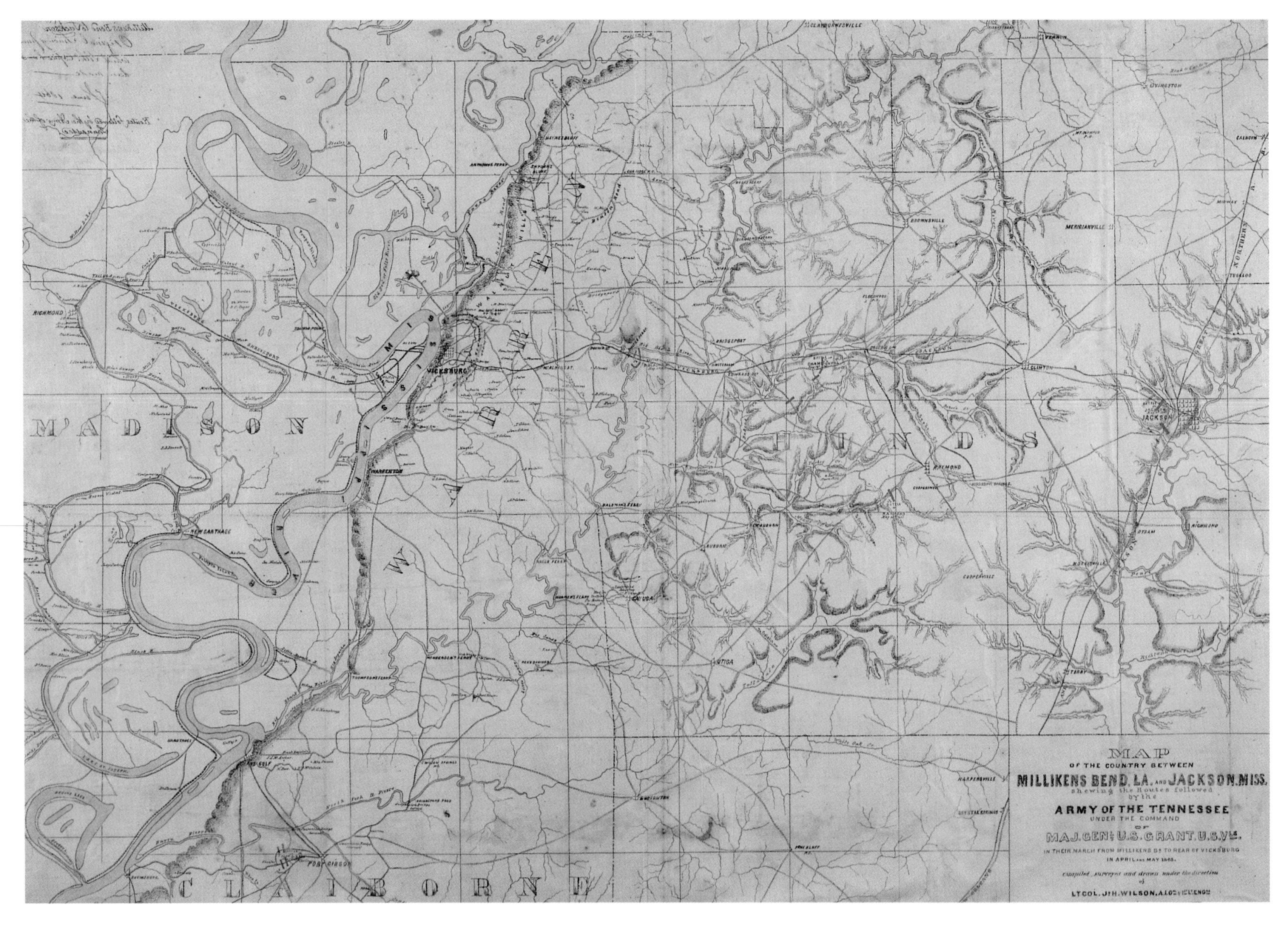

Grant's March on Vicksburg, Mississippi, April 1863

Above: Map showing the route followed by General Ulysses S. Grant's Army of the Tennessee during his march on Vicksburg. His line of march is indicated by orange lines, positions of the Union forces are marked in blue, Confederate troop positions and defenses in red, and drainage features in red. Also marked are the sites of some of the battles of the Vicksburg campaign. The note below the title describes geographical and man-made features.

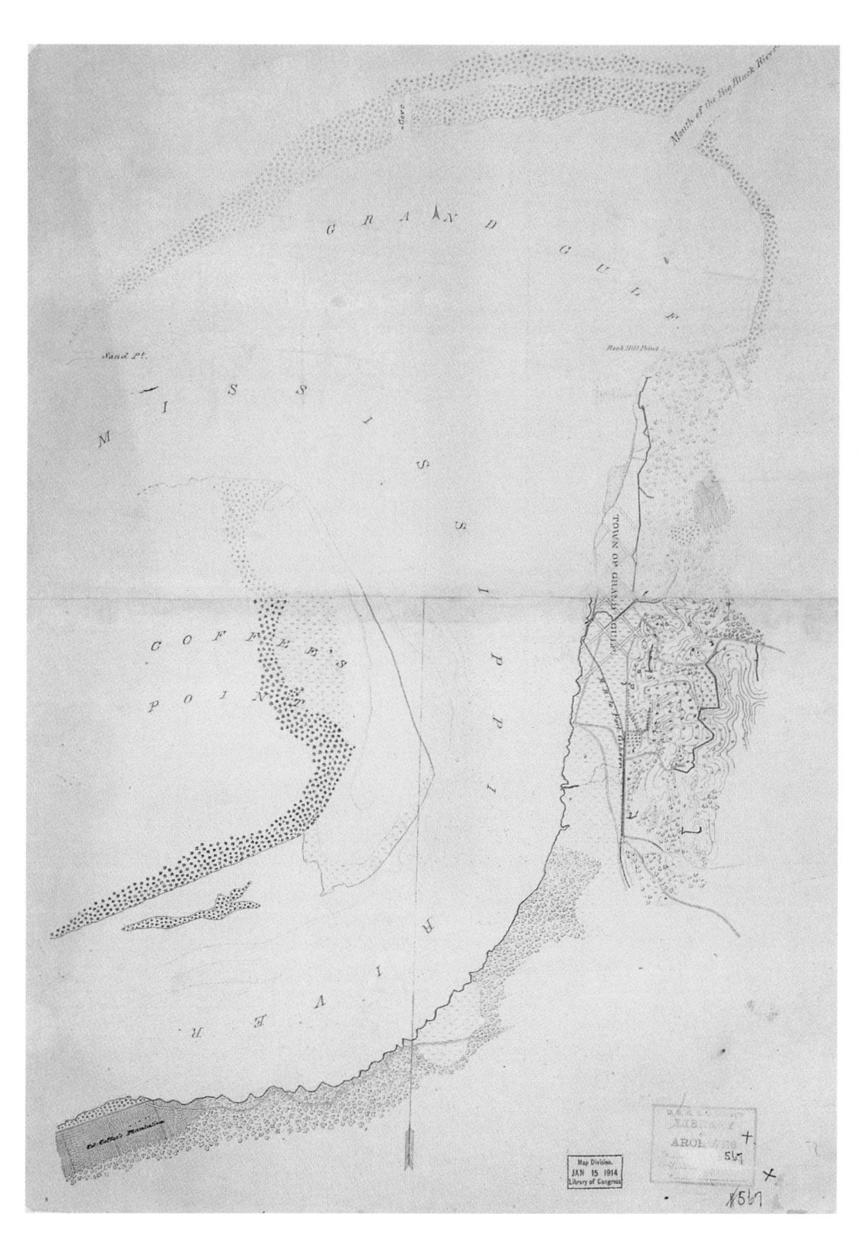

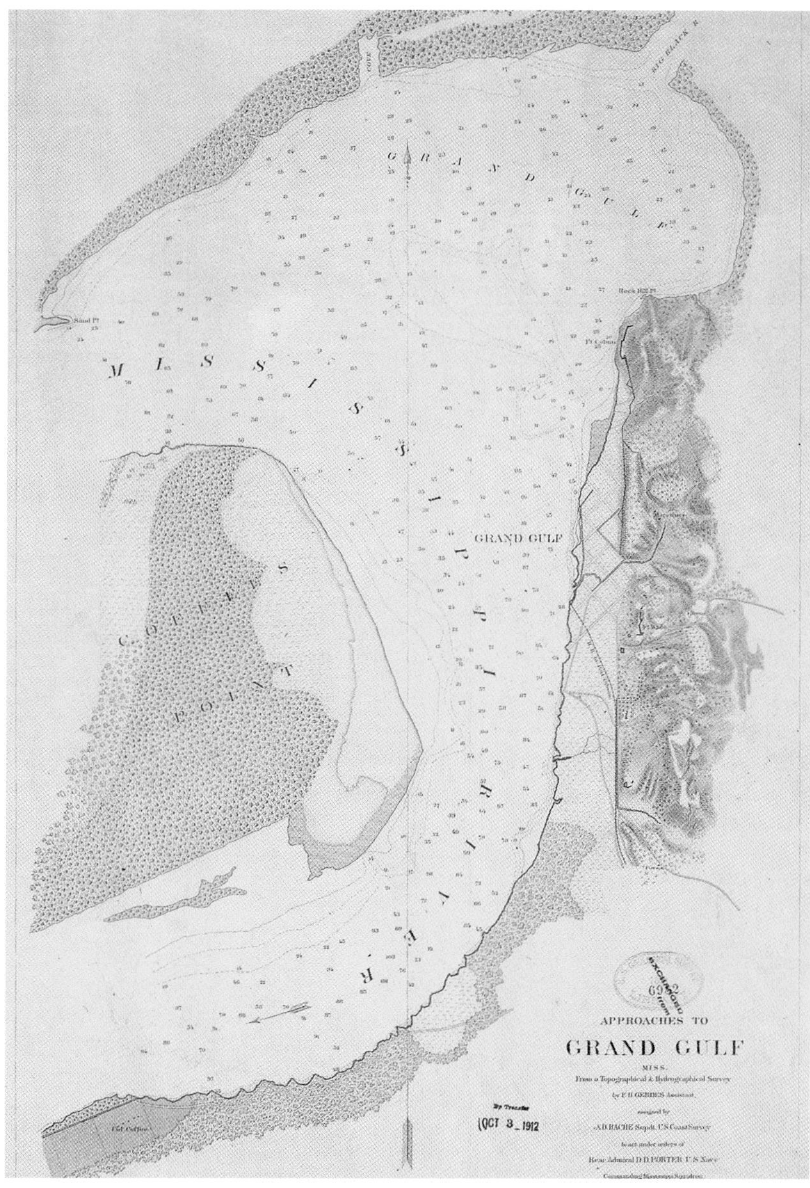

Grand Gulf, Missouri, 1863

Above, Left and Right: Two maps showing the approaches to Grand Gulf, Missouri; the first (**Left**) is a positive photocopy of the original sketch made by F. H. Gerdes of the U.S. Coast Survey during his topographical and hydrographical survey of the area, under orders of Admiral Porter, commander of the Mississippi squadron of the Federal Navy. This was used as a basis for the more detailed map that follows (**Right**), which gives soundings, fortifications overlooking the river, and detail of the vegetation. Note how Gerdes has elected to use contour lines on the original sketch, and haching on the published chart. Photocopying (or "sun-printing") as a process for the reproduction of maps was in its infancy, and the results were crude when compared to modern standards, but allowed mapmakers to reduce the time-consuming and costly techniques of tracing and lithographic printing.

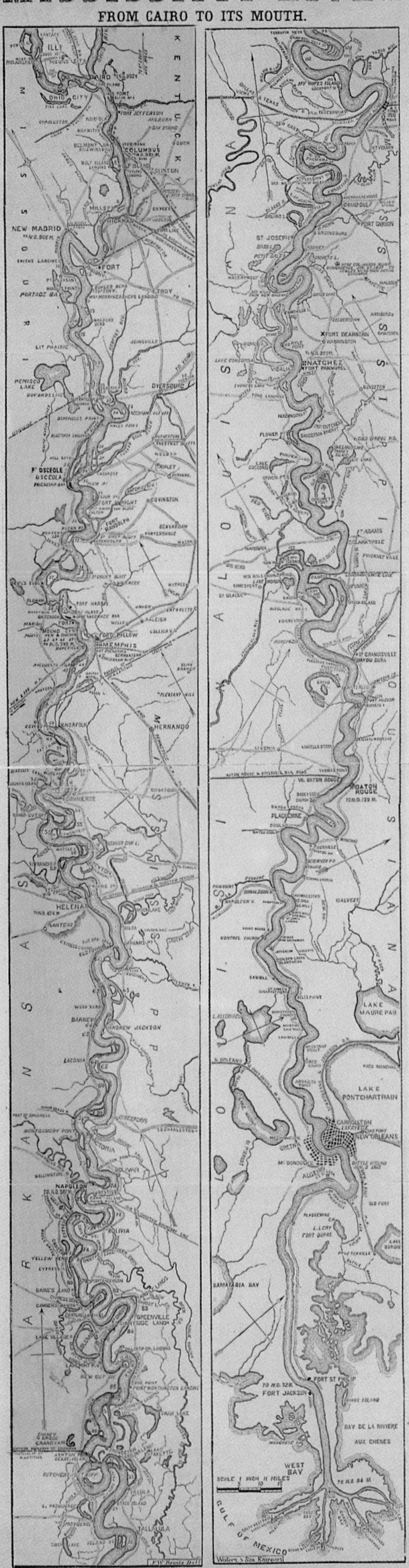

Mississippi River, 1863

Left and Right: H.H. Lloyd and Co. of New York and J. T. Lloyd of New York were rival commercial publishers who produced maps of the war. In 1863 both houses issued a map of the Mississippi River, which are shown here. H. H. Lloyd's map **(Left)** was printed from a wood engraving prepared by Waters and Co. and then colored by hand. This process was criticised by J. T. Lloyd, who had an acrimonious dispute with his rival, whom he accused of trading on his name. Lloyd comments on the lithographed map, undoubtedly the more detailed of the two: "This man's (Lloyd's) maps are engraved very coarsely on wood and very erroneous. He follows us with an imitation of every map we issue."

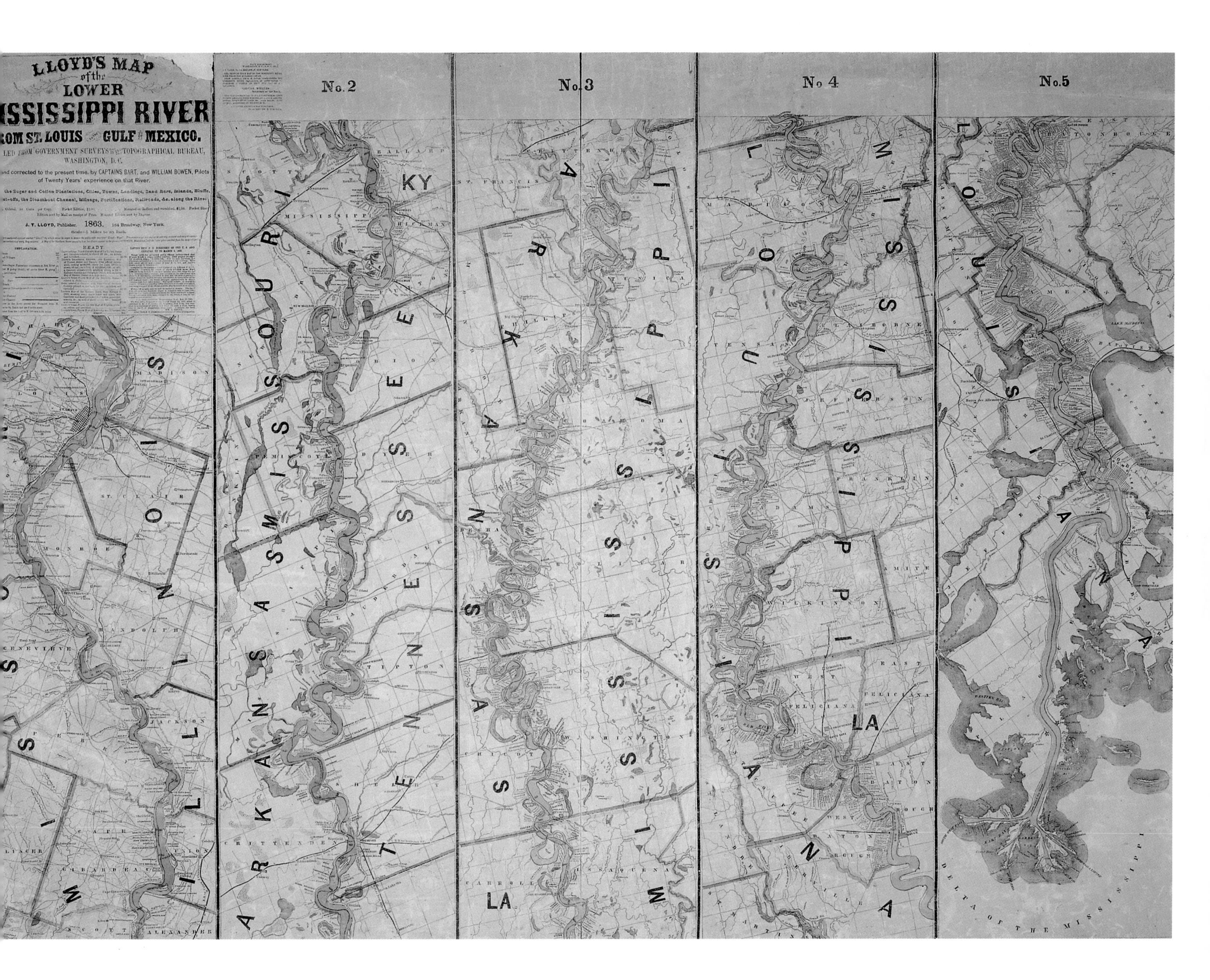
LLOYD'S MAP
of the
LOWER
ISSISSIPPI RIVER
OM ST. LOUIS GULF MEXICO.
LED FROM GOVERNMENT SURVEYS TOPOGRAPHICAL BUREAU,
WASHINGTON, D.C.
and corrected to the present time, by CAPTAINS BART. and WILLIAM BOWEN, Pilots
of Twenty Years' experience on that River.
J. T. LLOYD, Publisher. 1863. 164 Broadway, New York.
EXPLANATION.
READY
No.2
No.3
No 4
No.5
KY
LA
LA
LA

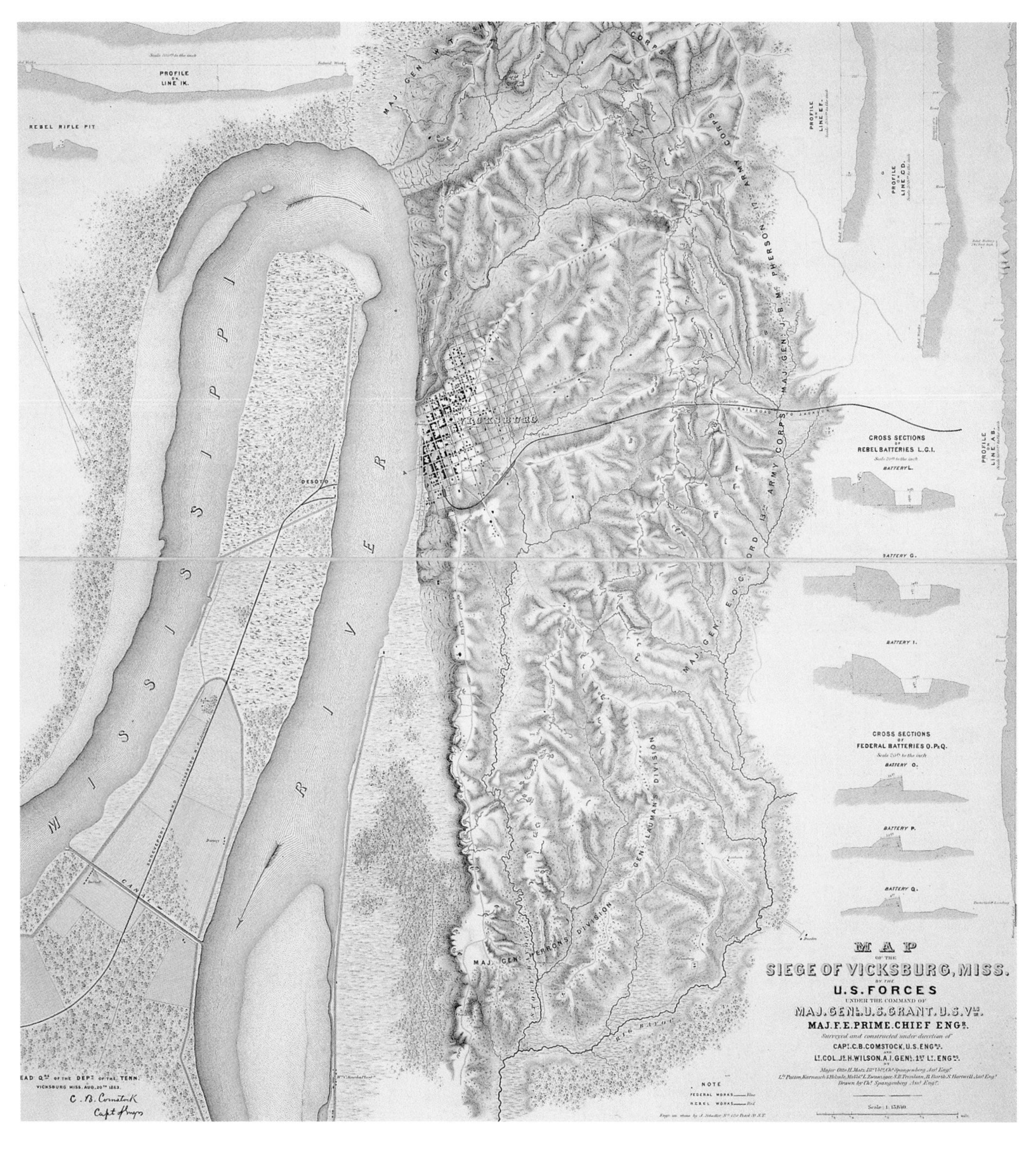

Siege of Vicksburg, Mississippi, May–July 1863

Left and Right: The siege of Vicksburg—an overview (**Right**) compiled at the U.S. Coast Survey Office of General Grants operations against the Confederate stronghold, with annotation showing the major battles, and Vicksburg (**Left**) itself. The names of some of the more prominent Union topographical engineers appear in the title, notably Captain Comstock and Major Matz. Drawn by Charles Spangenberg from a survey by Matz, it includes detailed information on the entrenchments, roads, streets, railroads, hachures, vegetation, houses, and drainage surrounding Vicksburg, and also gives five topographical profiles and cross-sections of artillery batteries.

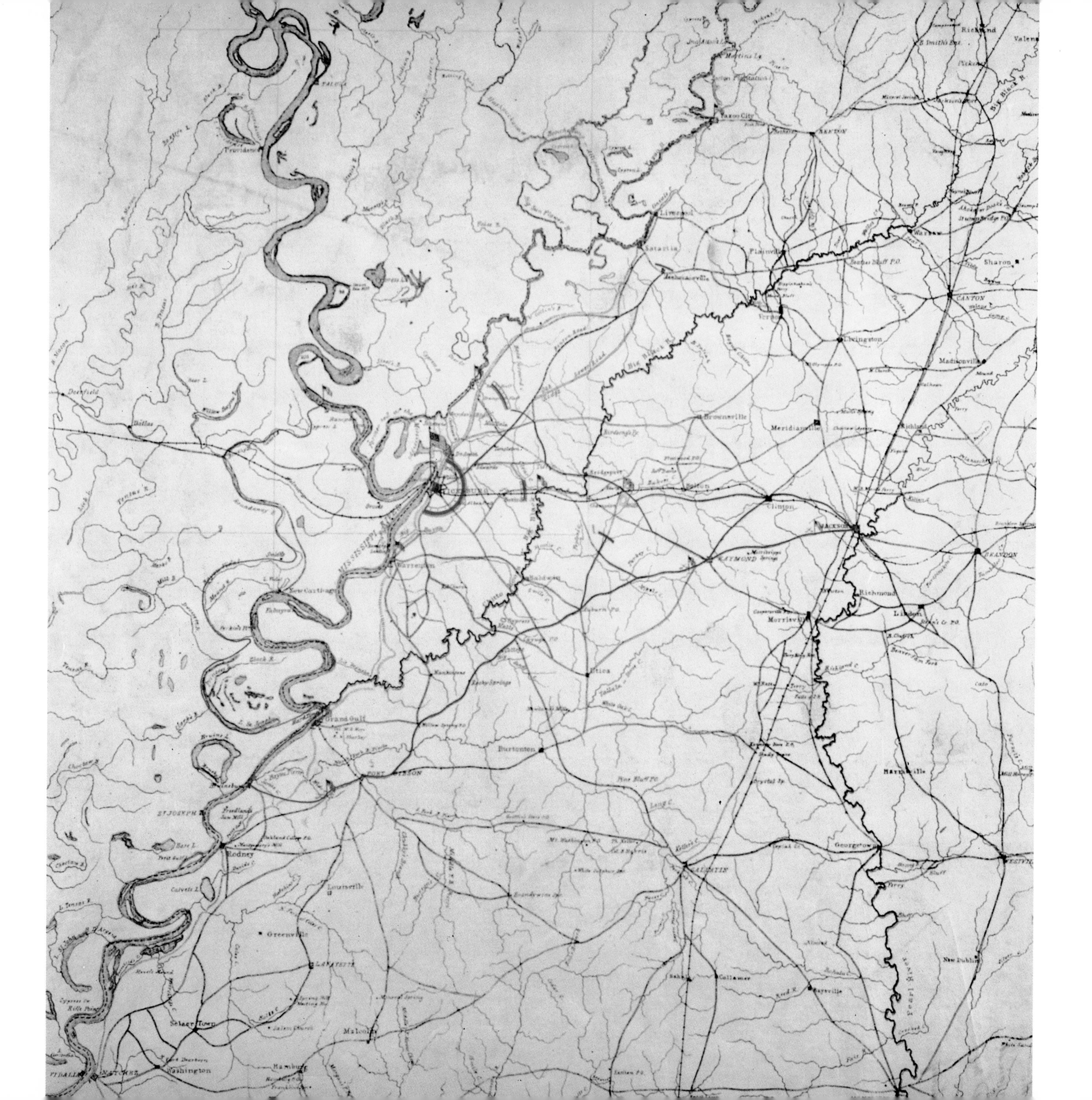

MISSISSIPPI
Providence
Yazoo City
Benton
Canton
Sharon
Livingston
Madisonville
Brownsville
Meridianville
Clinton
Raymond
Brandon
Richmond
Warrenton
New Carthage
Utica
Grand Gulf
Port Gibson
St Joseph
Rodney
Louisville
Greenville
Lafayette
Georgetown
Collamer
Selser Town
Washington
Natchez
Vidalia
New Dublin
Pearl River
Big Black R.
Dallas
Deerfield
Hamburg
Malcolm

Battle of Chancellorsville, Virginia, May 2–4, 1863

Right: This map shows Union and Confederate troop dispositions as at 4.00 p.m. on May 2, 1863, the first day of the three-day battle that ended in success for the Confederates. However, in the process "Stonewall" Jackson—Lee's "strong right arm" was wounded. He died a week later of infection.

Below Right: A sketch map of the three-day battle by Jedediah Hotchkiss for General Lee, with Confederate positions indicated in red and Union in purple. Last is a detailed map of Chancellorsville and the area immediately surrounding, showing the position of Howard's 11th Corps and Confederate entrenchments. At the top right-hand corner of this map is a small plan of the action at Dranesville, Virginia, on December 20, 1861.

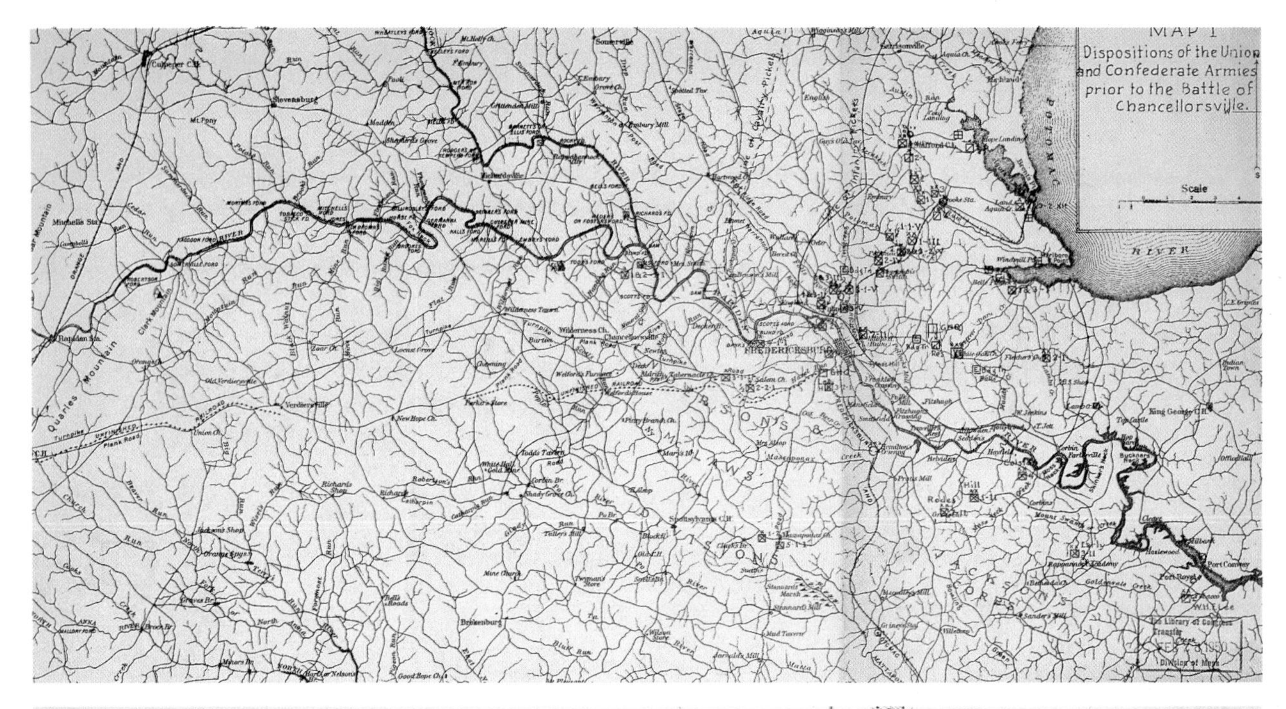

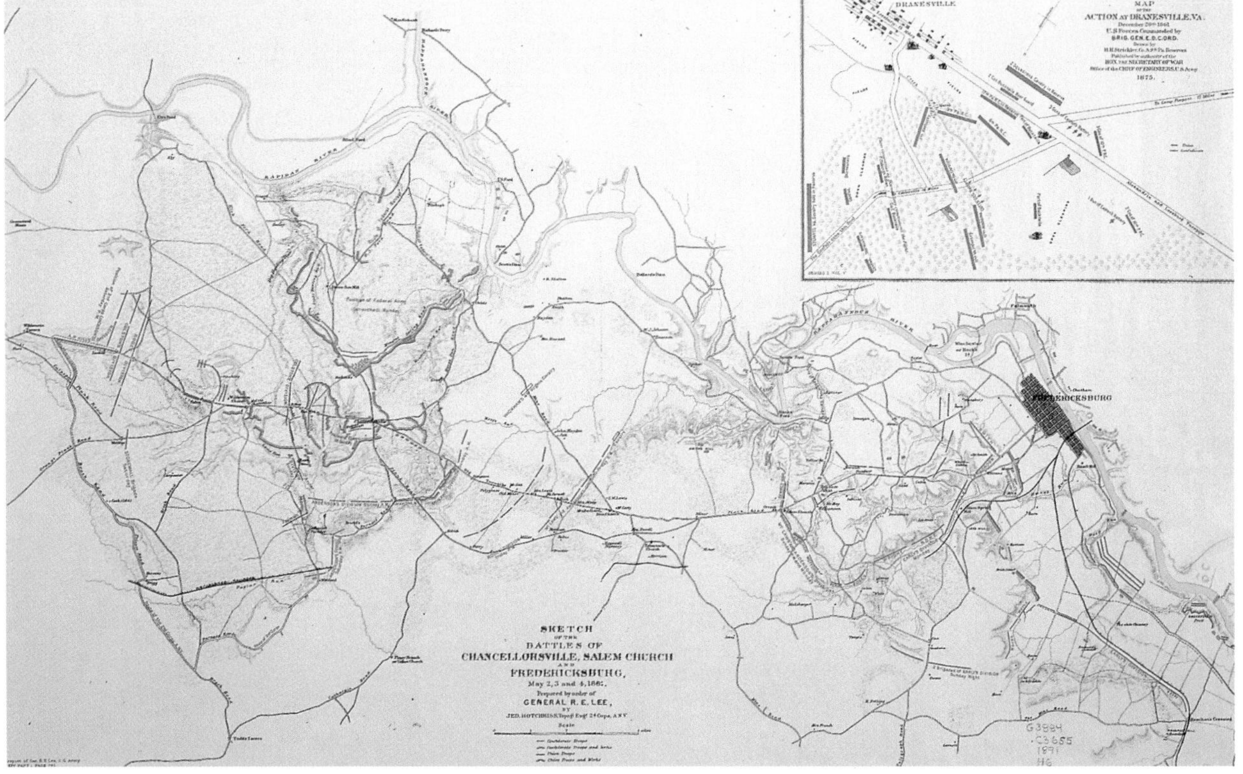

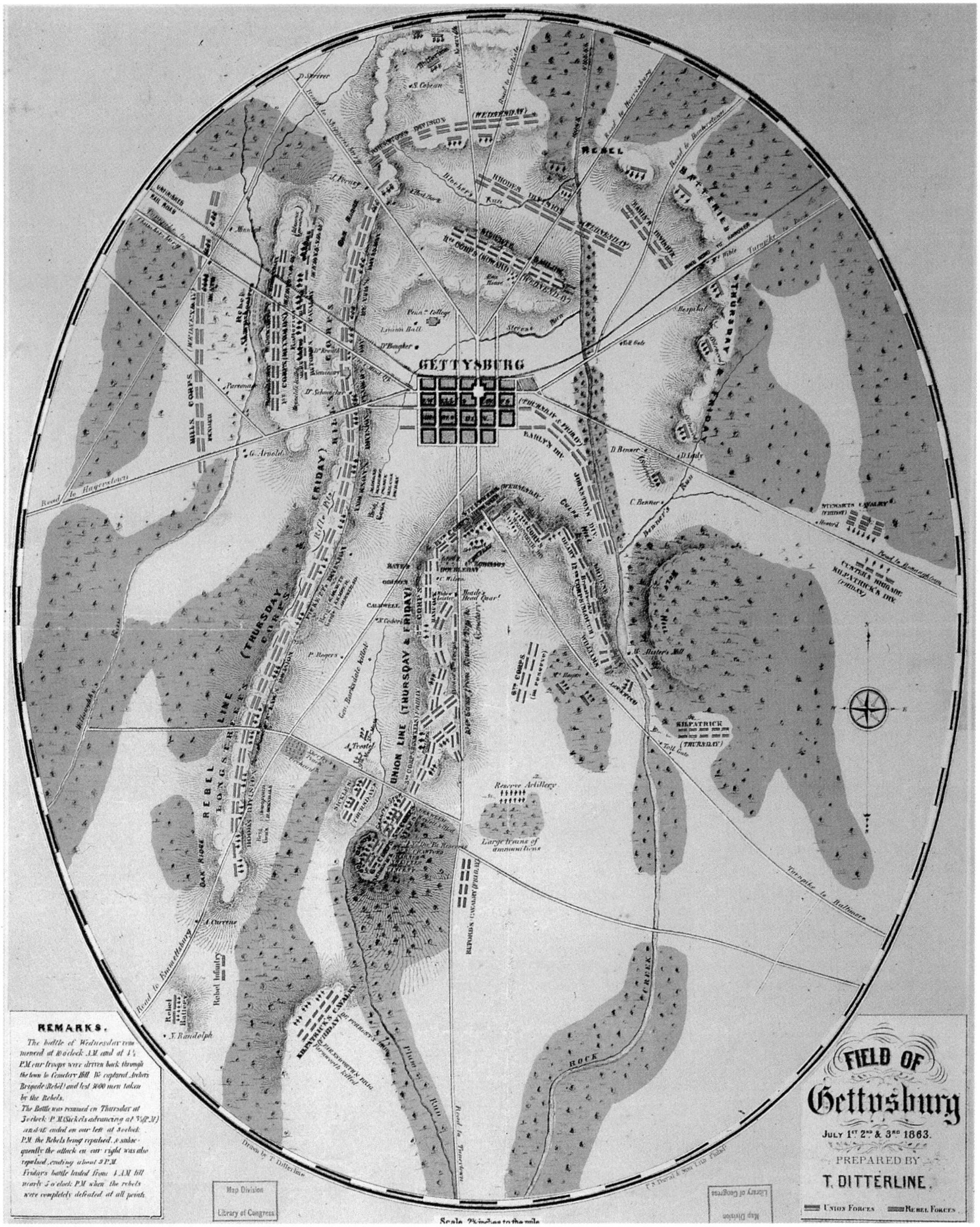

Battle of Gettysburg, Pennsylvania, July 1–3, 1863

Left and Pages 86 to 91: The Battle of Gettysburg was the culmination of a month-long campaign by General Robert E. Lee in which he attempted an invasion of the North. Gettysburg is often called the most important battle in American history, and at the end of its third day, after desperate fighting with over 50,000 casualties from both sides, Lee started to retreat back to Virginia.

Left: This attractive oval-shaped lithograph map of the battle was prepared by Theodore Ditterline to illustrate his 24-page pamphlet entitled *Sketch of the battles of Gettysburg*, published by C.A Alvord in New York in 1863.

Pages 86 (and details 87) and 88 (and details 89): Three years of research went into Bachelder's 1876 series of maps of the battlefield, covering each day of the battle (illustrated are July 1 and 2). Remarkably detailed and accurate, they were based on a postwar survey made by General G. K. Warren, General Meade's Chief Topographical Engineer during the battle, and are perhaps the finest maps to come out of the war. Note the use of complex contour lines to show relief.

Page 90 (and details 91): This is a colored bird's eye view of the battlefield by John B. Bachelder and features the signatures of the leading Union commanders, who have testified as to the accuracy of the lithographed map.

MAP OF THE
BATTLE FIELD OF GETTYSBURG.
Published by authority of the Hon. the SECRETARY OF WAR,
Office of the CHIEF OF ENGINEERS U.S. Army.
1876.
FIRST DAY'S BATTLE
GENERAL ROBERT E. LEE
MAJOR GENERAL GEORGE G. MEADE
POSITIONS OF TROOPS
OFFICIAL REPORTS
OFFICERS OF BOTH ARMIES.

W. ROSS
N. HOFFMAN
EWELL'S CORPS
W
E
S
N. BISELMAN
J. FORNEY
JOHN BLOCHER
SMITHY
I. BENDER
HERR TAVERN
CHAMBERSBURG
PIKE
SPANGLER
D. LEAFER
M. JOHNS
WADSWORTH'S DIV.
VON AMSBERG
DILGER
HAGY
SCHURZ'S DIVISION
COUNTY ALMSHOUSE
J. CRAWFORD
MEDICINAL SPRING
E. M'PHERSON
HECKMAN
PENN. COLLEGE
J. GRIMES
R. J. TATE
G E T T Y S B U
S. S. SCHMUCKER
M. SAYER
A. COLE
HOFFMAN
E. HARMAN
J. HERBST
HAGERSTOWN ROAD
D. FINNEFROCK
EAST CEMETERY

MAP OF THE
BATTLE FIELD OF GETTYSBURG.
JULY 1ST 2ND 3RD 1863.
Published by authority of the Hon. the SECRETARY OF WAR,
Office of the CHIEF OF ENGINEERS U.S. Army.
1876.
SECOND DAY'S BATTLE
GENERAL ROBERT E. LEE
MAJOR GENERAL GEORGE G. MEADE
Scale. 1 inch represents 1000 feet.
SCALES.
POSITIONS OF TROOPS
OFFICIAL REPORTS
consultations on the field, private letters, and
explanations
OF THE
OFFICERS OF BOTH ARMIES.
BOSTON MASS.
JOHN B. BACHELDER.
1876.

GEN. NEWTON
GEN. SEDGWICK
Com'd 6 Corps
THIS COLUMN
Not Engaged
ROUND TOP
HOOD'S DIVISION
HUMPHREYS
CALDWELL
HOWE
GRANT
WHEATON
SHALER
TORBERT
GEN. SYKES

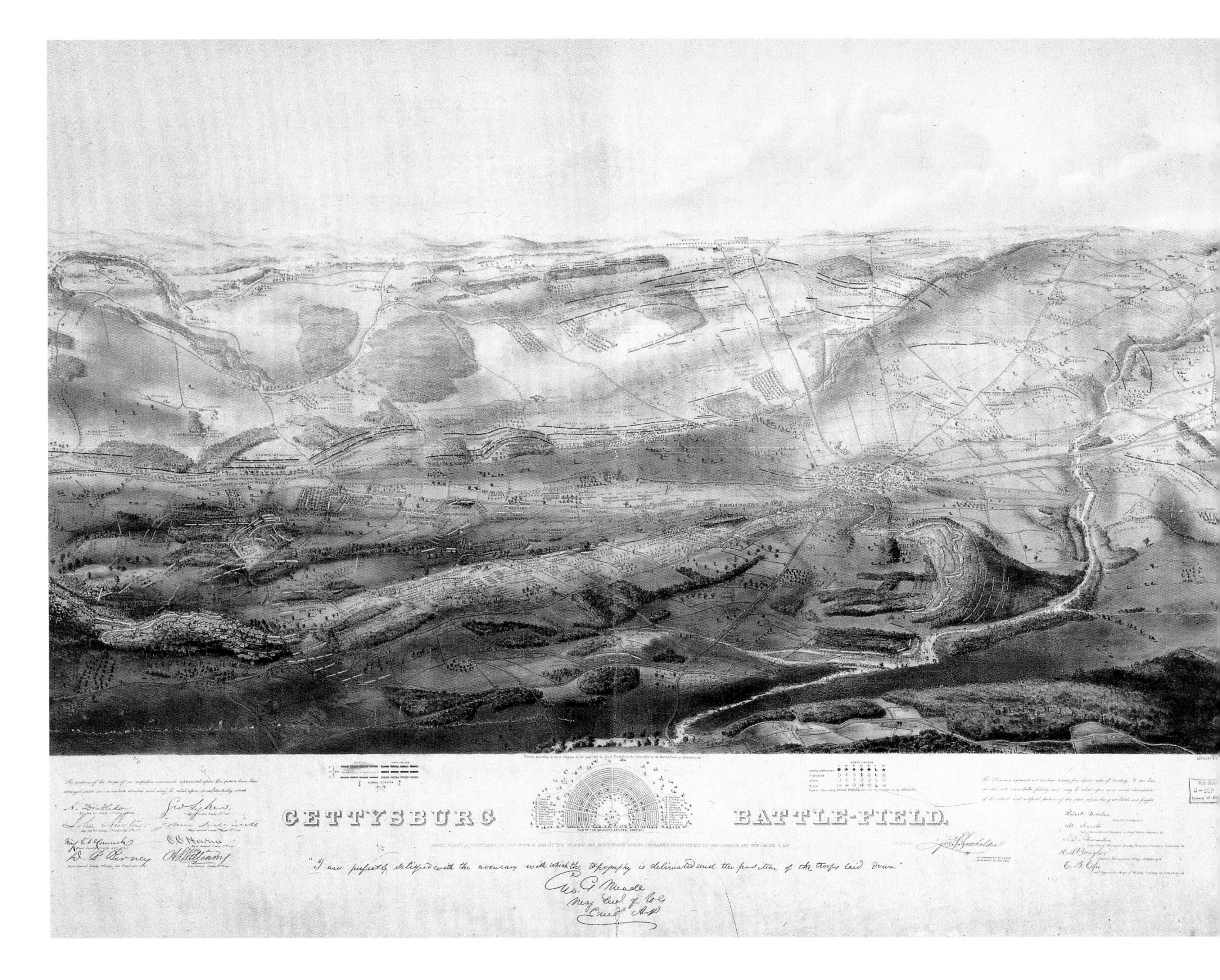
GETTYSBURG
BATTLE-FIELD.
PLAN OF THE SOLDIERS NATIONAL CEMETERY
SIGNAL STATION
CORPS BADGES
EMMITSBURG

GEN SCHURZ

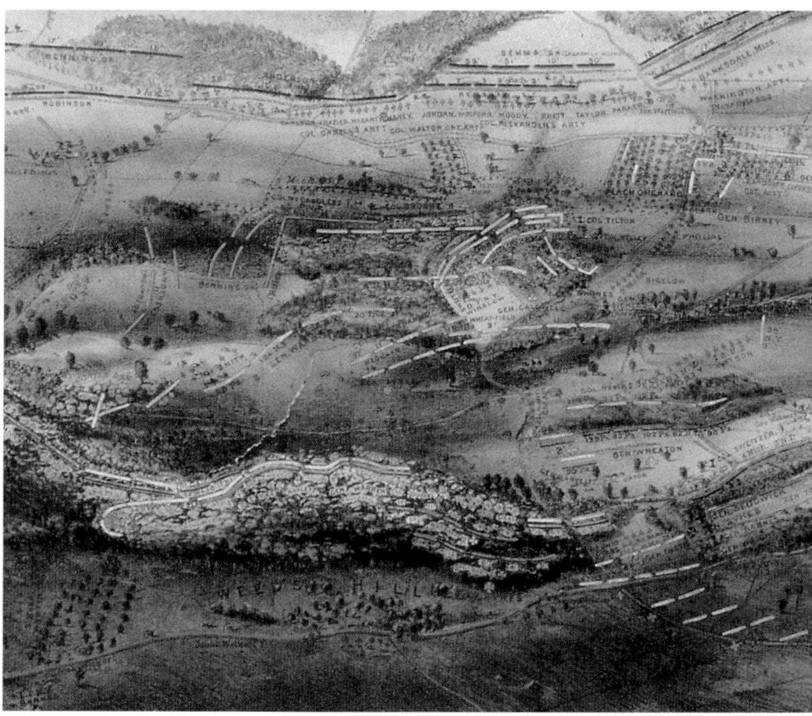
GEN BIRNEY

GEN SCHURZ
HARRISBURG ROAD
HANOVER ROAD
CULP'S HILL

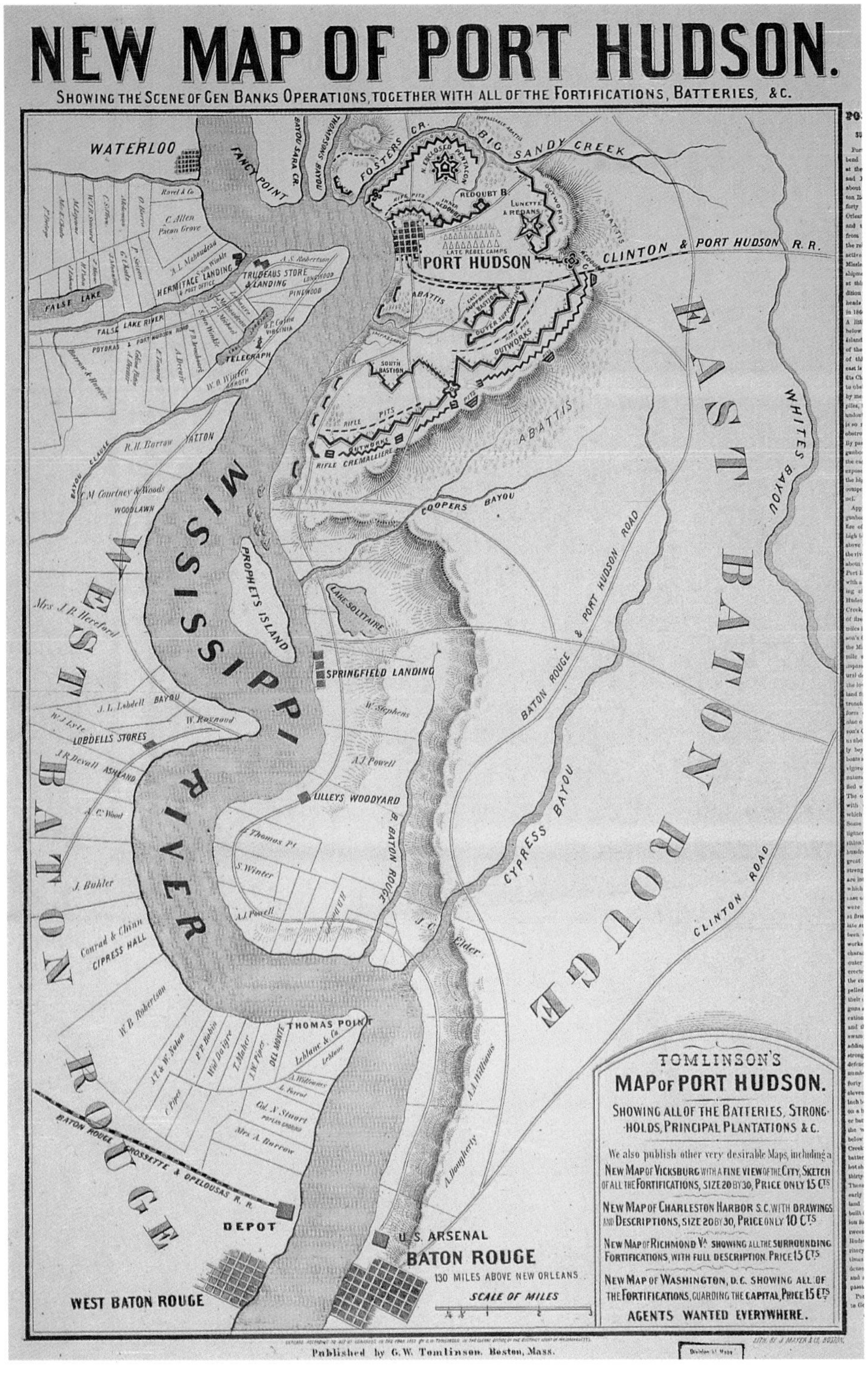

Port Hudson, Louisiana, July 23, 1863

Left: This commercial map of Port Hudson, Louisiana, from Boston publisher George W. Tomlinson was produced on July 23, 1863—only two weeks after the Federals took the town after besieging it from May 21 to July 8, 1863. The fall of Port Hudson left the whole of the Mississippi under Federal control, and gave the Union over 6,000 Confederate prisoners along with large quantities of ammunition. The besieged population of the city had been reduced to eating dogs and rats.

Louisiana, 1863

Right: Large scale map (dated January 14, 1863) of Louisiana from the papers of Federal Major-General Nathanial Banks. The wear to this map indicates that it was carried in the field. It covers the country from New Orleans to Vicksburg, and although it is annotated, there are no troop movements identified.

Department of the Gulf.
MAP No 13
STATE of LOUISIANA
showing Theatre of Operations of the Forces
under command of Maj. Gen. Banks
during the months of March, April, May, June and July and endin
with the Reduction of Port Hudson July 8th 1863.
Prepared by Order of
MAJ. GEN. N. P. BANKS.
D. C. HOUSTON
Major & Chief Engineer
AUGUST 1863.
PHOTOGRAPHED BY WALTER OGILVIE
DRAWN BY B. von REIZENSTEIN
SHREVEPORT
VICKSBURG
CLINTON
JACKSON
CANTON
WARRENTON
RAYMOND
GRAND GULF
PORT GIBSON
GALLATIN
HARRISONBURGH
TRINITY
COLUMBIA
NATCHITOCHES
ALEXANDRIA
OPELOUSAS
PORT HUDSON
BATON ROUGE
CLINTON
JACKSON
PLAQUEMINE
DONALDSONVILLE
NEW ORLEANS
LAKE PONTCHARTRAIN
LAKE BORGNE
VERMILLION BAY
COTE BLANCHE BAY
MONTICELLO
FRANKLINTON
NEW IBERIA
THIBODAUX
LAKE SALVADOR
BARATARIA BAY
TIMBALIER BAY

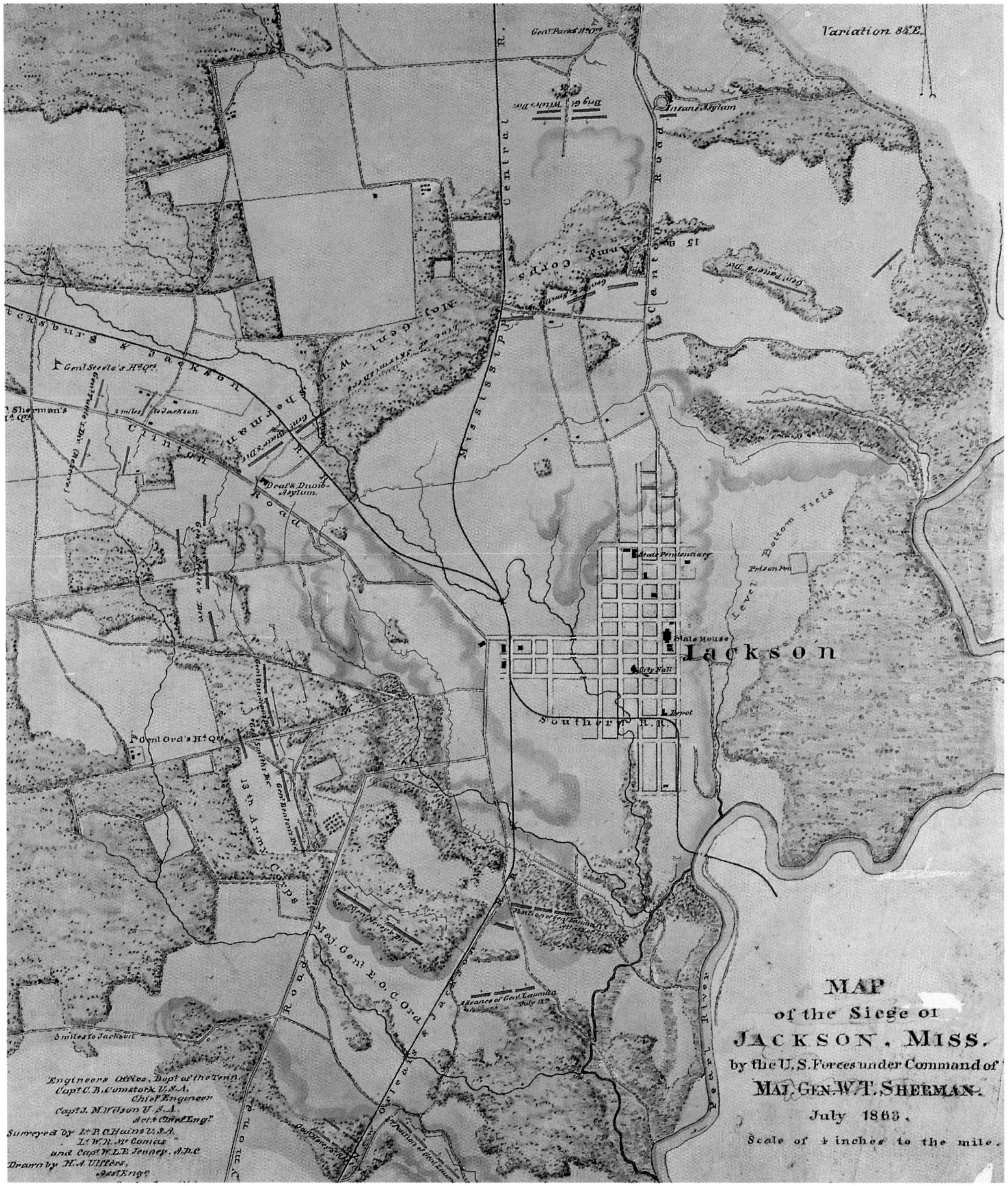

Siege of Jackson, Mississippi, July 1863

Left: Manuscript map of Jackson and vicinity drawn in September 1863, with information from a survey by Lt. P. C. Hains, by H. A. Ulffers, a topographical engineer with the Department of the Tennessee. Grant struck at Jackson in mid-May to prevent a concentration of reinforcements for Vicksburg and on July 16, General Johnston pulled out his Confederate forces, leaving Jackson to Union occupation.

MAP
of the Siege of
JACKSON, MISS.
by the U. S. Forces under Command of
MAJ. GEN. W. T. SHERMAN.
July 1863.
Scale of 4 inches to the mile.

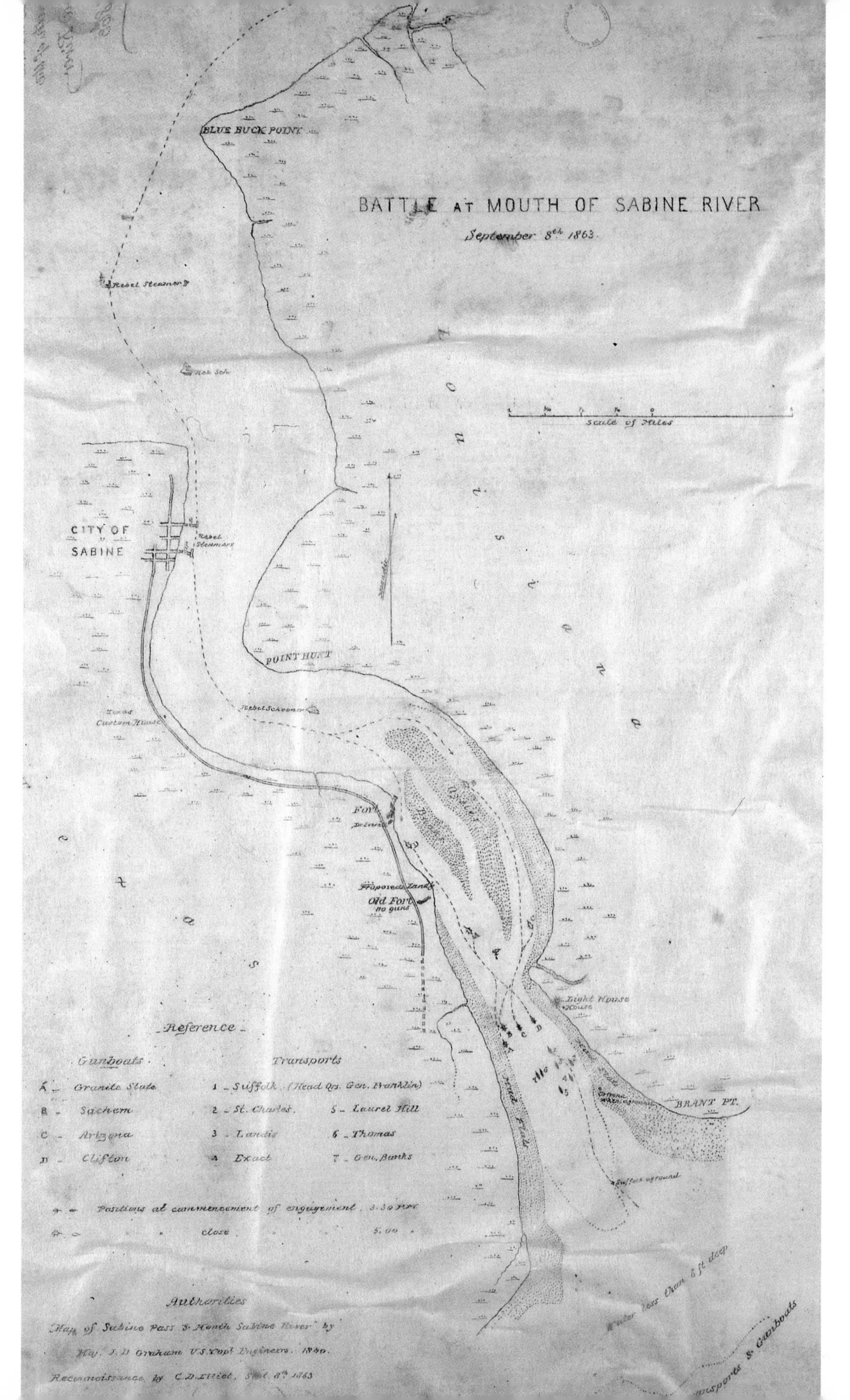

Battle at the Mouth of the Sabine River, Texas, September 5, 1863

Left: Positions of gunboats and transport vessels at 3.30 p.m. and 5.00 p.m. during the Battle of Mouth of Sabine River, September 8, 1863. The individual Federal ships are identified by letters and numbers keyed to a list of names. The positions of Confederate ships are shown upstream. The Federal transports and gunboats had sailed from New Orleans and entered the Sabine Pass in Texas to attack a small Confederate fort. Two of the Union ships were sunk and another forced to surrender, leaving the Union forces no choice but to abandon the operation.

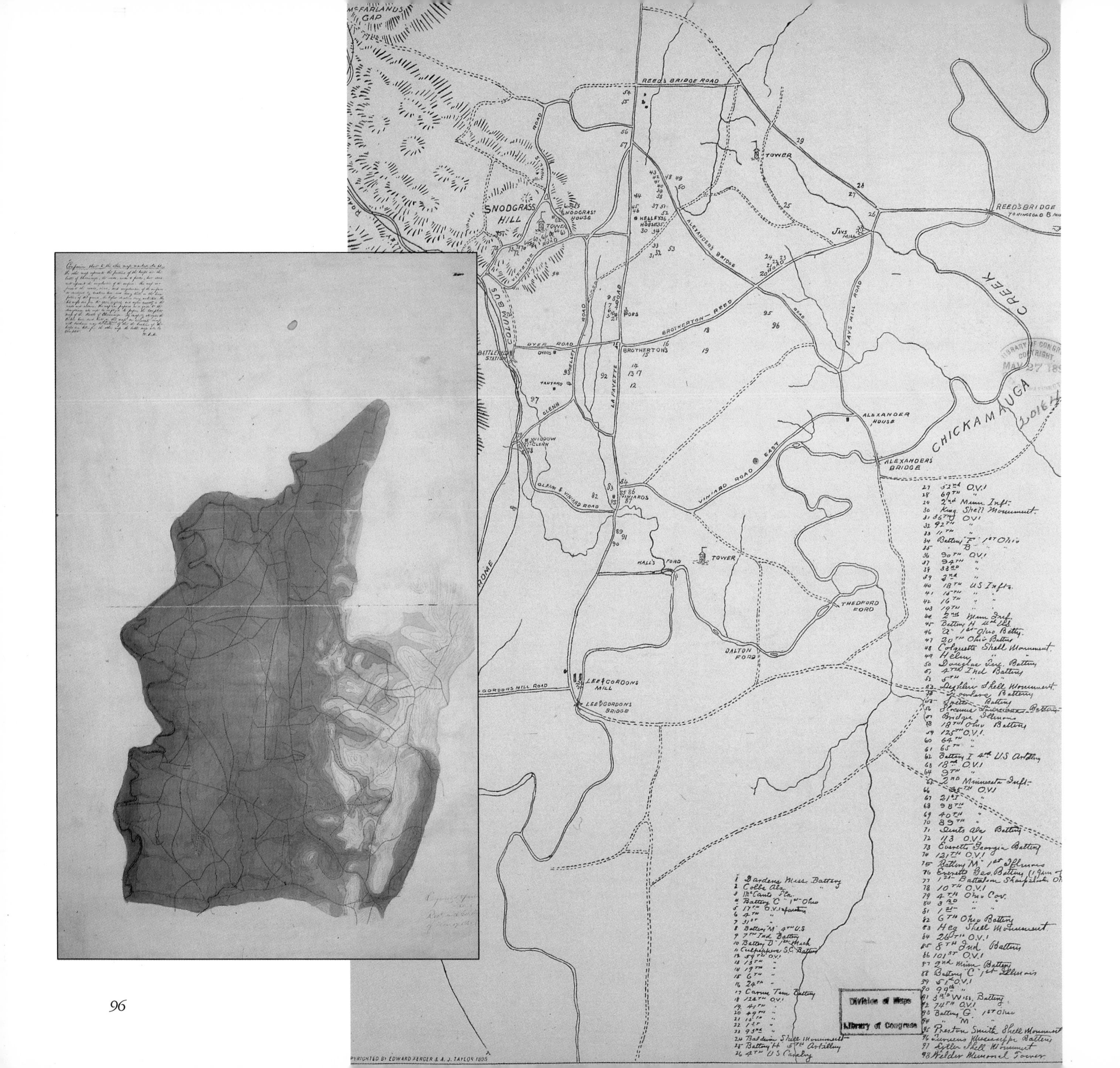

McFARLANDS GAP
REEDS BRIDGE ROAD
TOWER
SNODGRASS HILL
SNODGRASS HOUSE
KELLEYS HOUSE
ALEXANDERS BRIDGE ROAD
JAYS MILL
REEDS BRIDGE
CHICKAMAUGA CREEK
JAYS MILL ROAD
BROTHERTON - REED ROAD
POES
DYER ROAD
BATTLEFIELD STATION
BROTHERTONS
LA FAYETTE ROAD
COLUMBUS
TANYARD
GLENN
WIDOW GLENN
ALEXANDER HOUSE
ALEXANDERS BRIDGE
VINIARD ROAD EAST
VINIARDS
GLENN & VINIARD ROAD
HALL'S FORD
THEDFORD FORD
DALTON FORD
LEE & GORDONS MILL
LEE & GORDONS BRIDGE
GORDONS MILL ROAD
LIBRARY OF CONGRESS COPYRIGHT MAY 27 189
Division of Maps Library of Congress
COPYRIGHTED BY EDWARD FERGER & A. J. TAYLOR 1895
1 Swords Miss. Battery
2 Cobbs Ala.
8 Battery "M" 4th U.S.
9 7th Ind Battery
10 Battery "D" 1st Mich
17 Carnes Tenn Battery
24 Baldwin Shell Monument
25 Battery H 5th Artillery
26 4th U S Cavalry
27 52nd O.V.I
28 69th
29 2nd Minn Infty
30 King Shell Monument
31 36th O.V.I
32 92nd
33 11th
34 Battery "F" 1st Ohio
36 90th O.V.I
37 94th
38 33rd
39 2nd
40 18th US Infty
45 Battery H 4th U.S.
46 "A" 1st Ohio Battery
47 20th Ohio Battery
48 Colquitt Shell Monument
49 Helm
50 Douglas Tex. Battery
51 4th Ind Battery
53 Deshler Shell Monument
57 Bridges Illinois
58 18th Ohio Battery
59 125th O.V.I.
60 64th
61 65th
62 Battery I 4th U.S Artillery
63 18th O.V.I
64 9th
65 2nd Minnesota Infty
66 35th O.V.I
67 21st
68 98th
69 40th
70 89th
72 113 O.V.I
73 Everetts Georgia Battery
74 121st O.V.I
75 Battery "M" 1st Illinois
78 10th O.V.I
79 4th Ohio Cav.
82 6th Ohio Battery
83 Heg Shell Monument
84 26th O.V.I
85 8th Ind Battery
86 101st O.V.I
87 2nd Minn Battery
88 Battery "C" 1st Illinois
89 51st O.V.I
91 3rd Wiss. Battery
92 74th O.V.I
93 Battery "G" 1st Ohio
94 "M"
95 Preston Smith Shell Monument
97 Lytle Shell Monument
98 Wilder Memorial Tower

BATTLE FIELD
OF
CHICKAMAUGA
GEORGIA
Surveyed by command of Major Genl. G.H.Thomas
Commanding Department of the Cumberland
By Capt C.H.Boyd Sub-Asst U.S.Coast Survey
April and May 1864
Scale 1/20.000
Assisted in levelling by
Lieut Kuntze & Sergeant Wilson
Topl. Engineers 2nd Division 14th Army Corps
Note. "The tracing rolled with the Chickamauga map is from Major Morehart's survey of Mission Ridge, lying immediately N.E. of, and including Rossville Gap at which point it joins mine."
(See Boyd's letter of Oct. 22d 1864, No 1131)
Register No. 934
PLATE 15: BATTLE FIELD OF CHICKAMAUGA
When Confederate General Bragg was maneuvered out of Chattanooga in September 1863, he moved south into Georgia where he halted for regrouping near LaFayette, not far within the border. The pursuing Union General Rosecrans thought that Bragg was in full retreat, and split his forces. Whereupon, General Bragg turned and attacked General Rosecrans at Chickamauga Creek, just inside the Georgia line, in a two-day battle, September 19-20, 1863. General Bragg's army was reinforced by General Longstreet and his troops from Richmond. The Union army was driven back to Chattanooga, and would have been in complete rout had not there been some reinforcements on its side as well. Several months later the Confederates were driven from the area.
Early the next year, the territory now in Union hands again, Major General G. H. Thomas ordered that a detailed map be made of the Chickamauga battlefield. Captain C. H. Boyd, Sub-Assistant of the Coast Survey, was assigned the task. Assistant Boyd conducted the field surveys, assisted by personnel of the Army Topographic Engineers, and made this battle field map. The map depicts the terrain and cultural features in accurate detail, but does not show the actual battle conditions.
WEST CHICKAMAUGA CREEK
Scale Miles.

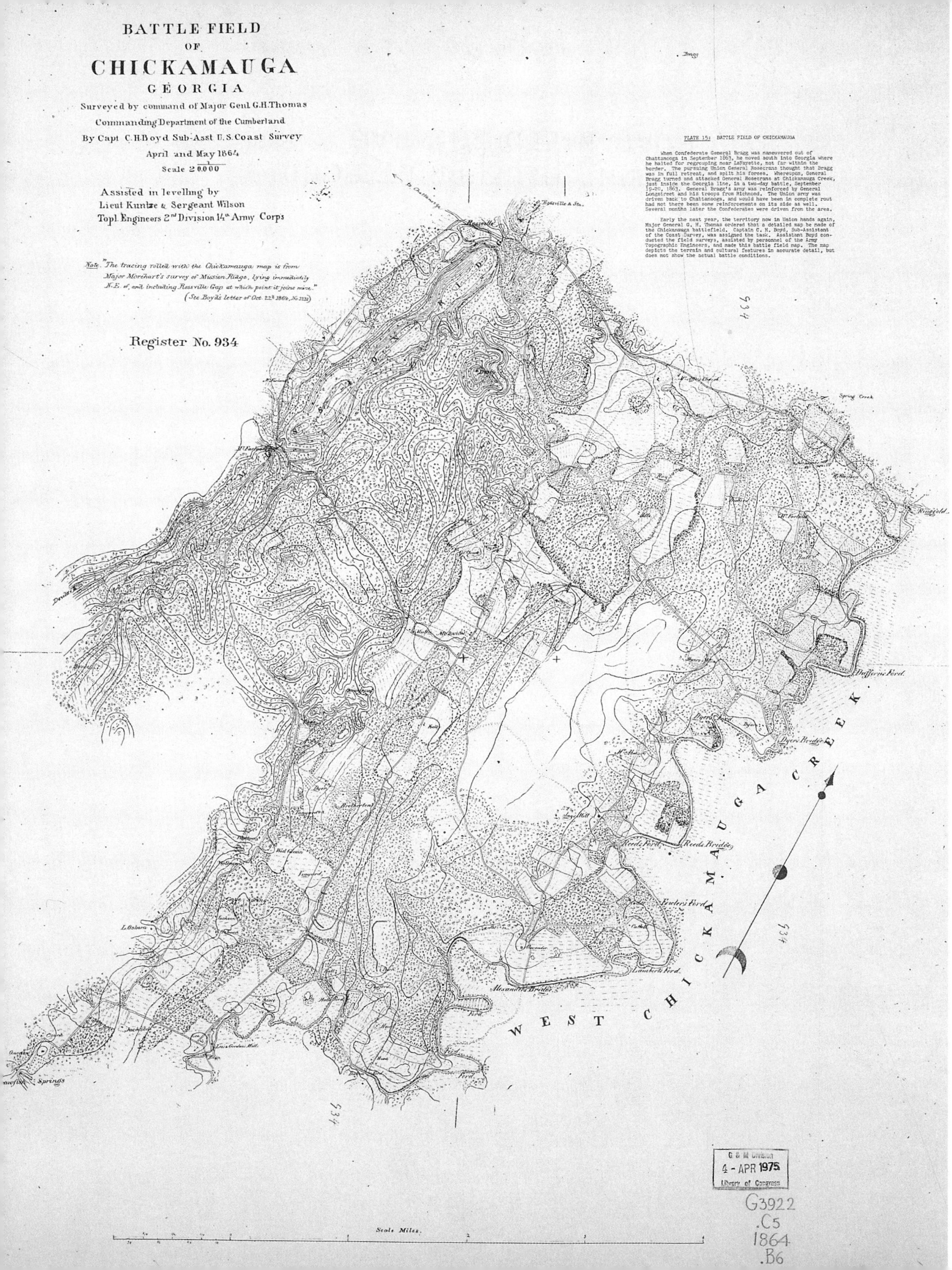

Battle of Chickamauga, Georgia, September 18–20, 1863

Far Left and Left: Various maps of the battlefield of Chickamauga, Georgia. Chickamauga (a Cherokee word meaning "River of Death") was the scene of the bloodiest battle in the Western Theater.

Far Left: The first map was produced by Edward Ferger and A. J. Taylor and published in 1895. Locations of various units and features are identified and keyed to a numbered list.

Left: Captain C. H Boyd's survey of the battlefield was conducted in April and May 1864 for General G. H. Thomas, who conducted a stout defense preventing the Union from being utterly routed at Chickamauga. The results were used to compile this map, a facsimile copy of the extensively detailed original manuscript.

Far Left, inset: Colonel William E. Merrill's manuscript map has also employed contour lines (at intervals of 20 feet) to depict relief features, and has also used tinting. Interestingly, Merrill notes that the map was only meant as a guide for the draftsmen employed to prepare the complete map, who he assumed would use the more familiar technique of haching to indicate relief. In fact, contour lines were generally adopted by cartographers after the war.

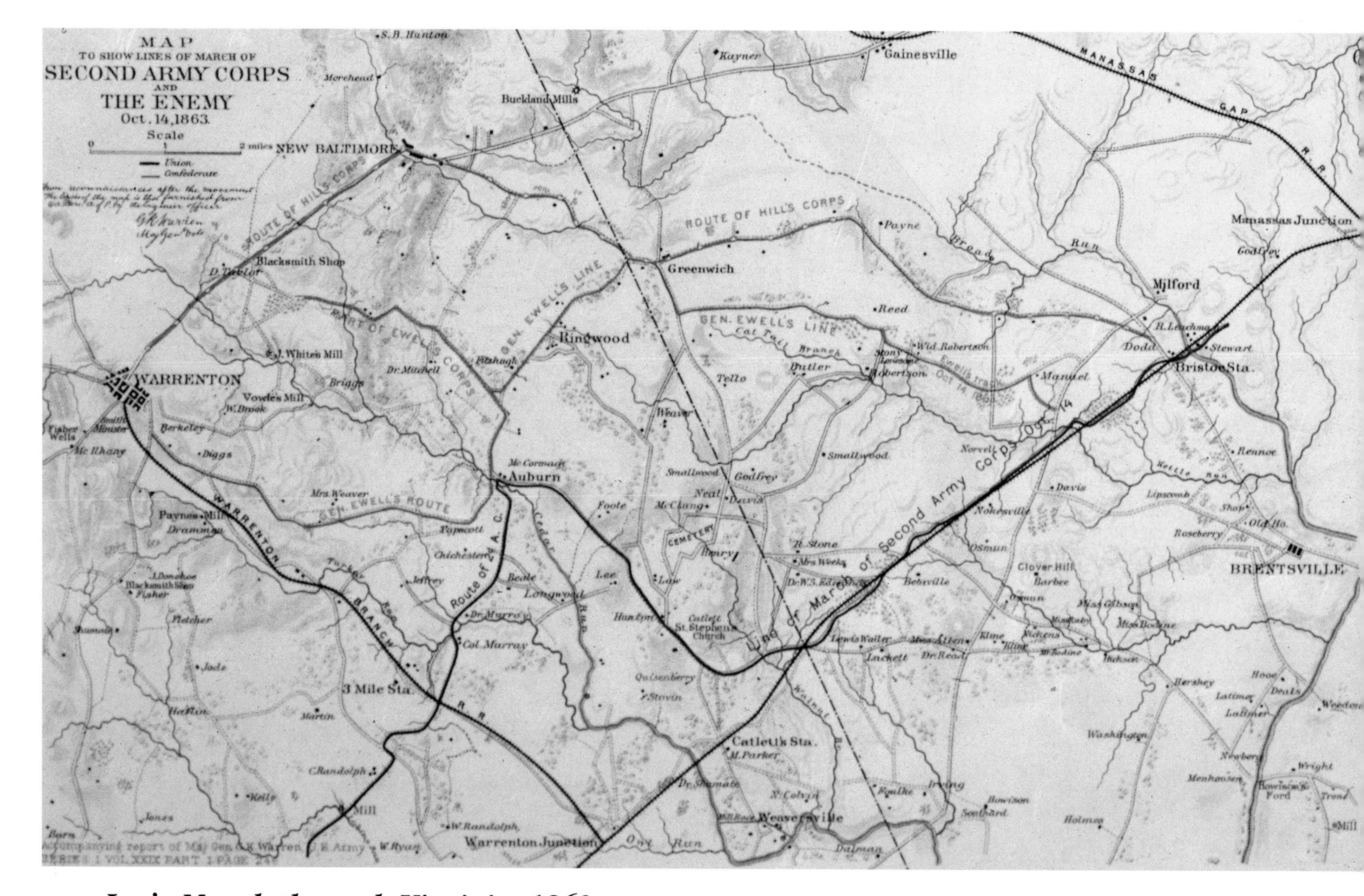

Lee's March through Virginia, 1863

Above: Map showing the line of march through Virginia of Lee's army and Warren's II Corps. Attempting to outflank Meade's Army of the Potomac and drive them from the west, Lee moved his Army of Northern Virginia from the Rapidan to the west and north. However, he failed to prevent Meade's withdrawal with an attack near Bristoe Station.

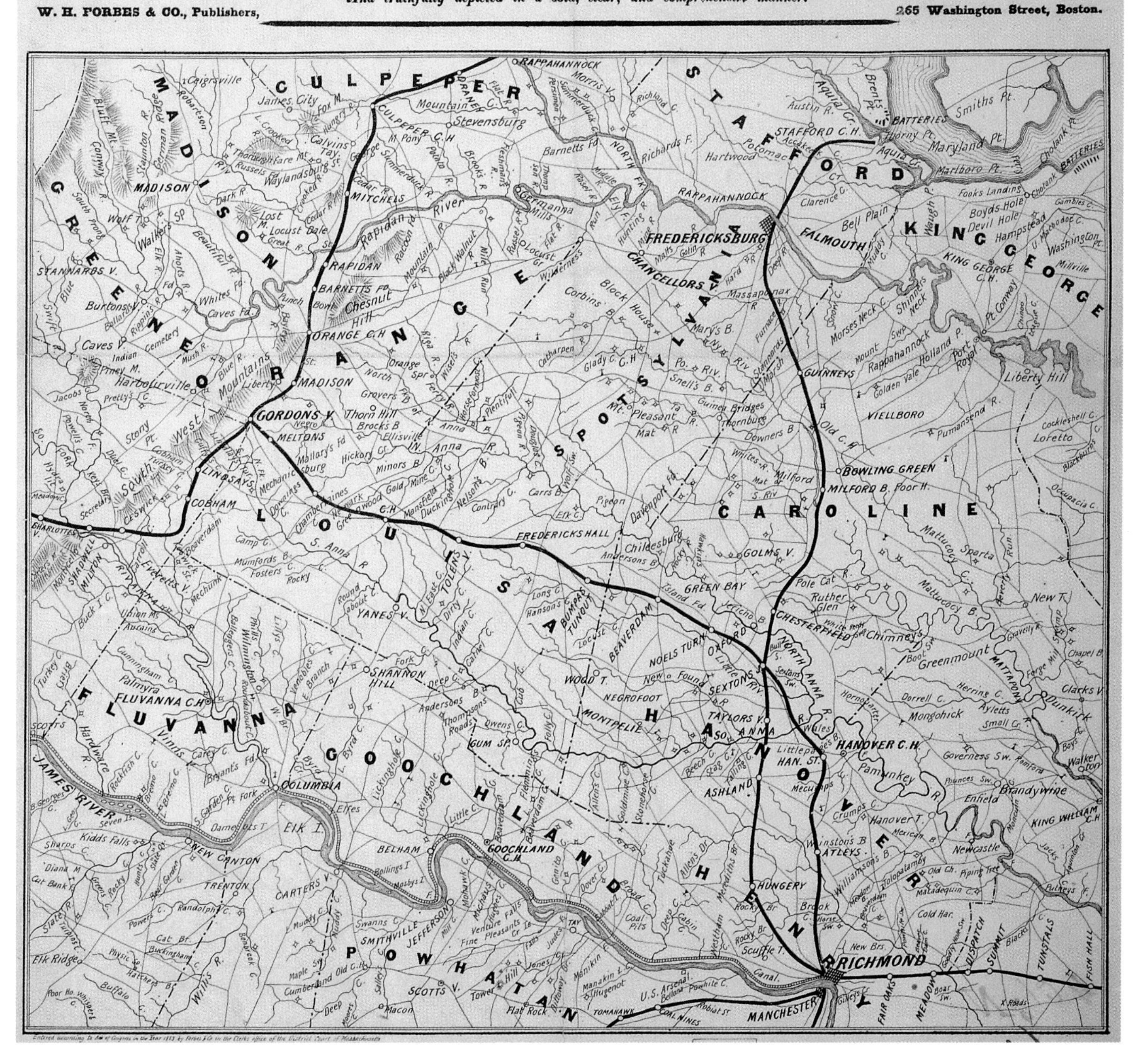

Approaches to Richmond, Virginia, 1863

Left: Boston-based W. H. Forbes and Co.'s strikingly titled map of "Theatre of War! A complete map of the battle-ground of Hooker's army!!" shows central Virginia north of Richmond. Major-General Joseph Hooker started well as commander of the Army of the Potomac, reorganizing it and renewing its confidence. "Fighting Joe"—whose name entered etymological dictionaries after he allowed camp followers into his soldiers' bivouacs—felt it was only a matter of time before he took Richmond, but he turned out to be a better organizer than battlefield commander.

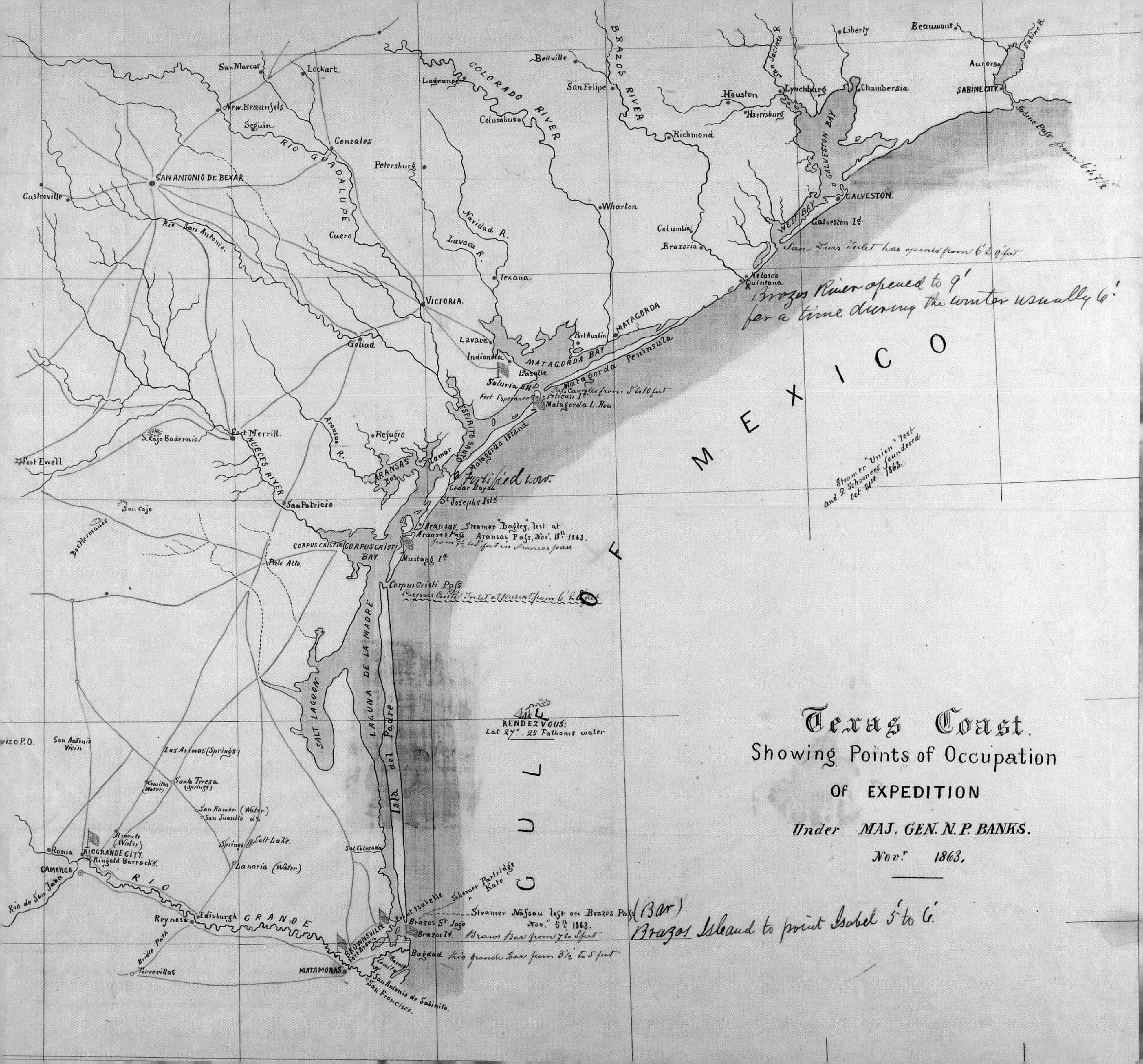

Texas Coast.
Showing Points of Occupation
OF EXPEDITION
Under MAJ. GEN. N. P. BANKS.
Novr. 1863.
GULF OF MEXICO
San Antonio de Bexar
Victoria
Galveston
Houston
Matagorda Bay
Corpus Cristi Bay
Laguna de la Madre
Isla del Padre
Brownsville
Matamoras
Brazos River opened to 9' for a time during the winter usually 6'
Brazos Island to point Isabel 5' to 6'
Rendezvous: Lat 27°. 25 Fathoms water
Streamer "Union" lost and 2 Schooners foundered Oct 31st 1863.
Steamer "Bagley" lost at Aransas Pass, Nov. 18th 1863.
Steamer Nassau lost on Brazos Pass (Bar) Nov. 5th 1863.
Fortified Work
Rio Grande

Texas Coast, November 1863

Left: Map of the Texas coast from Port Arthur (border with Louisiana) to Brownsville (border with Mexico) showing the points of occupation of the expedition led by Major-General Nathanial P. Banks during November 1863. The actual points of occupation are indicated by U.S. flags. The notes give details of events during the expedition, the navigability of certain passes and channels, and (in the south) the location of water supplies.

Aransas Pass, Texas, November 1863

Right: The Aransas Pass (to the north of Corpus Christi), guarding the entrance to Aransas Bay, was taken by Banks' forces on November 17, 1863. This map is a copy of the original sketch drawn by Charles Hosmer of the U.S. Coast Survey for the U.S. Engineer Department, and includes sailing directions for entering the pass.

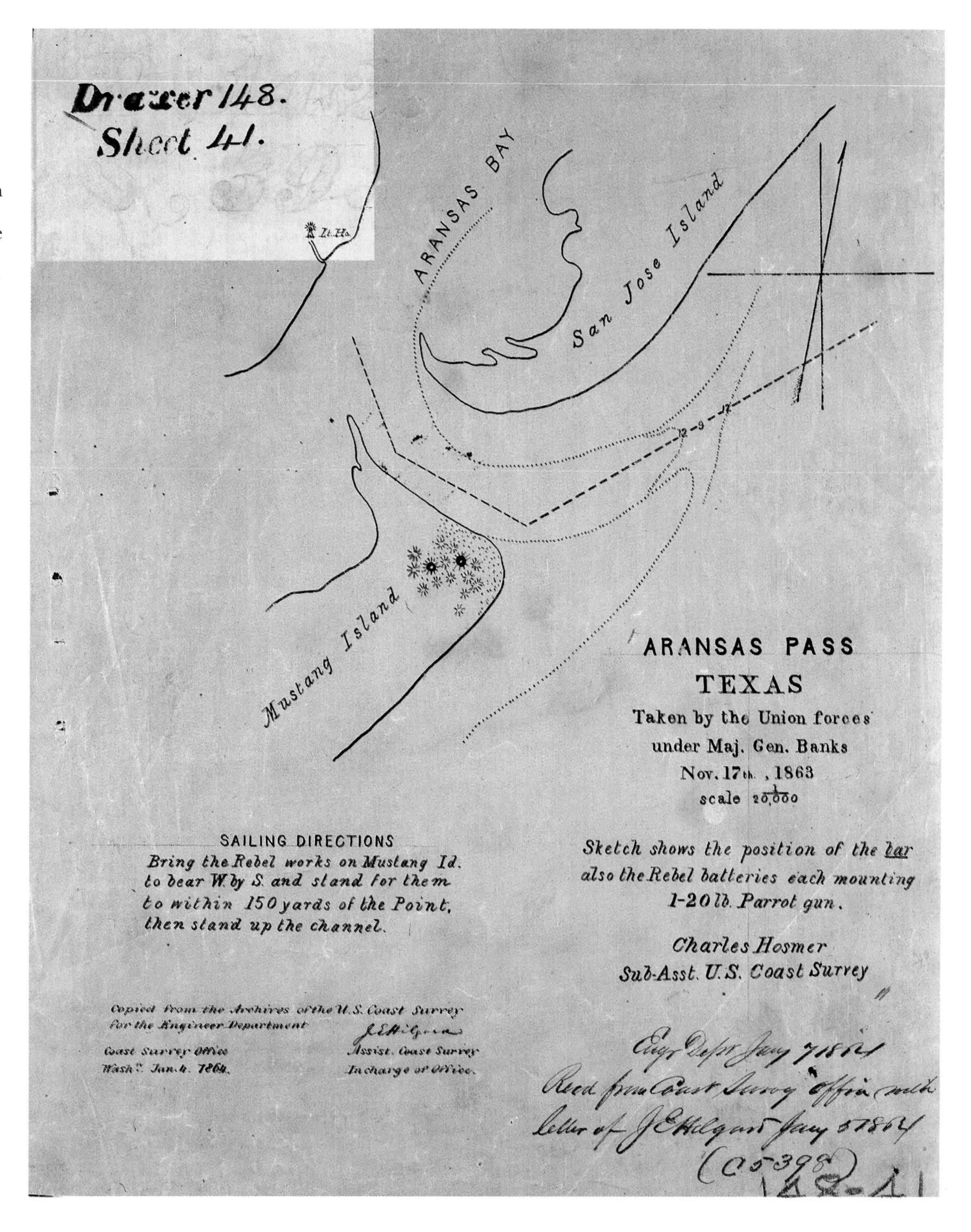

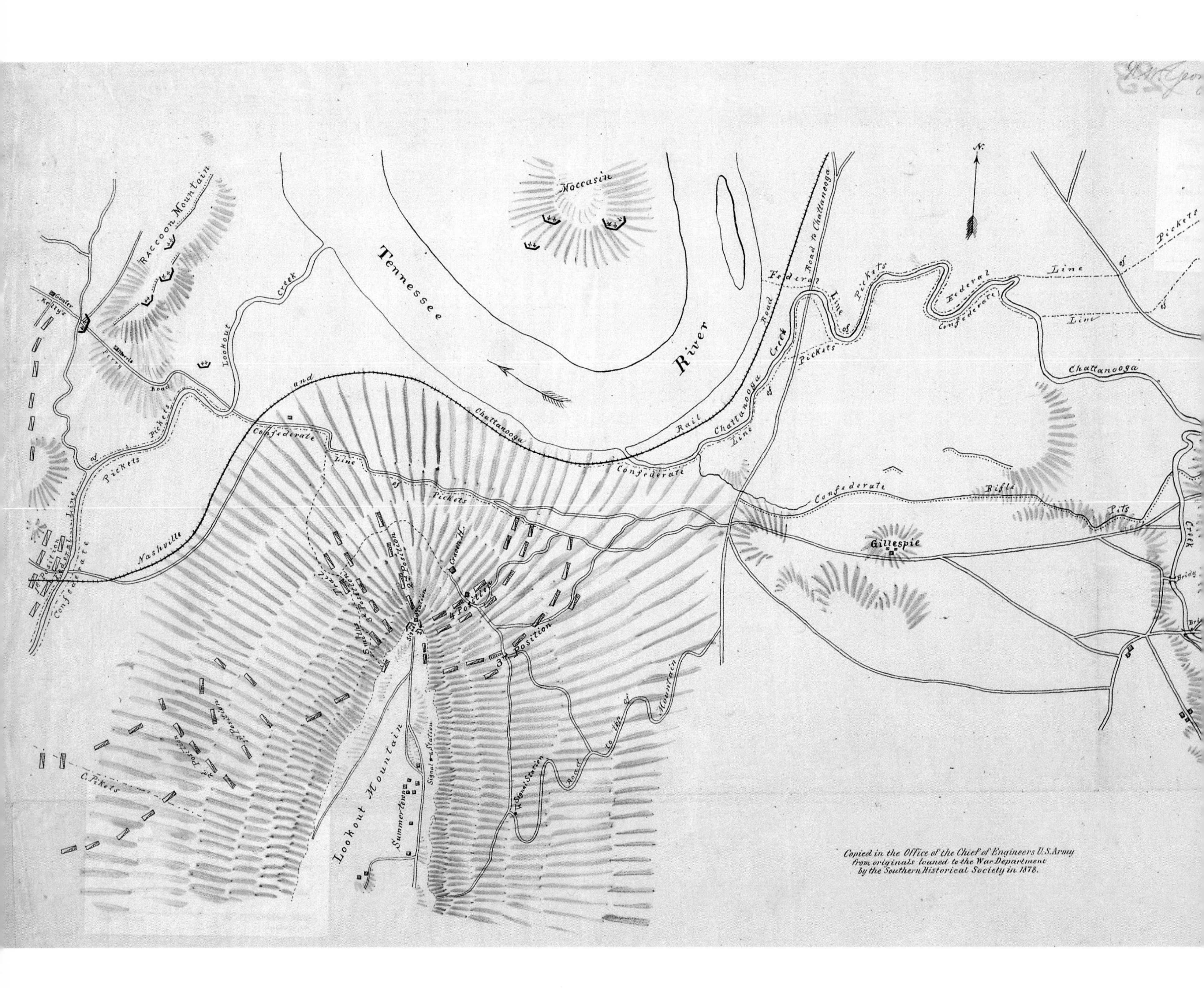
Raccoon Mountain
Moccasin
Tennessee
River
N.
Lookout
Creek
Nashville
and
Chattanooga
Rail
Road
Road to Chattanooga
Federal
Line
of
Pickets
Confederate
Line
of
Pickets
Confederate
Rifle
Pits
Chattanooga
Creek
Gillespie
Position
Lookout Mountain
Summertown
Signal Station
Road
to
top
of
Mountain
C. Pickets
Copied in the Office of the Chief of Engineers U.S. Army
from originals loaned to the War Department
by the Southern Historical Society in 1878.

Lookout Mountain, Tennessee, November 1863

Left: A copy of a Confederate map prepared to accompany the report of Brigadier-General William F. Smith showing rebel positions on Lookout Mountain. The hill was overrun in an assault on November 25, 1863.

Battle of Chattanooga, Tennessee, November 1863

Right, Pages 104, 105 (Details) and 106: Three maps depicting the daring and heroic Union attack on Missionary Ridge on November 25, 1863, the final action of the Chattanooga campaign. Sherman established a pontoon across the Tennessee river during the night of November 23–24 and his men entrenched on the opposite bank. After Sherman seized what his map told him is the northern end on Missionary Ridge, he was surprised to discover that he had only occupied an outlying hill and a large ravine lay between him and Missionary Ridge proper. On November 25, Grant, the Union commander, launched an all-out assault on the ridge, considered impregnable by General Bragg. Sherman attacked in the north and Hooker in the south, and at 3.00 p.m. Thomas's men got up the center of the ridge. They advanced at headlong pace through the Confederate lines, rapidly overtaking the retreating rebels. The Army of the Tennessee was subsequently forced to retreat to Ringgold in Georgia.

Right: Map of the battlefield with the operations of the Union forces.

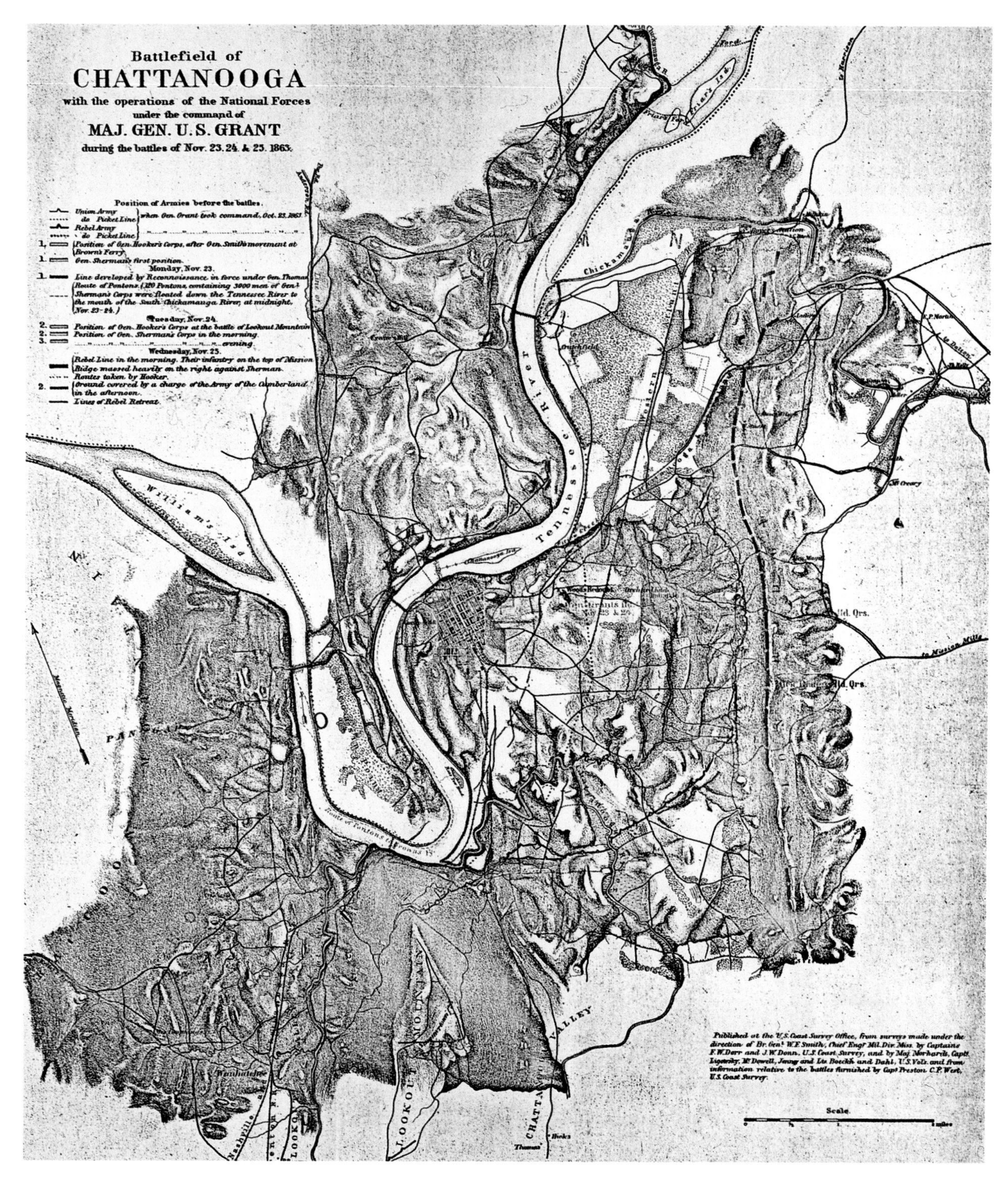

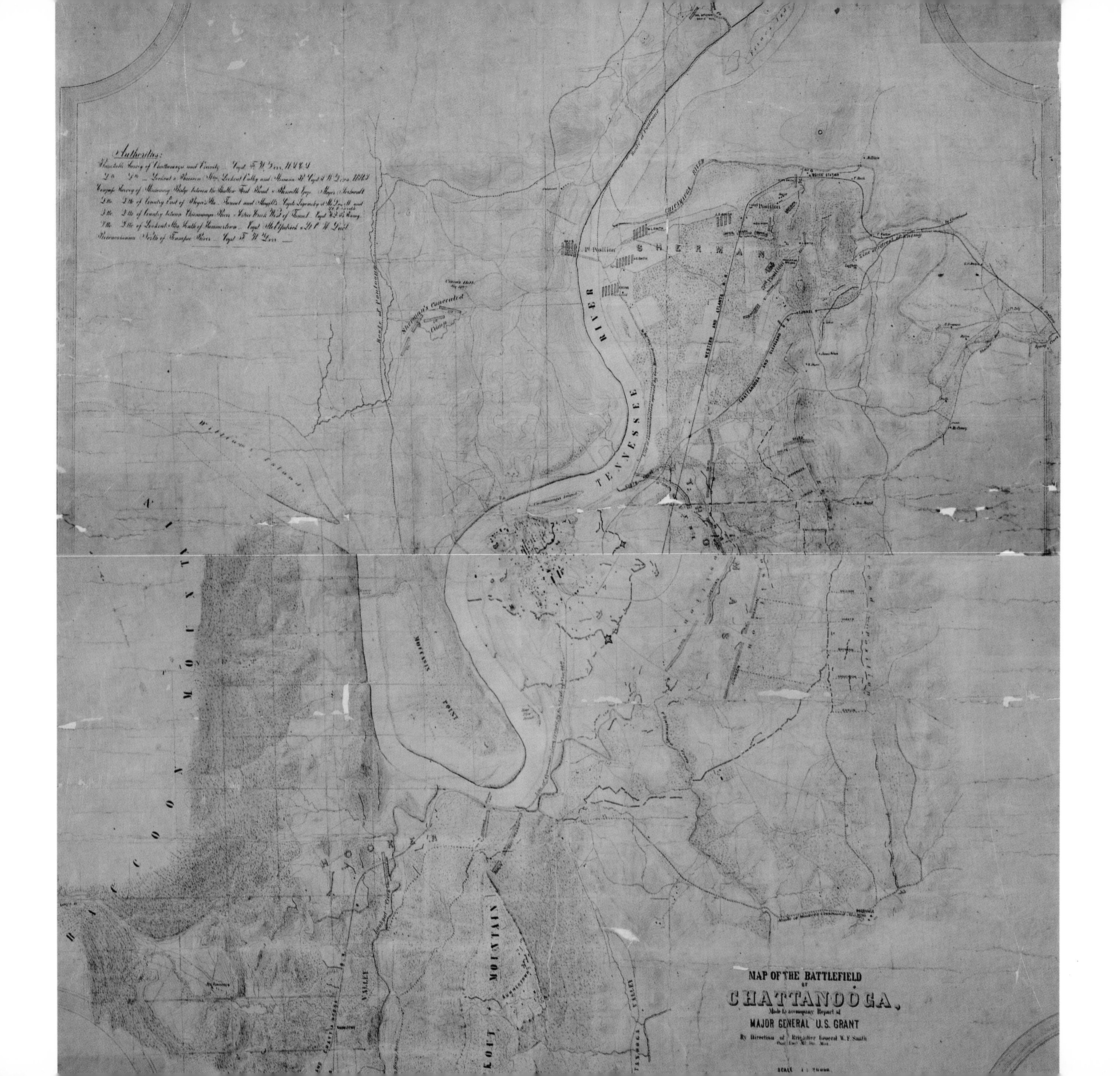
Authorities:
1st Position
2nd Position
SHERMAN
TENNESSEE
RIVER
Sherman's Concealed Camp
MOCCASIN
POINT
RACCOON MOUNTAIN
HOOKER
MOUNTAIN
VALLEY
MAP OF THE BATTLEFIELD
OF
CHATTANOOGA,
Made to accompany Report of
MAJOR GENERAL U.S. GRANT
By Direction of Brigadier General W. F. Smith

Left and Right (Detail): Map of the battlefield prepared to accompany Grant's report and published in 1875. Union forces are in blue; Confederates in red.

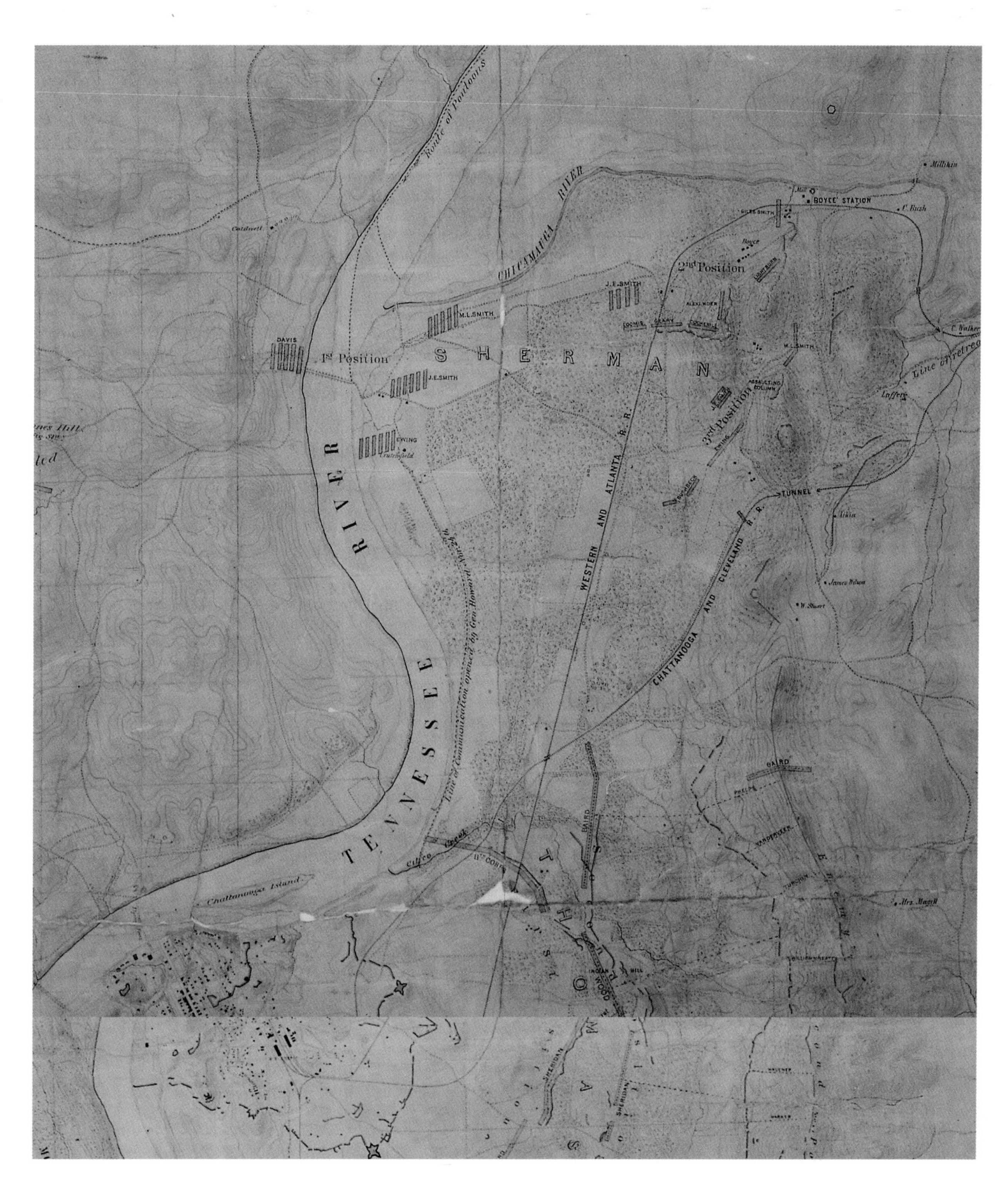

Right: Sketch by G. H. Blakeslee of the area around Chattanooga, including topographical locations (note Lookout Mountain at left), picket lines, Confederate General Bragg's headquarters on Missionary Ridge, and Grant's headquarters to the east of the town.

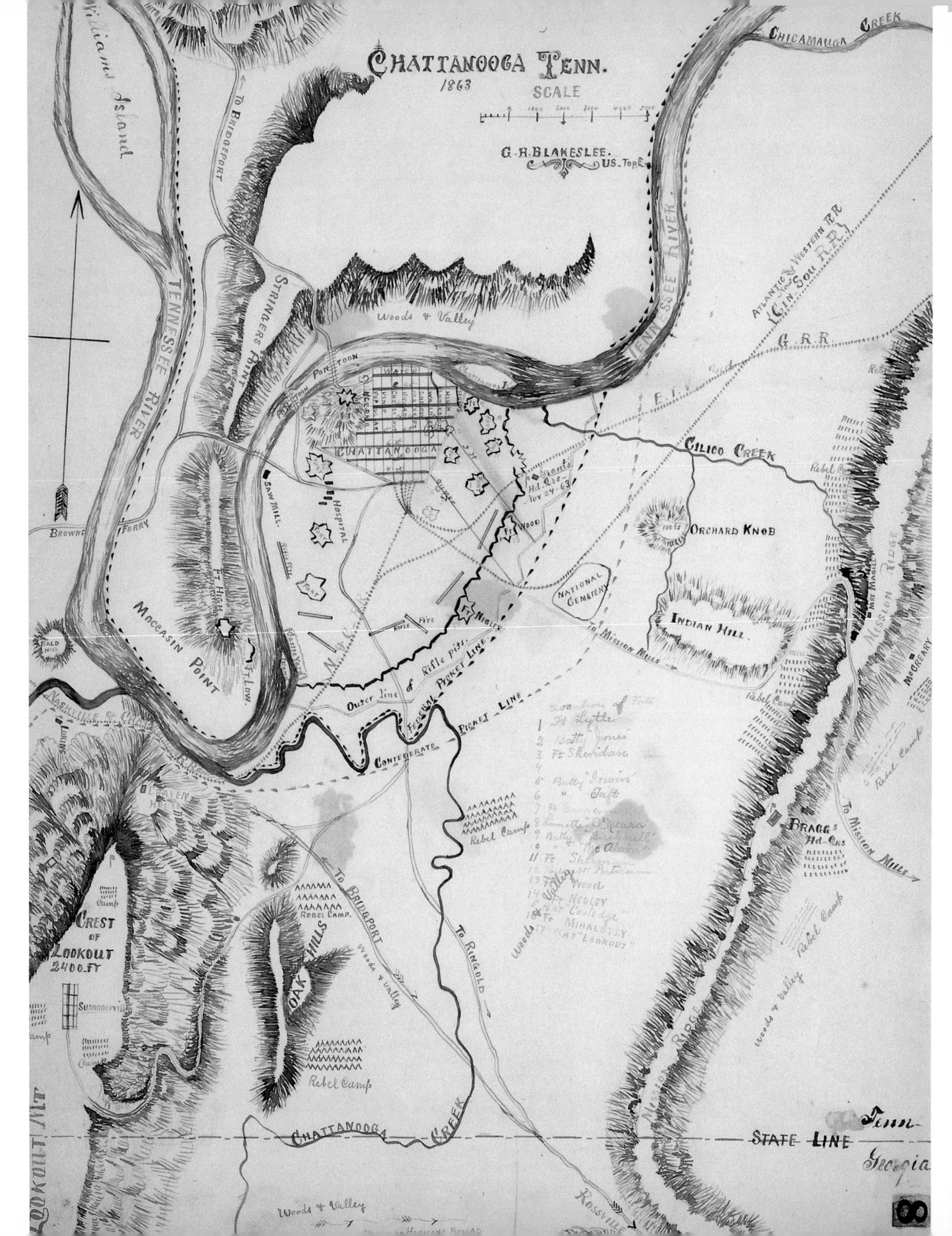

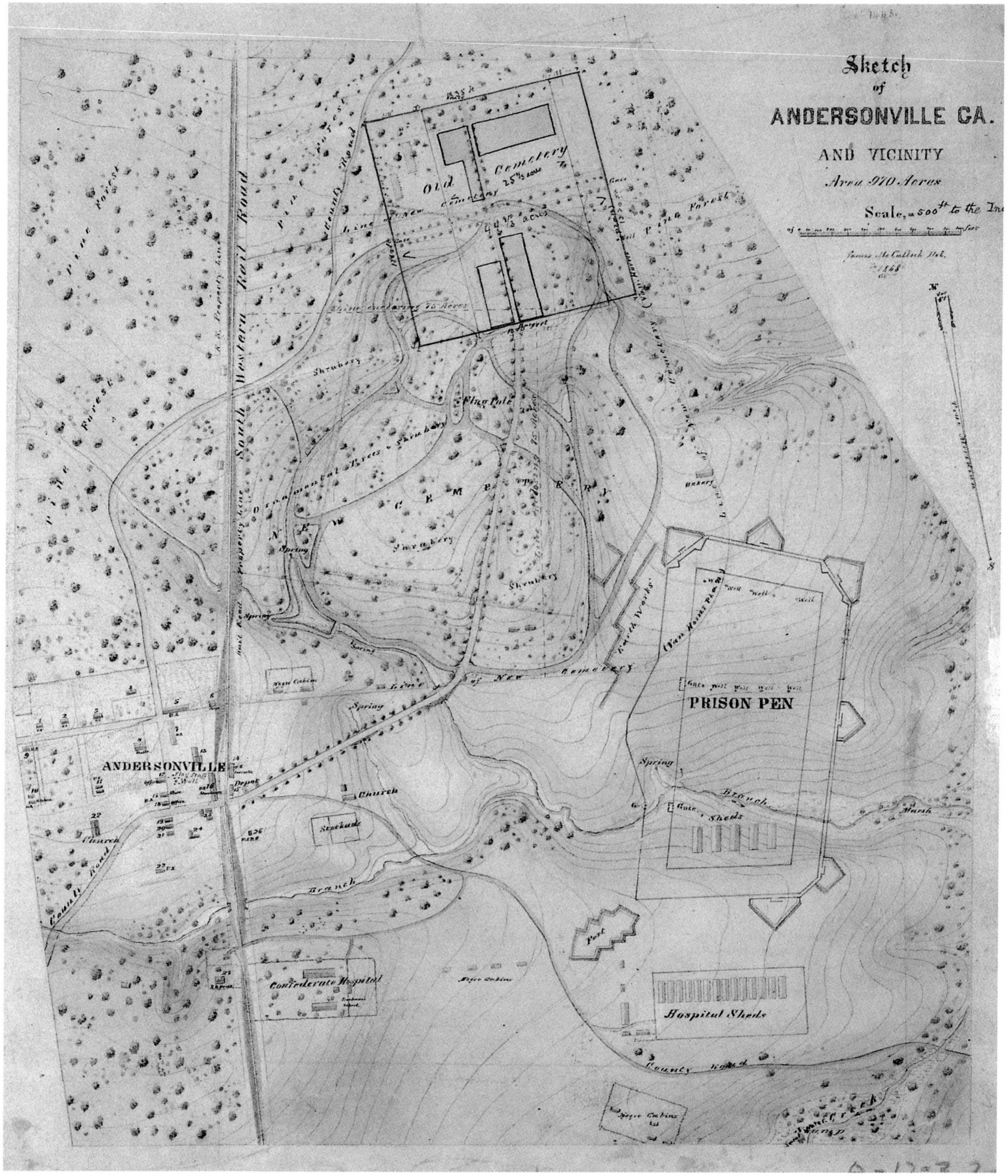

Andersonville, Georgia, 1863

Left: The prison camps that housed the many prisoners of war from both sides were atrocious hell holes where nearly 50,000 prisoners would die from disease, neglect, and malnutrition. This is a sketch from the records of the Office of the Quartermaster General of Andersonville, Georgia, showing the fort, prison camp, sheds, and Confederate Hospital. Union troops began to arrive at the hastily constructed prison camp, known as Camp Sumter, in February 1864, after the camps at Richmond became overcrowded. It would house over 30,000 men in squalid conditions.

Central Virginia, 1864–65

Right and Below (detail): Lithographed map showing the routes of Sheridan's cavalry raids in Central Virginia in 1864–65, each one of the seven indicated by a different color, as is General Lee's line of retreat. Attached to the map is a printed description of each one of the raids, which were designed to disrupt Southern supply lines and harass the enemy rear. The map was published in 1865 by the War Department.

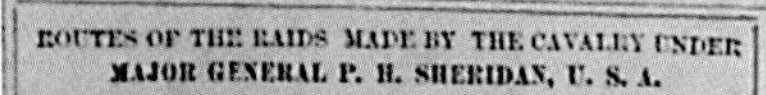

ROUTES OF THE RAIDS MADE BY THE CAVALRY UNDER MAJOR GENERAL P. H. SHERIDAN, U. S. A.

FIRST RAID.

From Todd's Tavern, starting May 9, 1864, via. Chilesburgh, Anderson's Ford, Beaver Dam, Ground Squirrel Bridge, Yellow Tavern, Richmond, Meadow Bridge, Mechanicsville, Bottom's and White Oak Bridges, and Malvern Hill, to Haxall's Landing, arriving May 14, 1864.

Returning May 17, 1864:

Via. St Mary's Church, Jones' Bridge, Baltimore Cross Roads, White House, Lanesville, King William C. H., Ayletts, and Reedy Swamp, to Pole Cat Station, arriving May 25, 1864. Rejoining the army at this point and proceeding in its advance via. Chesterfield Station, Mangohick Church, and Hanover Town, to New Castle, arriving May 29, 1864.

SECOND RAID.

From New Castle, starting June 7, 1864, via. Ayletts, Reedy Swamp, Pole Cat Station, Chilesburgh, Brock's Bridge, and Miner's Bridge, to Trevillian Station, arriving June 11, 1864.

Returning June 12, 1864:

Via. Carpenter's Ford, Shady Grove Church, Spottsylvania C.H., Bowling Green, Newtown, Clarksville, King and Queen C. H., and back to Clarksville, thence via. Dunkirk, King William C.H., Lanesville, White House, Tanstalls Station, Baltimore Cross Roads, Jones' Bridge, Charles City C. H.,—crossing the James River at two points,—Prince George C. H., Lee's Mills, and back through Prince George C. H., to Light House Point, arriving June 28, 1864.

THIRD RAID,

UNDER COMMAND OF BRIGADIER GENERAL JAMES H. WILSON.

From Lee's Mills, starting June 22, 1864, via. Ream's Station, Dinwiddie C. H., Mount Level, Blacks and Whites, to Nottaway C. H.; thence diverging into two columns, the right proceeding via. Burke's Station, the left via. Hungry Town, to Meherrin Station: from Meherrin the entire column moved via. Keysville, to Roanoke Station, arriving June 25, 1864:

Returning June 25, 1864.

Via. Willesburg, Christianville, Greensborough, and Bolling's Bridge, to Ream's Station, and back to Bolling's Bridge, thence via. Jarrett's Station, Peters' Bridge, and Cabin Point, to Light House Point, arriving July 2, 1864.

FOURTH RAID,

UNDER COMMAND OF BREVET MAJOR GENERAL W. MERRITT.

From Winchester, starting November 28, 1864, via. Ashby's Gap, and Middleburg, to Fairfax, Centreville, and other points in London Valley.

Returning:

Via. Goose Creek, Snicker's Gap, and Berryville, to Winchester, arriving December 3, 1864.

FIFTH RAID,

UNDER COMMAND OF BREVET MAJ. GENERAL A. T. A. TORBERT.

From Winchester, starting December 19, 1864, via. Stoney Point,

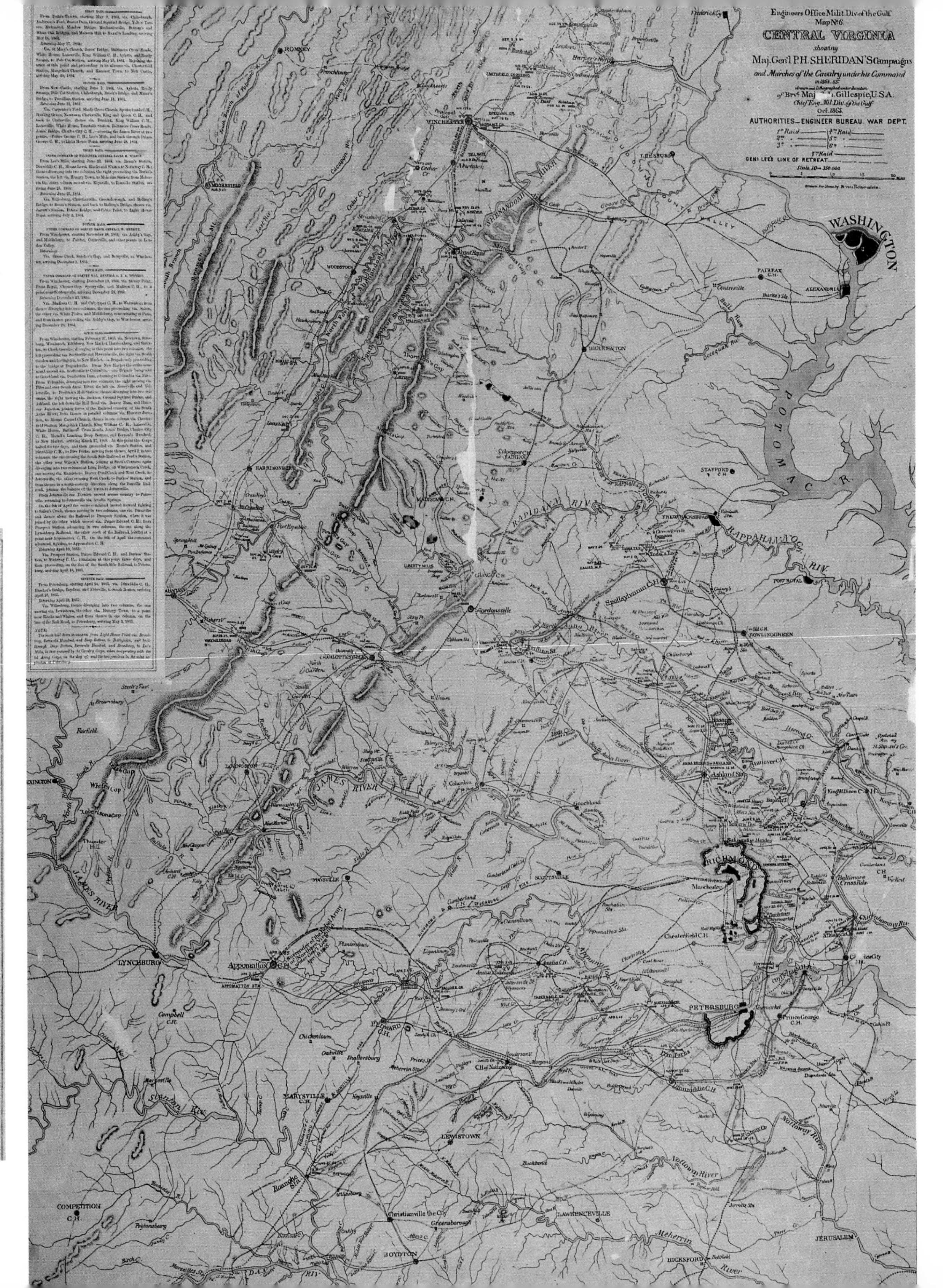

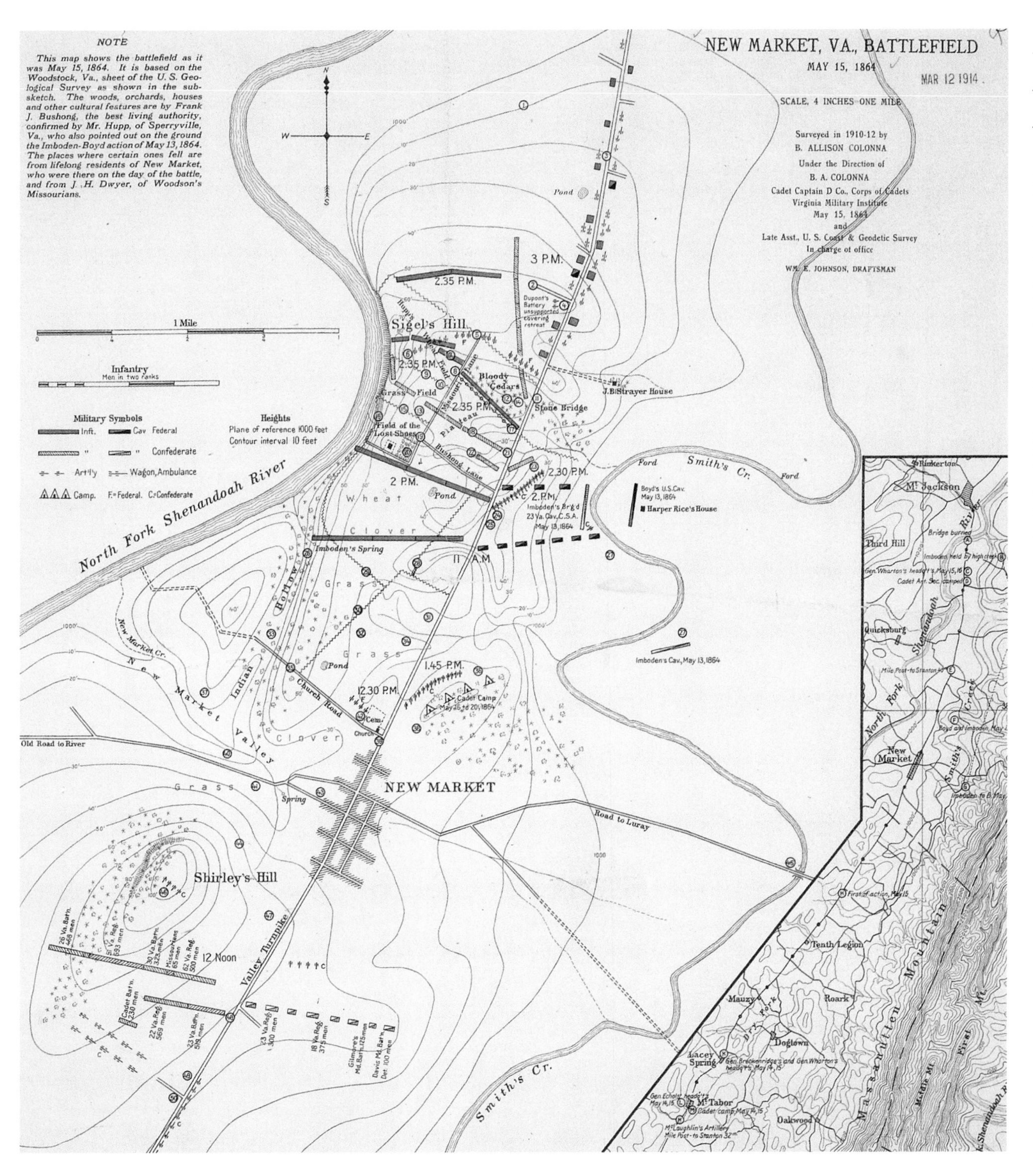

Battle of New Market, Virginia, May 15, 1864

Left A 1914 map of the battlefield of New Market, Virginia, typical of the many battlefield maps produced after the war, compiled and drawn under the direction of Cadet Captain B. A. Colonna, one of 247 Virginia Military Institute cadets who fought with distinction in the engagement. The inset shows New Market's general location. Colonna was later the assistant director of the U.S Coast and Geodetic Survey, the forerunner of the National Ocean Service. The battle took place on May 15, 1864, when Union commander Franz Sigel, moving up the Shenandoah Valley, met a Confederate force and was routed.

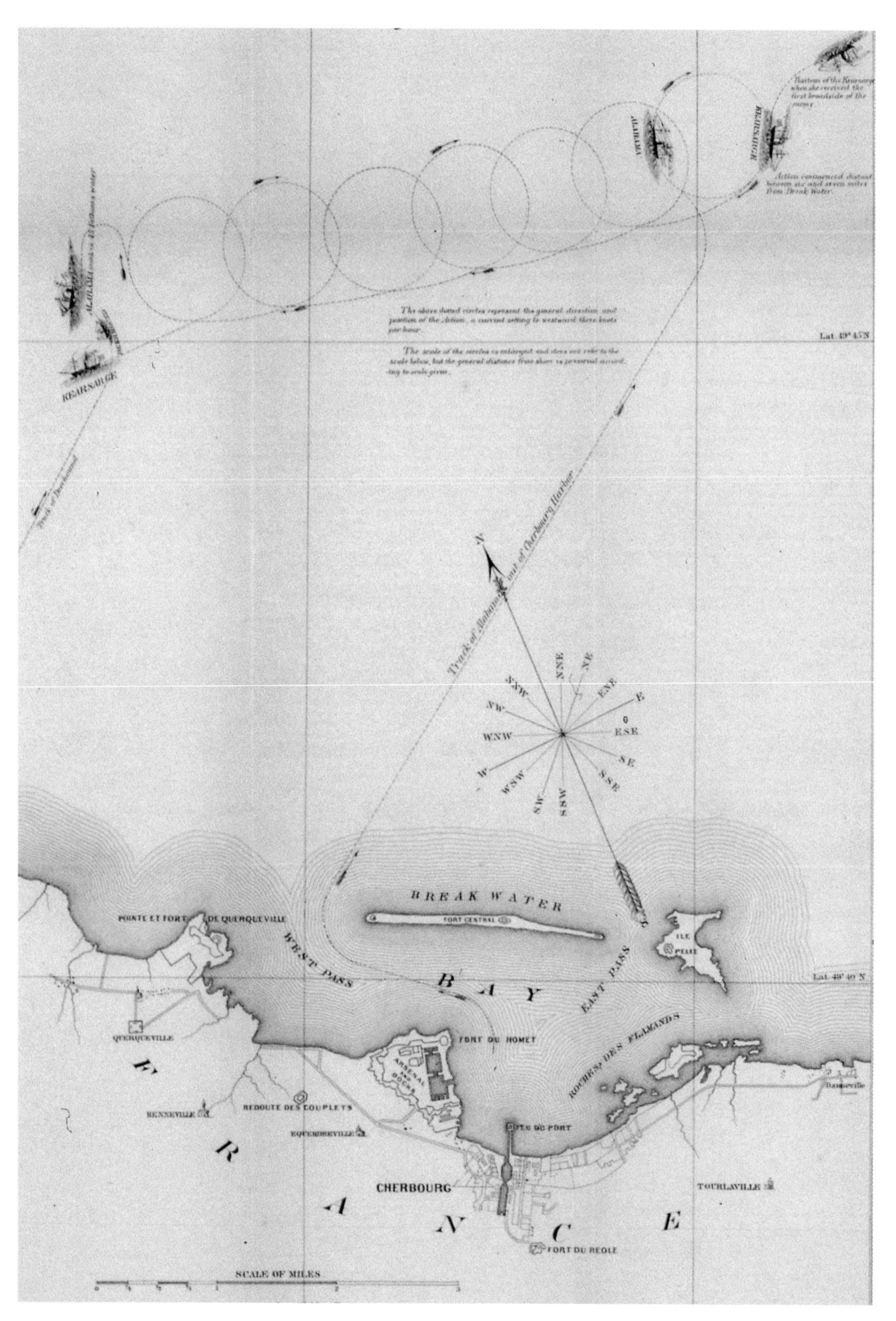

Cherbourg, France, June 19, 1864

Left: Map of the Cherbourg Peninsula in northwestern France, scene of a naval engagement in which the Confederate commerce raiding ship *Alabama* was sunk by the U.S. steamer *Kearsage*. The action, which ended the career of the *Alabama*, was watched by crowds of observers on nearby cliffs and from a British yacht. This lithograph map was produced to accompany the official report of Captain John A. Winslow, commander of the *Kearsage*.

Fort McPherson, Kentucky, 1864–65

Right: Union map of Fort McPherson, one of nine such forts defending the city of Louisville, Kentucky. Note the use of contour lines to show relief, and annotation indicating distance to neighbouring forts. The map is annotated just below the scale to indicate that it was presented with a report of Union operations in Kentucky between July 1, 1864, and May 1865.

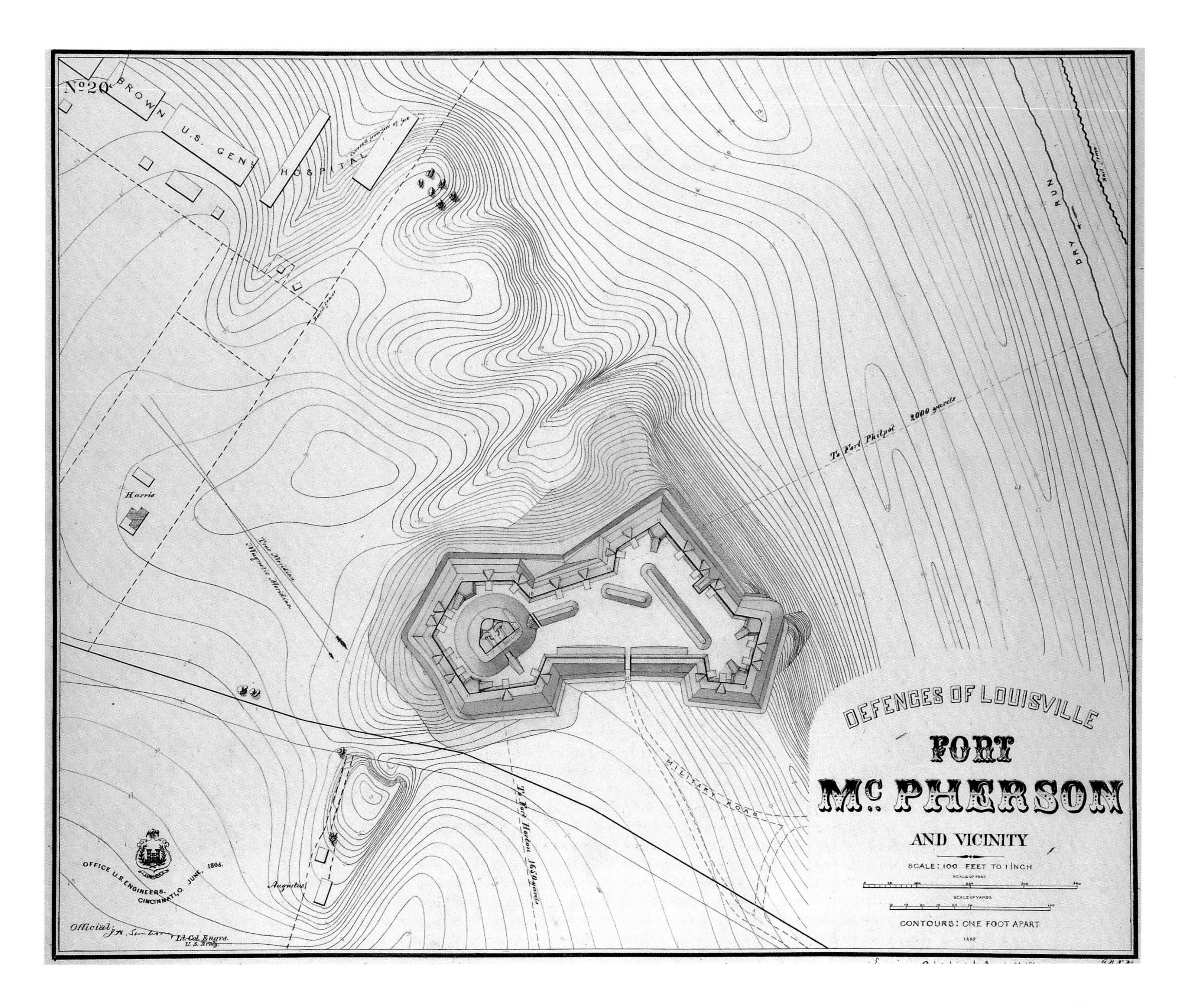

DEFENCES OF LOUISVILLE
FORT
Mc PHERSON
AND VICINITY
SCALE: 100 FEET TO 1 INCH
CONTOURS: ONE FOOT APART
No 20
BROWN
U.S. GENL
HOSPITAL
DRY RUN
To Fort Philpot 2000 yards
Harris
True Meridian
Magnetic Meridian
MILITARY ROAD
To Fort Horton 1650 yards
Augustus
OFFICE U.S. ENGINEERS. CINCINNATI, O. JUNE, 1865.
Official
Lt. Col. Engrs.
U. S. Army.

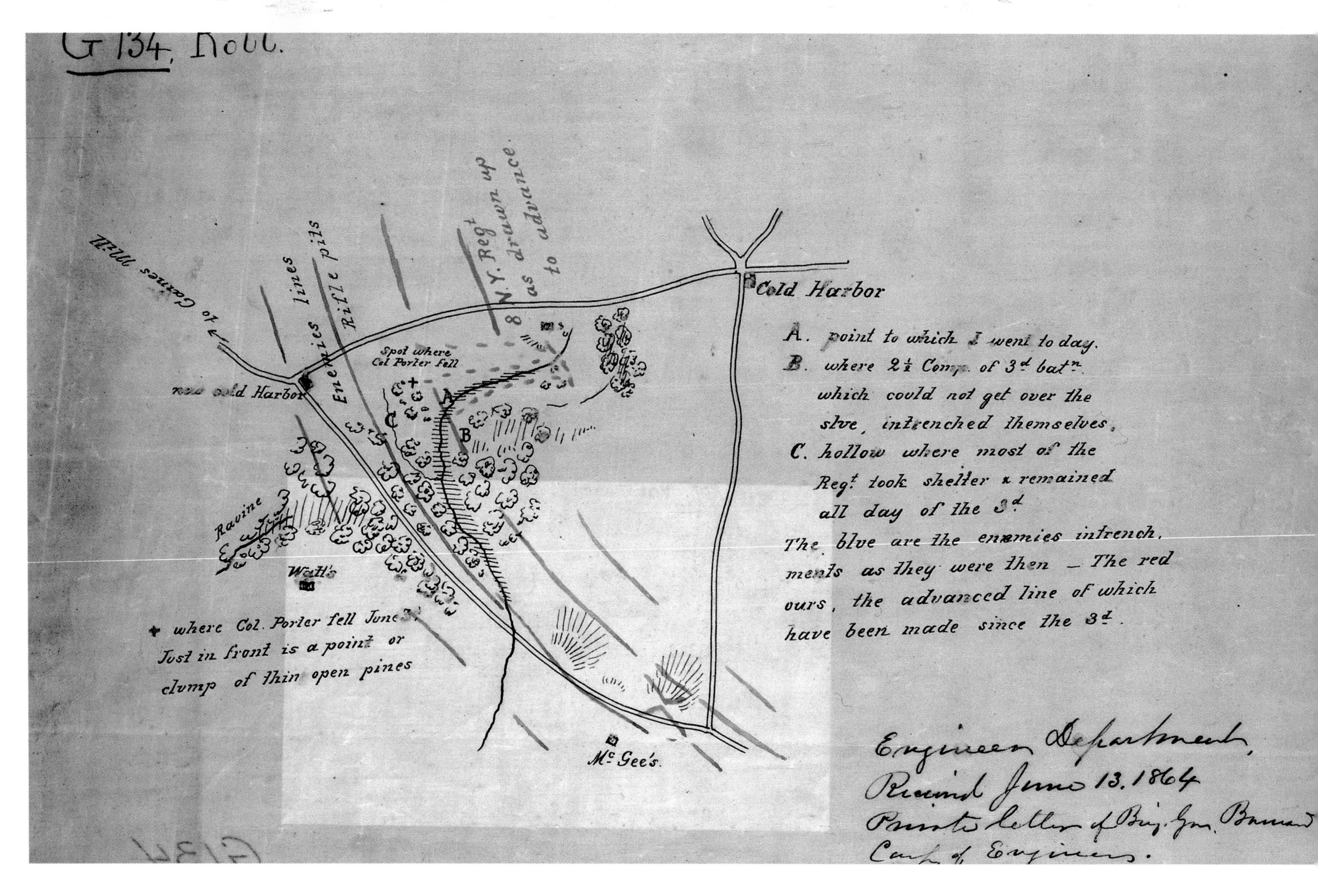
G 134. Roll.
to Gaines Mill
Enemies lines
Rifle pits
8 N.Y. Regt as drawn up to advance
Cold Harbor
Spot where Col Porter fell
A
B
C
Ravine
Watt's
McGee's
A. point to which I went to day.
B. where 2½ Comp. of 3d batn. which could not get over the slve, intrenched themselves.
C. hollow where most of the Regt took shelter & remained all day of the 3d.
The blue are the enemies intrench. ments as they were then – The red ours, the advanced line of which have been made since the 3d.
+ where Col. Porter fell June 3d. Just in front is a point or clump of thin open pines
Engineer Department,
Received June 13. 1864
Private letter of Brig. Gen. Barnard
Corps of Engineers.

Battle of Cold Harbor, Virginia, June 1–3, 1864

Above: Manuscript sketch map on the action at Cold Harbor. It was contained in a letter from General Barnard of the Corps of Engineers. Confederate positions are marked in blue and Union in red. Notes by Barnard also indicate where Colonel Porter fell and detail the positions where companies entrenched. At Cold Harbor, outside Richmond, the bloodiest charge in the war took place as 8,000 Union troops died in eight minutes.

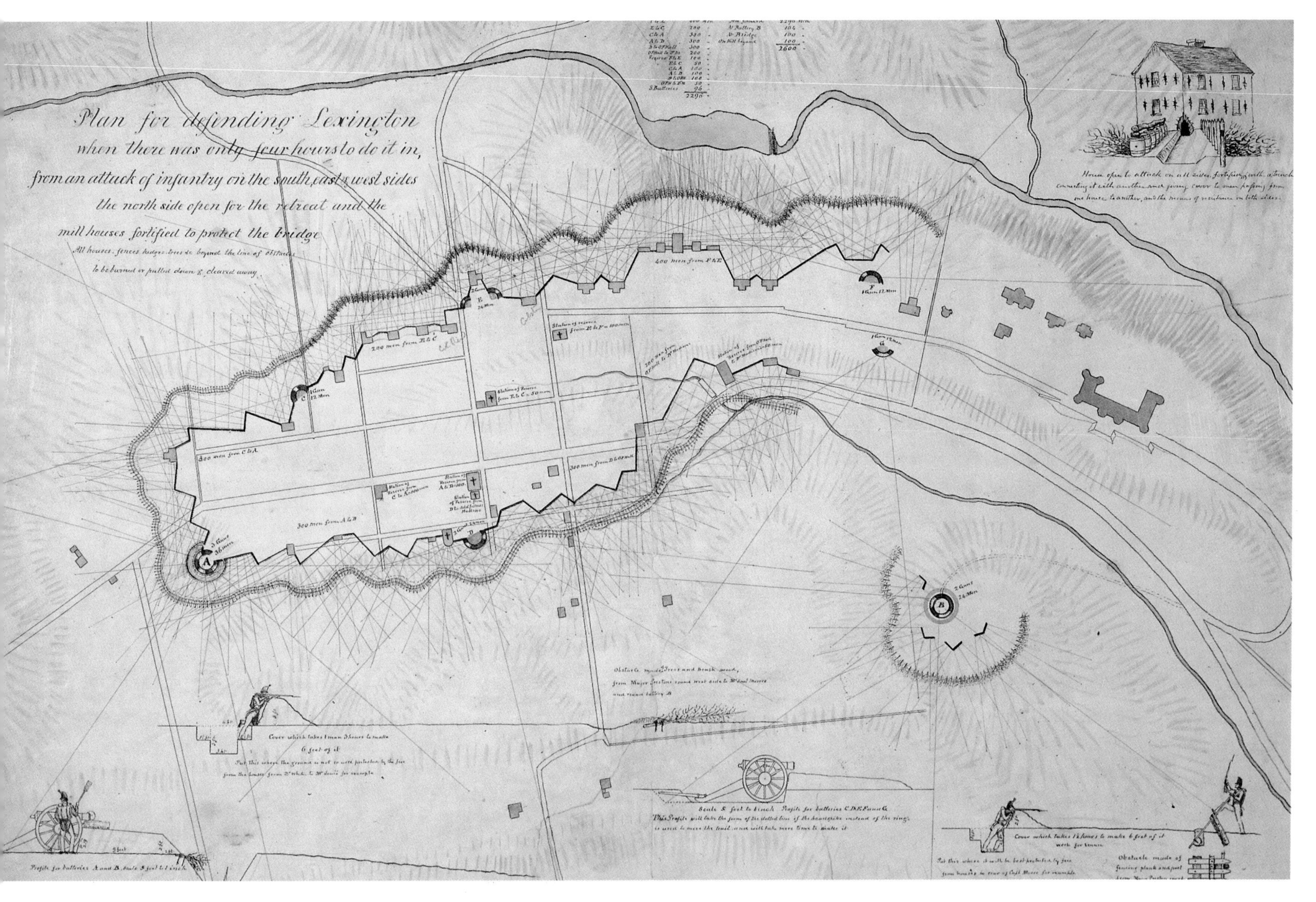

Defenses at Lexington, Virginia, 1864

Above: Plan for defending Lexington, Virginia, from attack. Buildings and fortifications are shown in orange and drainage features in blue. Yellow hachures and shading indicate relief, and interestingly, the cartographer had also included the lines of fire for individual riflemen. Disposition of men and guns along the line of defense are given in numbers. Accompanying sketches (of curiously antiquated military figures) show cross-sections of rifle pits, profiles of batteries, details of obstacles, and defense of a house open to attack on all sides.

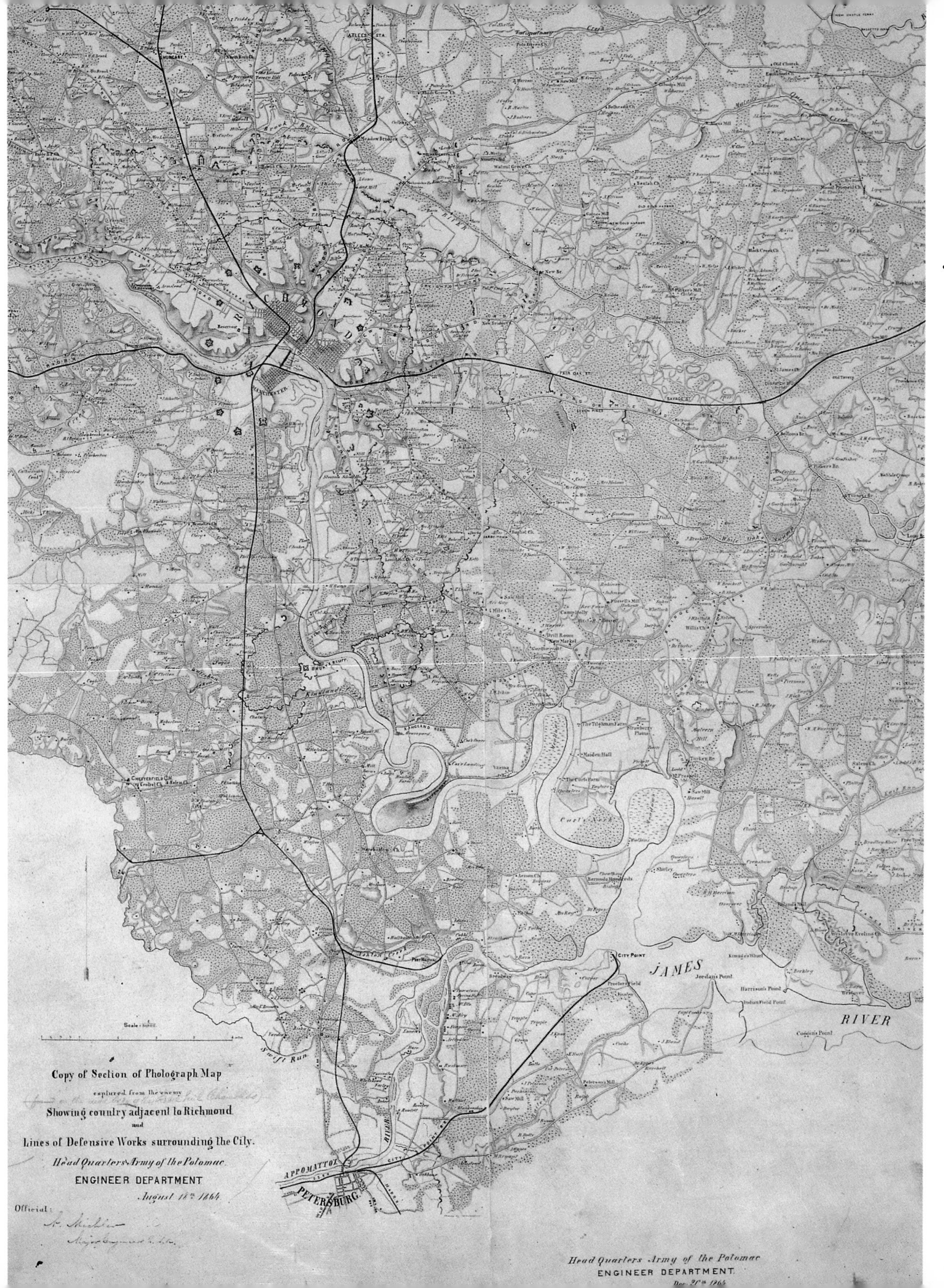

Grant's Petersburg Campaign, Virginia, June–August 1864

Pages 114–120: The next seven pages provide a series of commercial and military maps and sketches relating to Grant's Petersburg campaign, June–August 1864, which aimed at destroying General Lee's army and capturing Richmond, the heart of the Confederacy. By spring of 1864, almost every able-bodied man in the South was in uniform, whereas the North could issue a draft call for 600,000 more men. Added to this, shortages of food and other basic supplies were becoming endemic, and during the year the advancing Federal armies adopted a strategy of systematically destroying the industrial and agricultural capacity of the South, a concept later called "Total War."

Left: "Section of photographic map captured from the enemy showing country adjacent to Richmond and lines of defensive works surrounding the city." 1864. An annotation declares that the note was "found on the dead body of the Rebel Gen'l. Chambliss."

Right: A commercial map, by D. van Nostrand of New York, of Richmond and its defenses, with concentric circles to indicate distance from the city center.

MAP OF
RICHMOND, Va.
AND SURROUNDING COUNTRY
showing Rebel Fortifications.
From the latest and most authentic surveys
Published by D. VAN NOSTRAND
192 Broadway
NEW YORK.
1864.
Entered according to act of Congress A.D. 1864, by D. Van Nostrand, in the clerks office of the district court of the United States for the south. dist. of N.Y.
RICHMOND
MANCHESTER
ROCKETTS
OREGON HILL
UNION HILL
CHIMBORAZO HILL
ACADEMY HILL
TOLL GATE
FT. JOHNSON
FT. JACKSON
RACE COURSE
CHESNUT GROVE
BROOK BRIDGE
MEADOW BRIDGE
BROOK R.
TURNERS TAVERN
HUNGARY BRANCH STA.
SHADY GROVE CHURCH
POPOPATOMOY CR.
MECHANICSVILLE
MECHANICSVILLE BR.
WALNUT GROVE CH.
GAINES MILL
COLD HARBOR
NEW COLD HARBOR
U. TRESTLE BR.
L. TRESTLE BR.
NEW BRIDGE
FORT BR.
DUANE'S BR.
WOODBURY BR.
SUMNER'S U. BR.
SUMNERS L. BR.
SAVAGE'S STA.
BOTTOMS BR.
NINE MILE ROAD
NEW BRIDGE ROAD
Dr. FRENCH
RICHMOND & YORK RIVER R.R.
FAIR OAKS St.
SEVEN PINES
WHITE OAK SWAMP
WILLIAMSBURG
CHARLES CITY ROAD
CENTRAL ROAD
SOUTH BR.
JAMES RIVER
KANAWHA CANAL
COAL MINES
BROAD ROCK
PAWHITE STA.
RICHMOND & DANVILLE R.R.
RAIL ROAD
PLANK ROAD
TURNPIKE
FALLING CR.
GOODES CR.
MANCHESTER & CHESTERFIELD R.R.
PETERSBURG TURNPIKE
FORT MAGRUDER
ALMOND CR.
WATKINS
CHESTER HILL
WILTON
CHAPIN'S BLUFF
FALL'S BLUFF
FORT DARLING
DRURY'S BLUFF
HALF WAY HOUSE
REBEL EARTHWORKS
COX
COX FERRY
JONES NECK
NEWMARKET ROAD
VARINA
KINGSLAND ROAD
FOUR MILE CREEK
TREE MILE CREEK
DEEP BOTTOM
BAILYS RUN
TURKEY CR.
QUAKER ROAD
WESTERN RUN
SAMS RUN
LONG BRIDGE ROAD
MALVERN HILL
3 MILES
4 MILES
5 MILES
6 MILES
7 MILES

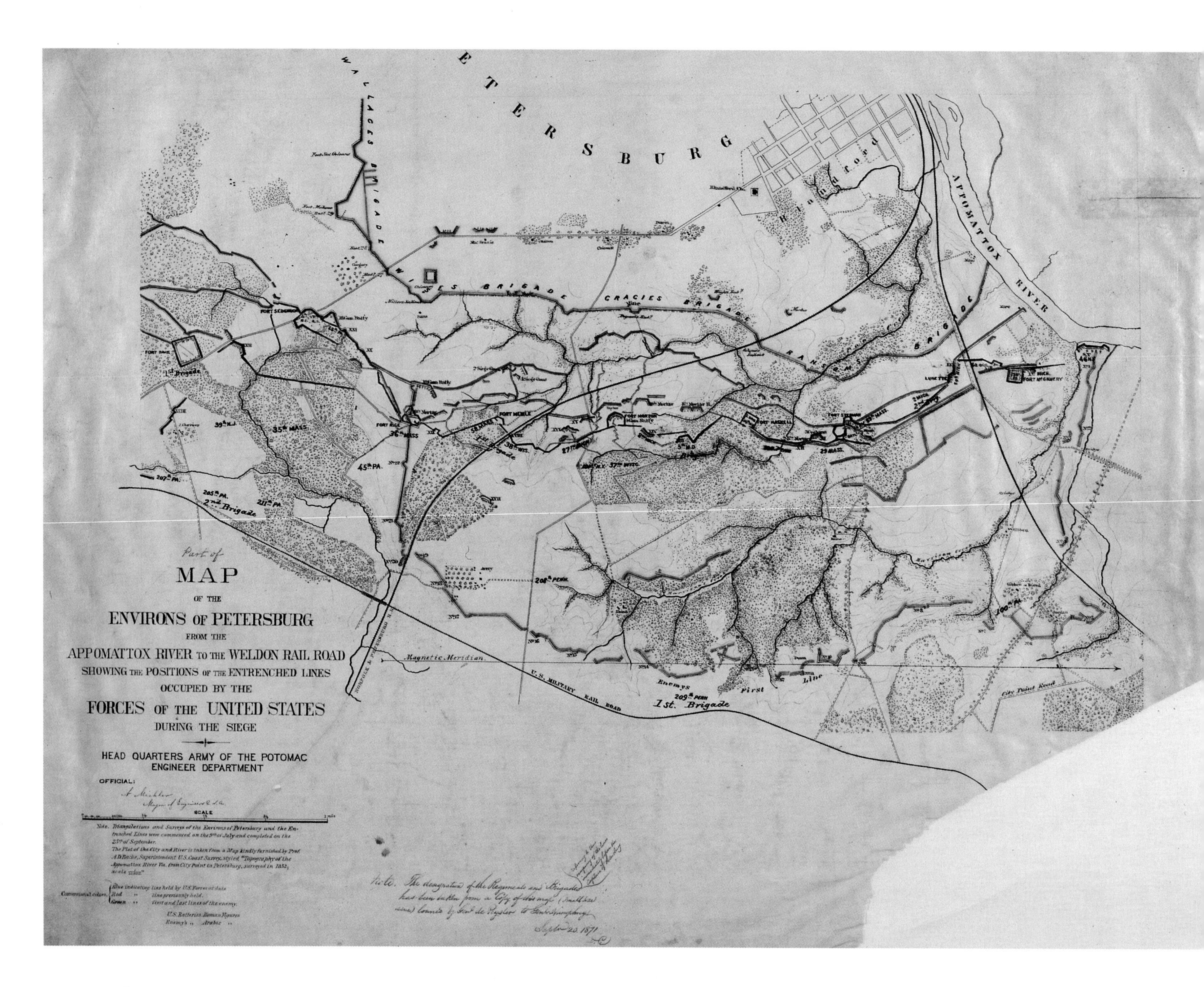
Part of
MAP
OF THE
ENVIRONS OF PETERSBURG
FROM THE
APPOMATTOX RIVER TO THE WELDON RAIL ROAD
SHOWING THE POSITIONS OF THE ENTRENCHED LINES
OCCUPIED BY THE
FORCES OF THE UNITED STATES
DURING THE SIEGE
HEAD QUARTERS ARMY OF THE POTOMAC
ENGINEER DEPARTMENT
OFFICIAL:
SCALE
Note. Triangulations and Surveys of the Environs of Petersburg and the Entrenched Lines were commenced on the 9th of July and completed on the 25th of September.
The Plot of the City and River is taken from a Map kindly furnished by Prof. A.D. Bache, Superintendent U.S. Coast Survey, styled "Topography of the Appomattox River Va. from City Point to Petersburg, surveyed in 1852,"
Conventional colors.
Blue indicating line held by U.S. Forces at date
Red ,, line previously held.
Green ,, first and last lines of the enemy.
U.S. Batteries Roman Figures
Enemy's ,, Arabic ,,
PETERSBURG
APPOMATTOX RIVER
WALLACES BRIGADE
WISES BRIGADE
GRACIES BRIGADE
RANSOMS BRIGADE
FORT SEDGWICK
FORT DAVIS
FORT RICE
FORT MEIKLE
FORT MORTON
FORT HASKELL
FORT STEDMAN
FORT MCGILVERY
1st. Brigade
2nd. Brigade
35th MASS.
36th MASS.
39th N.J.
45th PA.
207th PA.
205th PA.
211th PA.
208th PENN.
209th PENN.
29 MASS.
37th WISC.
38th WIS.
27th MICH.
100th PA.
Magnetic Meridian
U.S. MILITARY RAIL ROAD
NORFOLK & PETERSBURG R.R.
Enemys First Line
City Point Road
Note. The designation of the Regiments and Brigades has been taken from a Copy of this map (small size) loaned by Genl de Peyster to Genl Humphreys
Septr 20. 1871

Left: Map of the environs of Petersburg, from the Appomattox River to the Weldon Railroad showing positions of Union forces immediately before the capture of Petersburg, June 19, 1864.

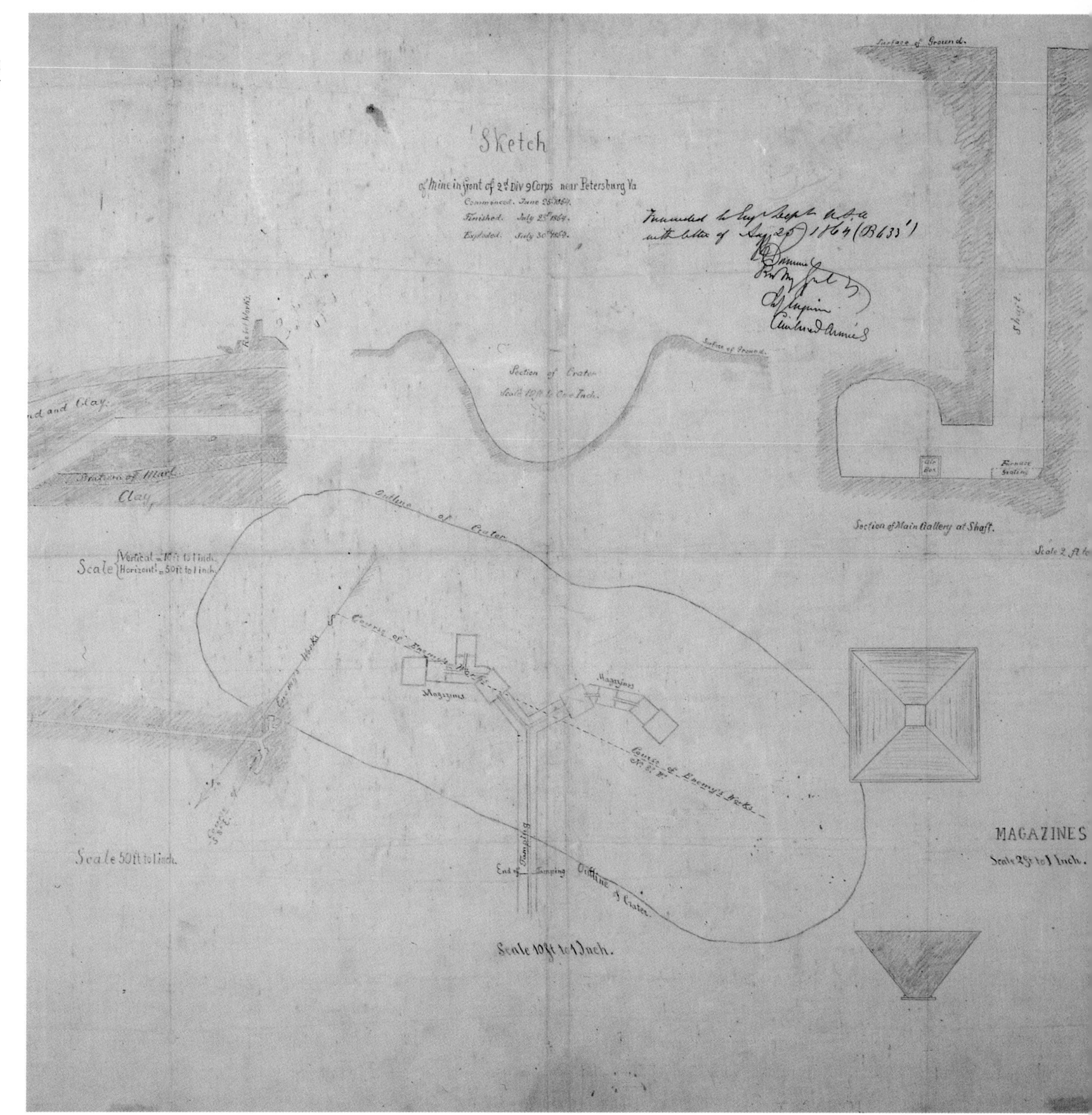

Right: This rough sketch is a plan of the mine shaft that was excavated under the Confederate lines near Petersburg by Union engineers. The work commenced on June 25, 1864, and was finished on July 23. The explosive packed into the mine was detonated on July 30, creating the crater that the artist has depicted in the center of his plan.

Right and Below (detail): This is a commercial map produced by a Boston publisher, John H. Bufford. His "angle" was to aim at those serving in the Union armed forces—a sizable market—and provide a grid system so that they could tell people of their location or actions. Bufford even had the temerity to add authenticity to his map by advertising it as "Genl. Grant's Campaign War Map." Note the use of a grid system.

Far Right: Petersburg and Five Forks—an extremely detailed topographic map produced from a survey by Brigadier-General Nathaniel Michler and published in 1867. Union positions are given in blue and Confederate in red.

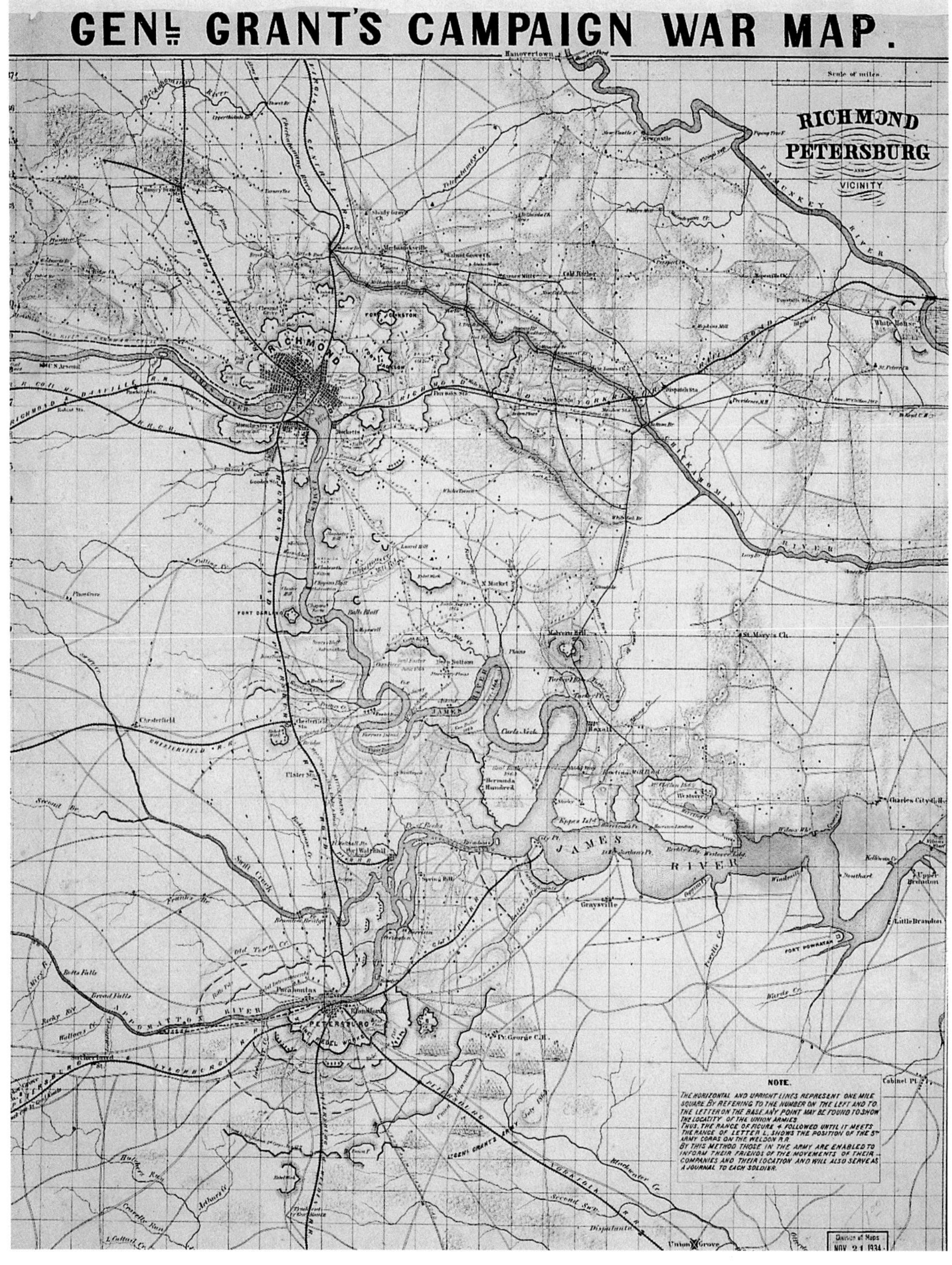

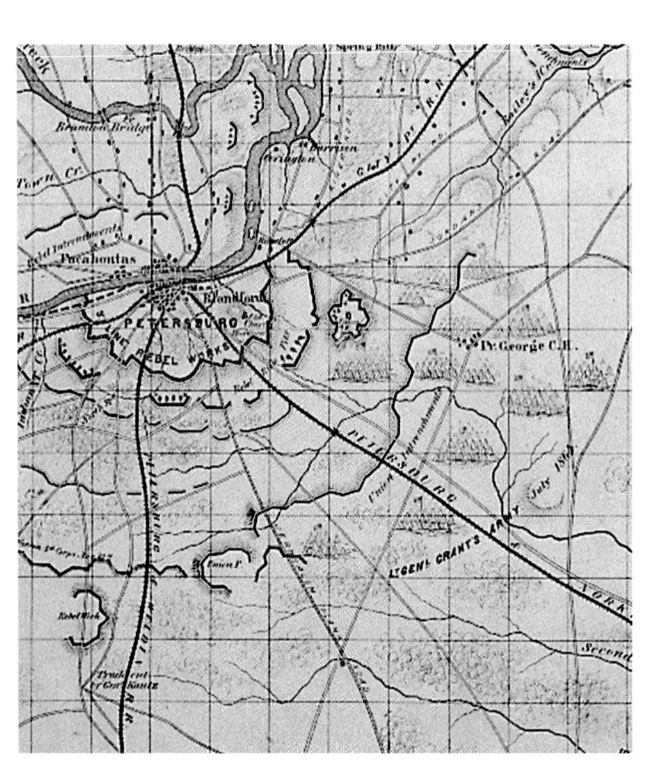

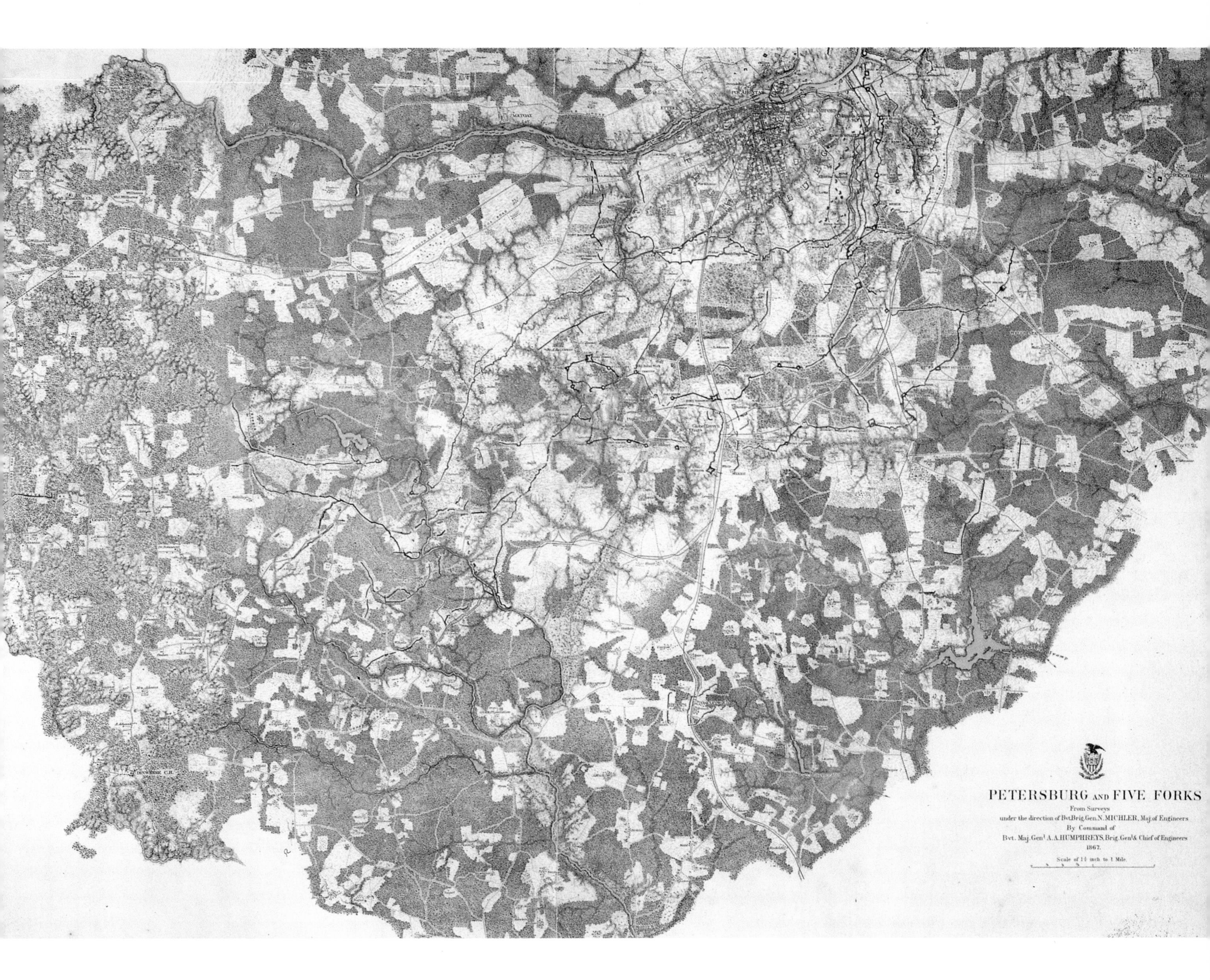
PETERSBURG AND FIVE FORKS
From Surveys
under the direction of Bvt.Brig.Gen.N. MICHLER, Maj.of Engineers
By Command of
Bvt. Maj.Genl A.A.HUMPHREYS, Brig.Genl & Chief of Engineers
1867.
Scale of 1½ inch to 1 Mile.
DINWIDDIE C.H.

CHIEF ENGINEERS OFFICE D.N.V.
MAJ. GEN. J. F. GILMER CHIEF ENGINEER.
MAP OF THE
VICINITY OF RICHMOND
AND PART OF THE
PENINSULA
FROM SURVEYS MADE
UNDER THE DIRECTION OF A. H. CAMPBELL, CAPT. P.E.C.S.A.
IN CHARGE TOPOGRAPH^L DEP^T D.N.V.
1864

Albermarle County, Virginia, 1864

Left: Confederate map of Albermarle County, Virginia. The map was prepared in 1864 on tracing linen by Lieutenant C. S. Dwight from a survey conducted by Albert H. Campbell, the Chief of the Topographical Department of the Department of North Virginia.

Far Left: Another Confederate map, this one by Albert H. Campbell of the Department of North Virginia, depicts the Virginia Peninsula from Round Squirrel Church to Williamsburg. It was prepared for use in the field by Confederate engineers from a photocopying of the original. The copy was then sectioned and mounted on cotton muslin. Note the fold marks to allow the user to reduce the map to a more manageable size (16 x 13cm).

Battle of the Monocacy, Maryland, July 9, 1864

Right: This map of the Battle of the Monocacy formed part of Jedediah Hotchkiss's report and atlas for the camps, marches and engagements of 1864–65 of II Corps, Army of North Virginia. When time permitted, army topographers were required to prepare maps of the fields of battle for use in official reports. This is one of 38 such maps in the report. Early left Lee at Cold Harbor and linked with Major-General John Breckinridge's forces at Lynchburg, Virginia. Thrusting toward Washington D.C. to draw as much of Grant's strength away from Petersburg, he was confronted on the banks of the Monocacy River by a small force of Union troops—some 7,000 strong, led by Major-General Lew Wallace. Early brushed these troops aside on Saturday, June 9; Wallace lost 1,800 men, most captured.

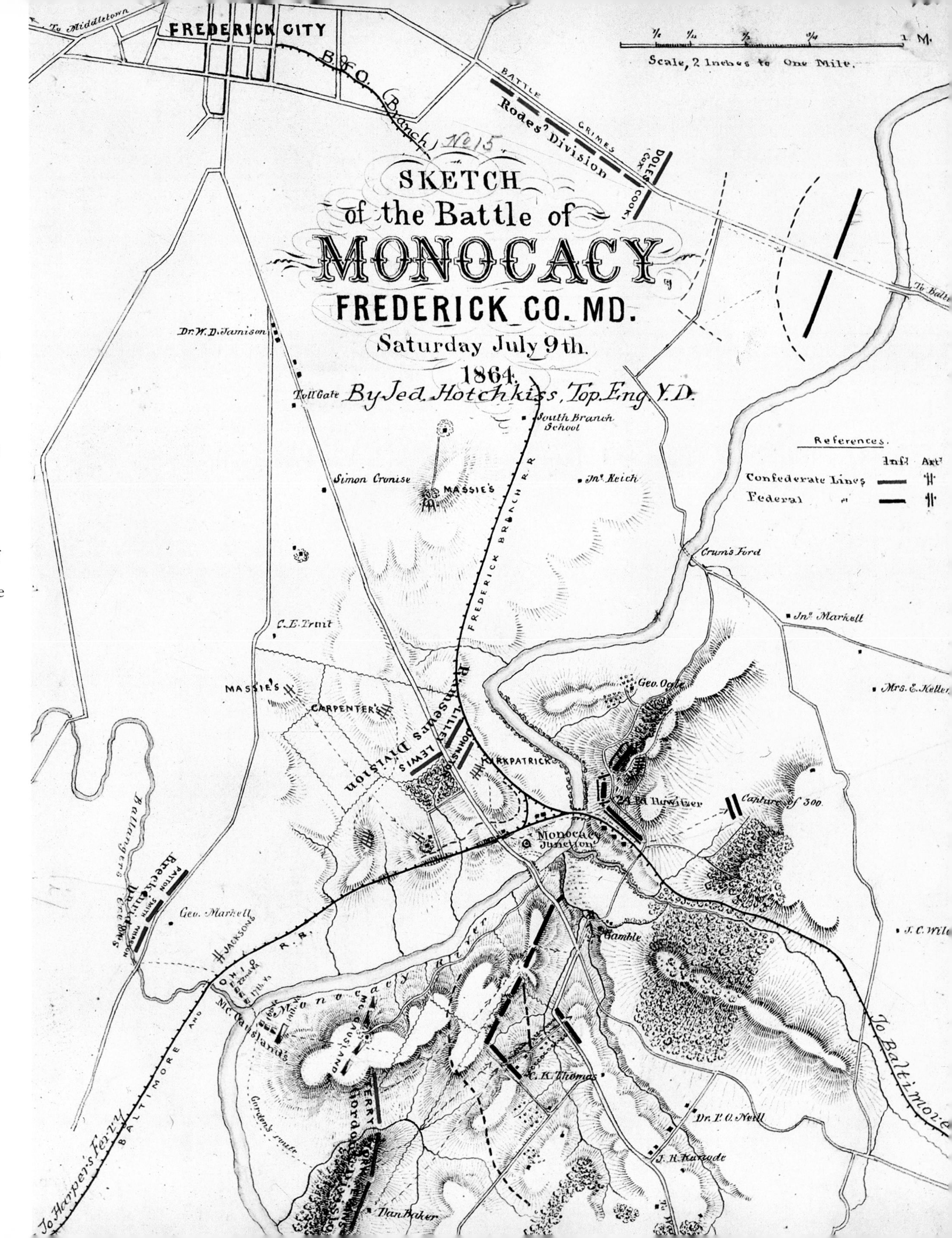

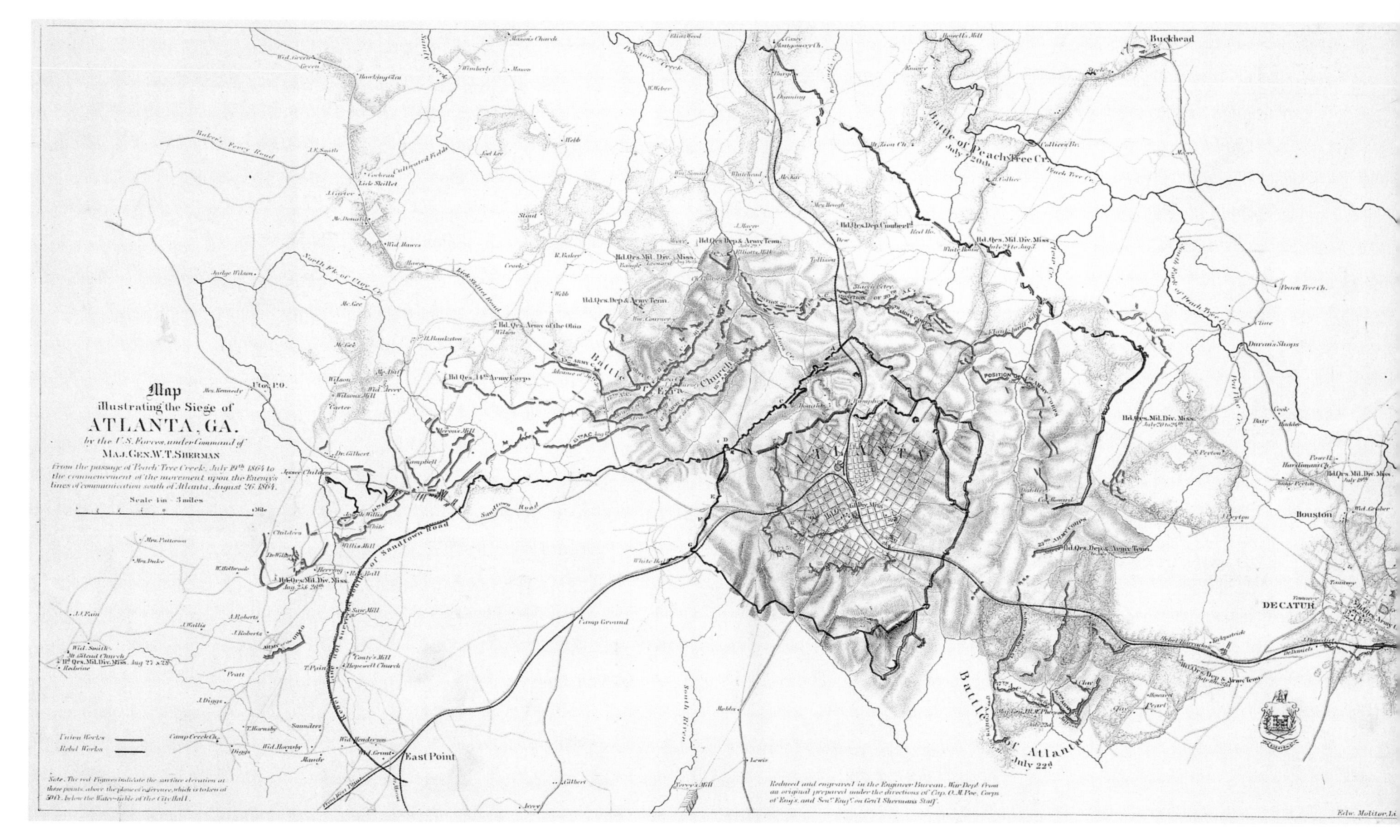

Advance on Atlanta, Georgia, July–September 1864

Above and Pages 124 and 125: Sherman began his advance on Georgia on July 19, 1864, and successfully fought off a Confederate counterattack on the 22nd. Sherman subsequently moved to surround the city, hoping to force its abandonment. On August 27 he delivered a telling blow by cutting the final rail links into the city. On September 1, Hood and the Army of the Tennessee evacuated; Union troops moved into the city the next day. This map (**Above**) illustrates the military operations in front of Atlanta, Georgia from the passage of Peach Tree Creek, July 19, 1864, to the commencement of the movement upon the enemy's lines of communication, south of Atlanta, August 26, 1864. Compiled 1875.

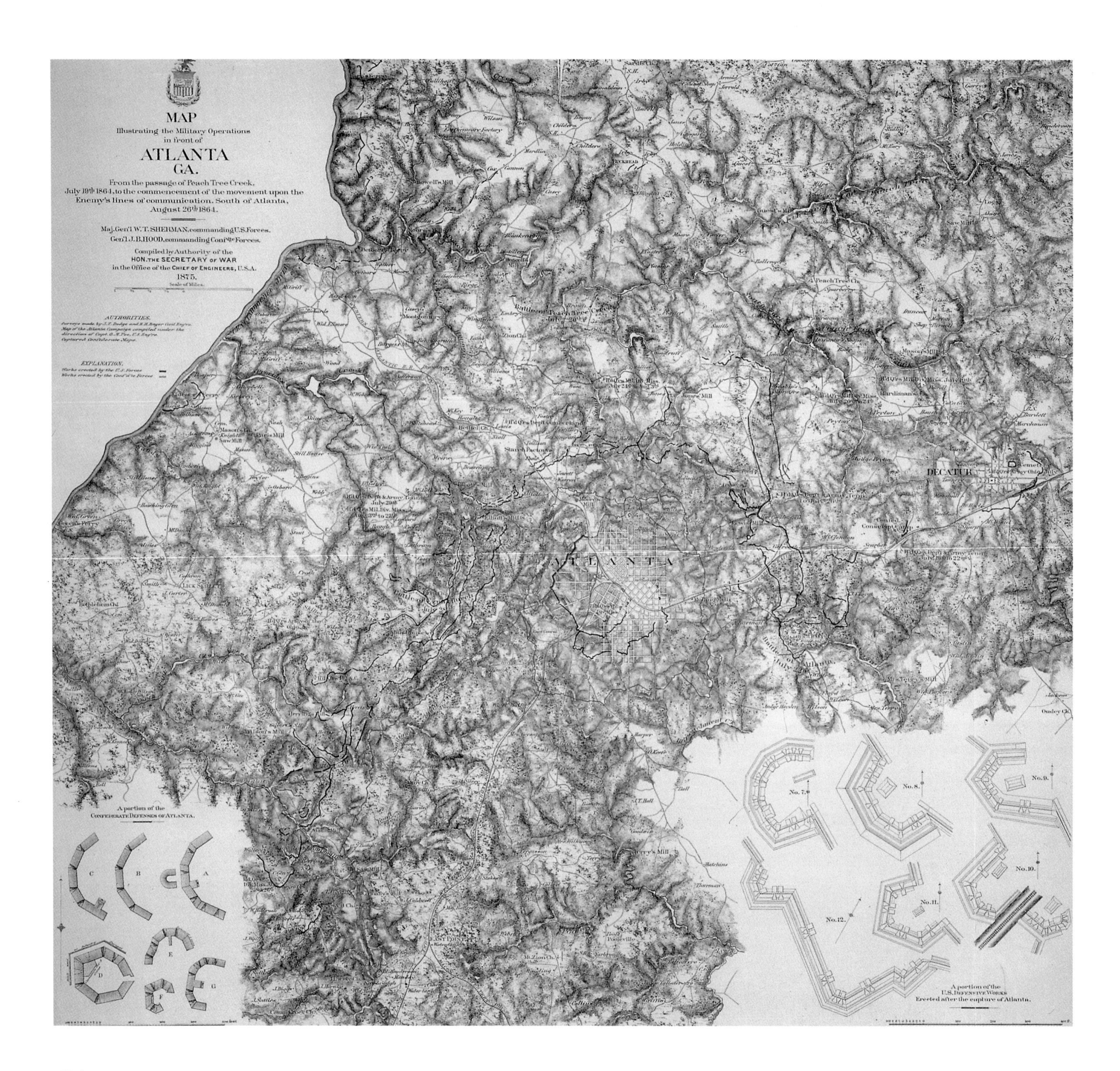
MAP
Illustrating the Military Operations
in front of
ATLANTA
GA.
From the passage of Peach Tree Creek,
July 19th 1864, to the commencement of the movement upon the
Enemy's lines of communication, South of Atlanta,
August 26th 1864.
Maj. Gen'l W. T. SHERMAN, commanding U.S. Forces.
Gen'l J. B. HOOD, commanding Conf'ate Forces.
Compiled by Authority of the
HON. THE SECRETARY OF WAR
in the Office of the CHIEF OF ENGINEERS, U.S.A.
1875.
Scale of Miles.
AUTHORITIES.
EXPLANATION.
ATLANTA
DECATUR
A portion of the
CONFEDERATE DEFENSES OF ATLANTA.
A portion of the
U.S. DEFENSIVE WORKS
Erected after the capture of Atlanta.

Left and This Page (details): Another map showing the siege of Atlanta. The insets are examples of the Confederate defensive works (left of map and shown **Below**) and the Union defenses erected after the capture of the city (right of map and shown **Below Right**).

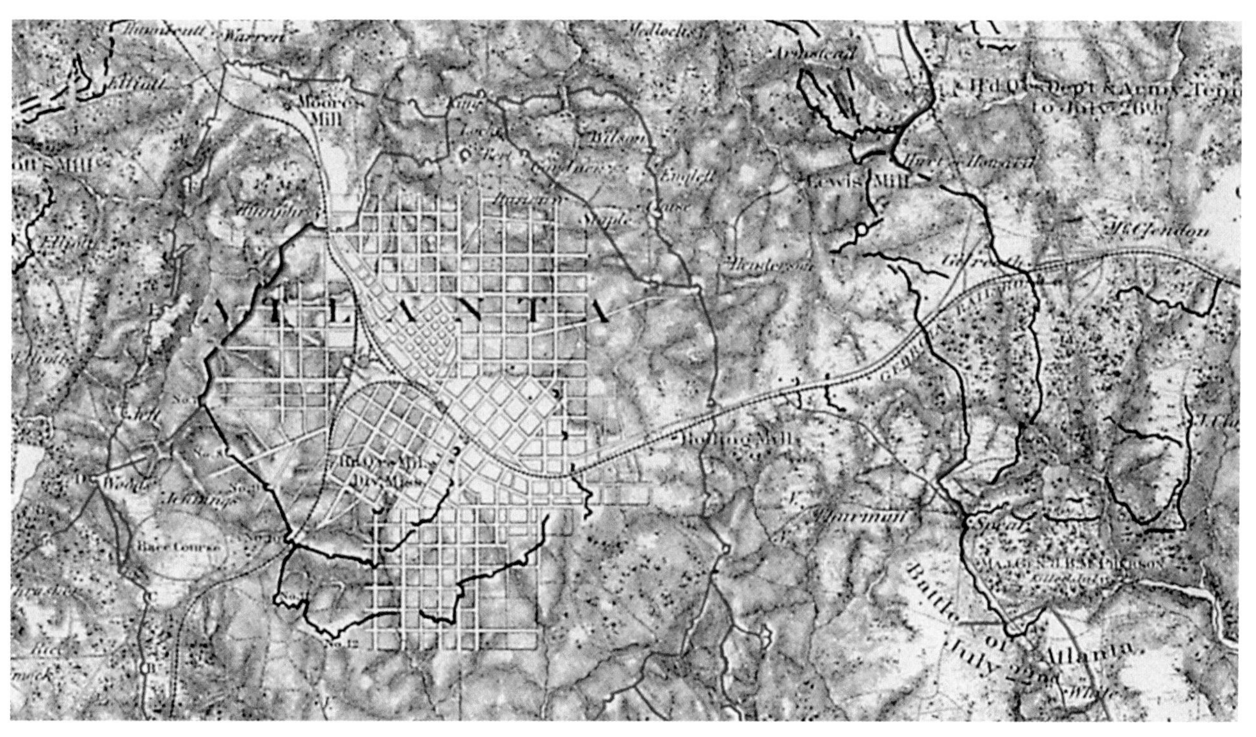

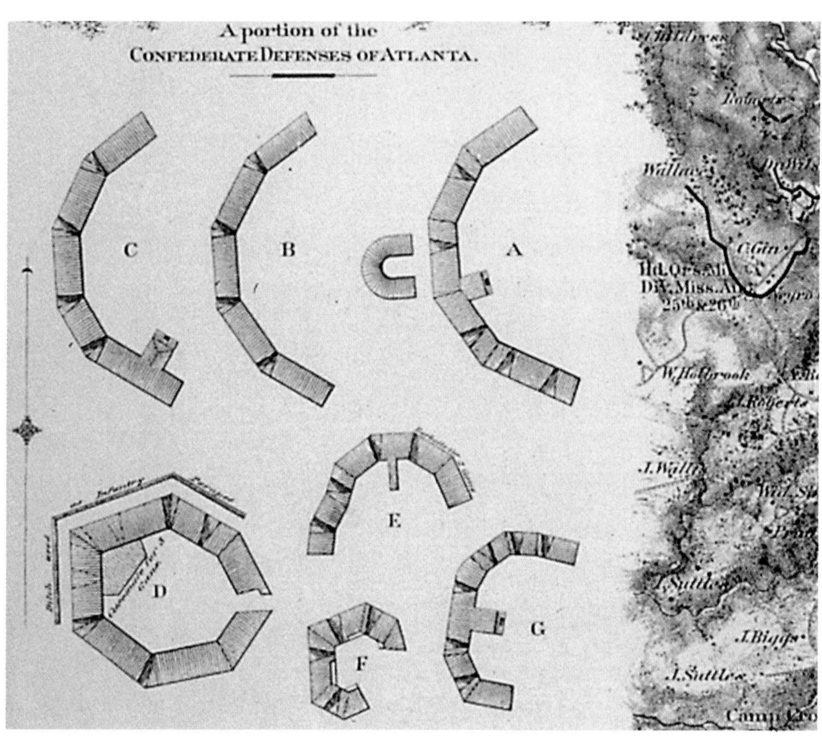

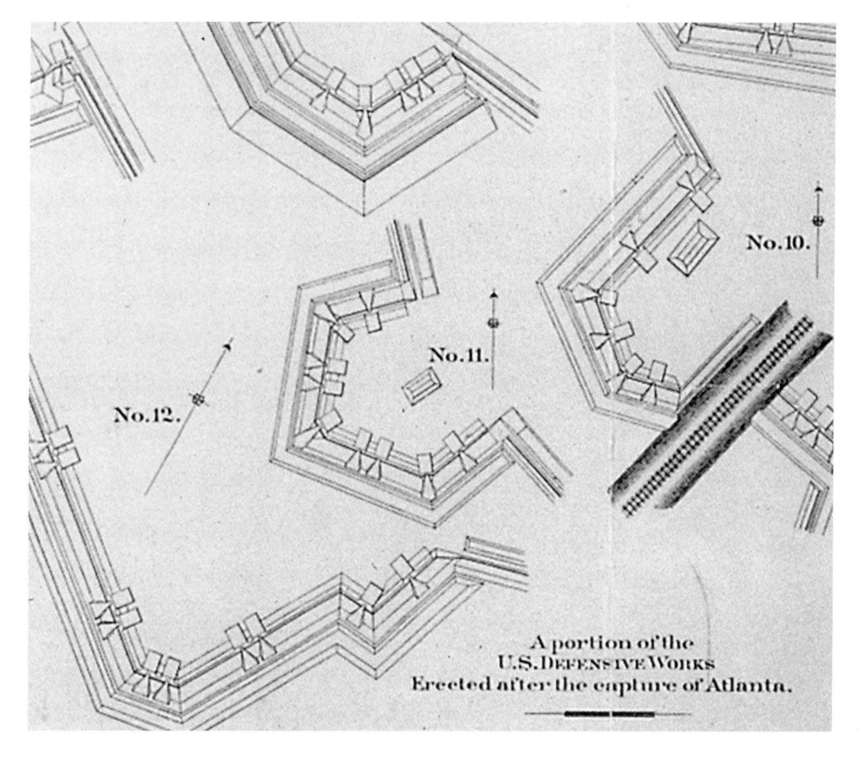

Battle of Mobile Bay, Alabama, August 5, 1864

Right: Detailed chart compiled and drawn by Robert Weir for Admiral David Farragut after the Battle of Mobile Bay, Alabama. The chart shows the positions and tracks of the vessels during the sea battle, obstructions, channels, banks, and shoals. Small views show the iron-clad *Tennessee*, a Federal ship colliding with the ram *Tennessee*, a general view of the battle and a vessel passing Mobile Point. Besides removing a valuable port from the Confederacy, the action gave the Union army a base from which to launch attacks on Mobile.

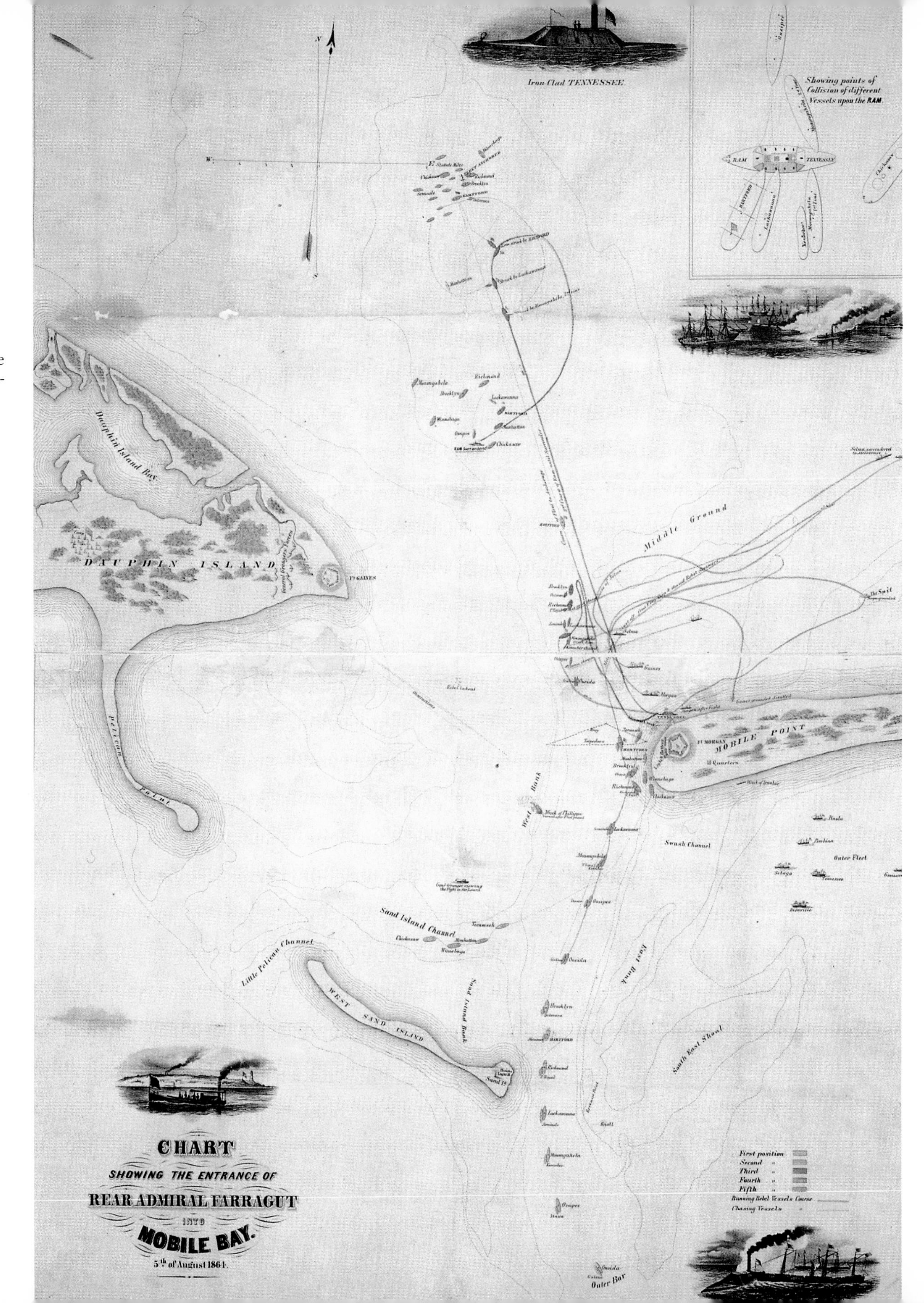

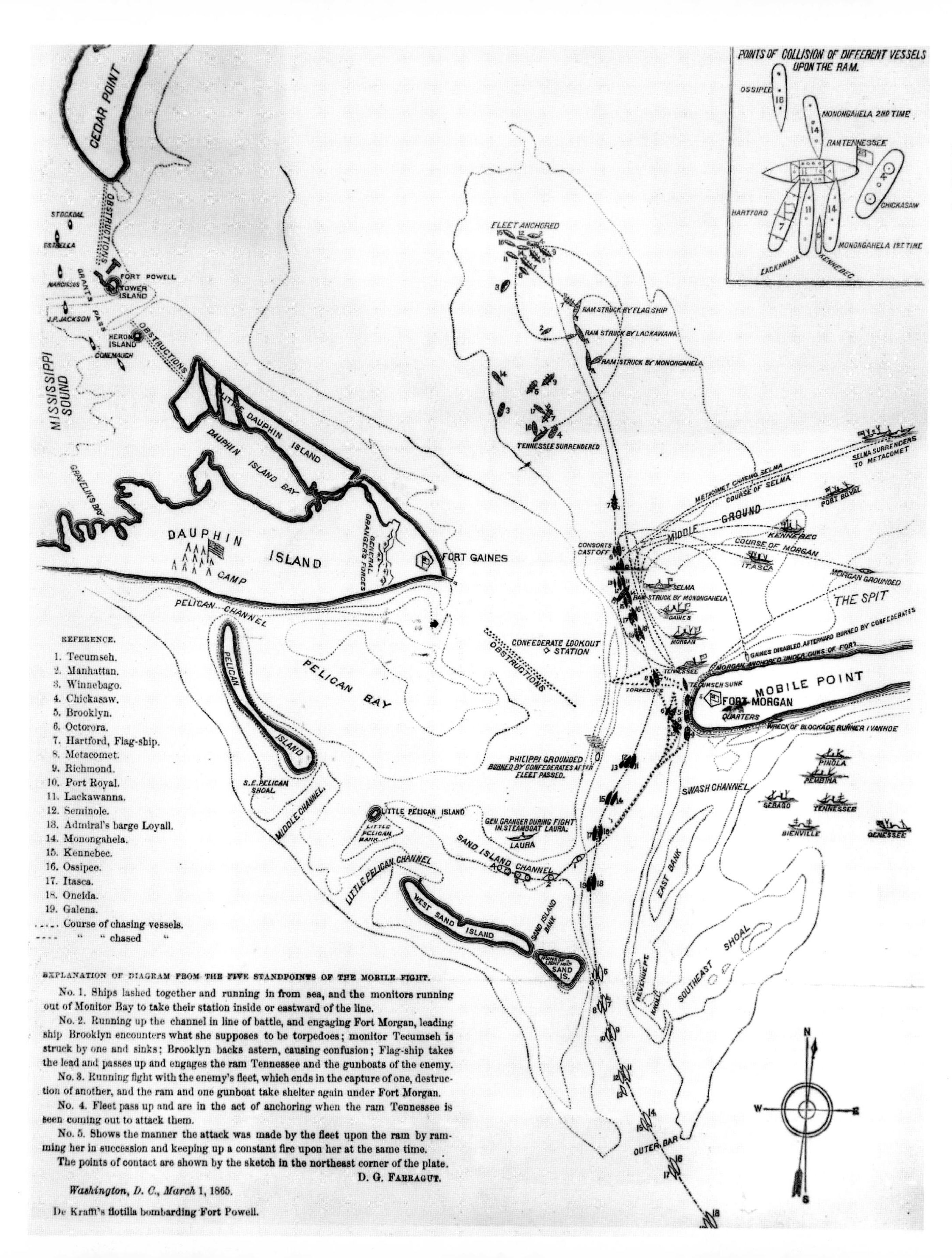

Left: Another view of the battle with a report signed by Rear Admiral Farragut and dated March 1, 1865.

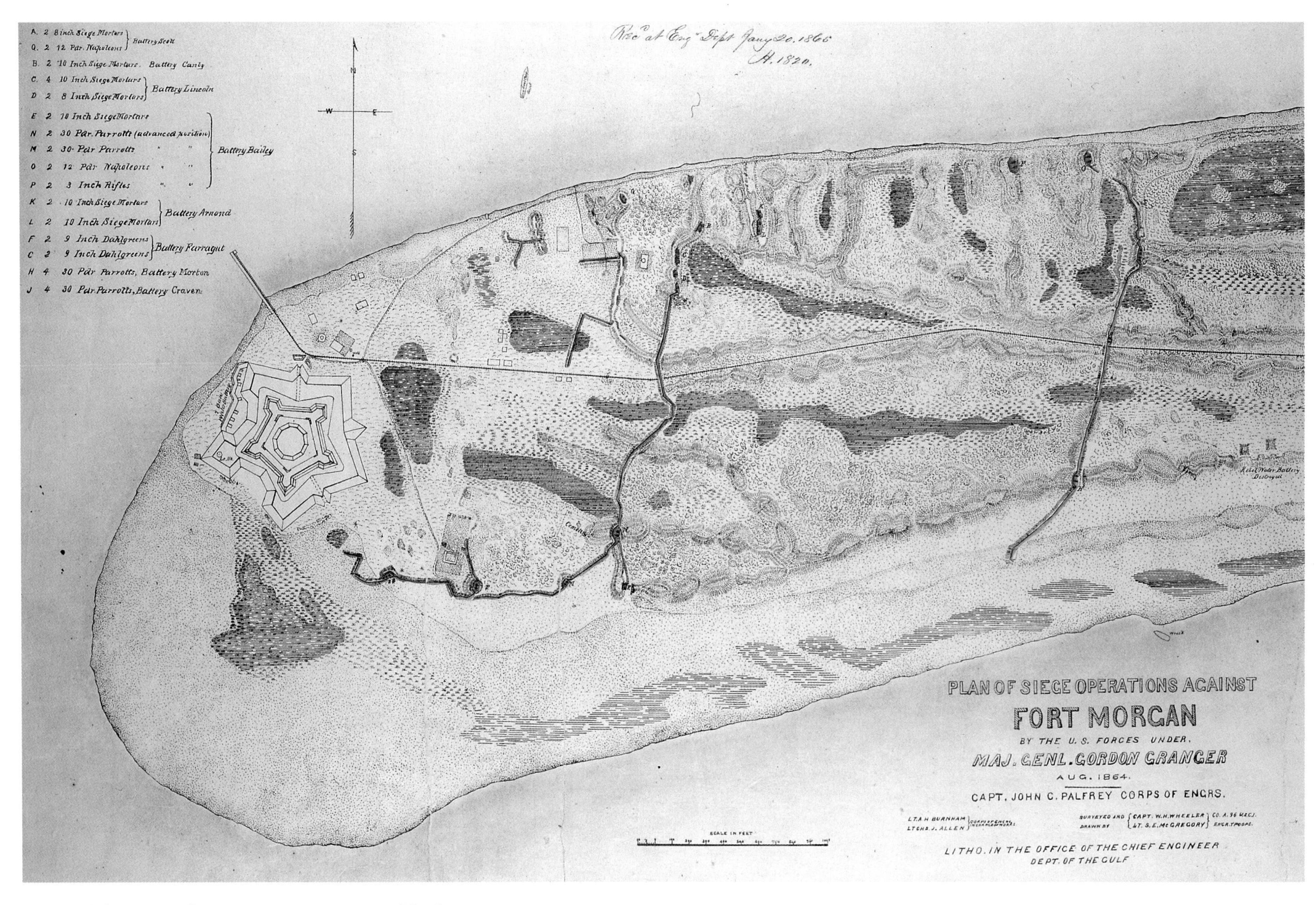

Siege of Fort Morgan, Alabama, August 1864

Above: Plan of the siege operations against Fort Morgan, as surveyed and drawn by Captain Wheeler and Lieutenant Gregory, engineers with the Department of the Gulf. The defensive lines and works are shown, and the number and type of armament along the line of works are listed with letters keyed to positions on the map. Fort Morgan, at the entrance to Mobile Bay, was blockaded after the naval battle by Union ships and fell on August 23, 1864. Thereafter, the only port remaining in Confederate hands is Wilmington, North Carolina.

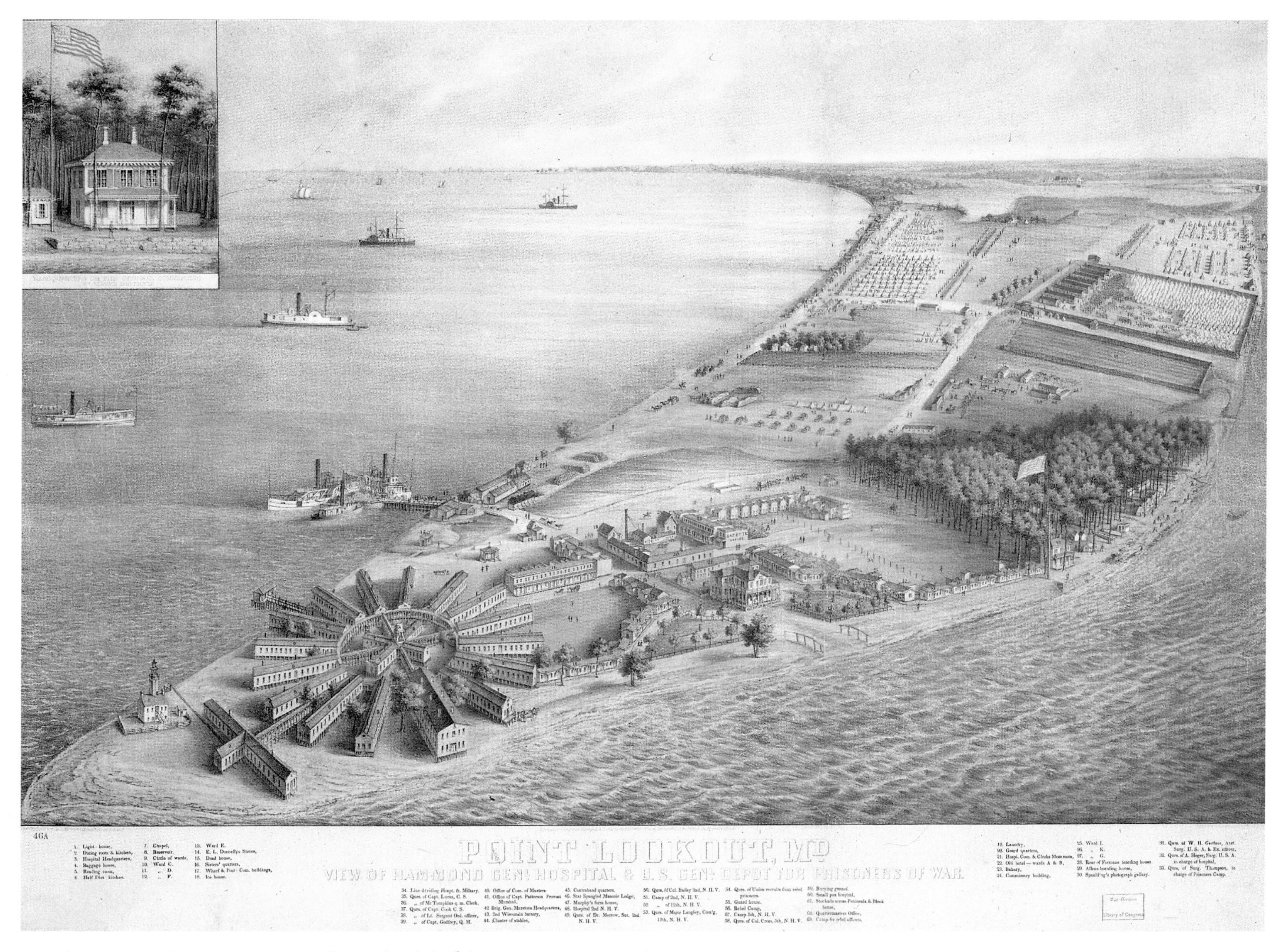

Point Lookout, Maryland, 1864

Above: Edward Sachse used the popular panoramic or bird's eye view in this lithographed depiction of Point Lookout, Maryland, published in 1864 in the town by George Everett. It shows Hammond General Hospital and the U.S. General Depot for prisoners of war; 63 other sites are listed in the margin and keyed by numbers to the appropriate position in the view. The inset image is the headquarters of the commanding general.

Battle of Franklin, Tennessee, November 30, 1864

Right: This photo-lithograph is an issue of a map compiled under the direction of Colonel William E. Merrill depicting the battlefield in front of Franklin, where Union General Schofield stood to halt Hood's advance from Alabama.

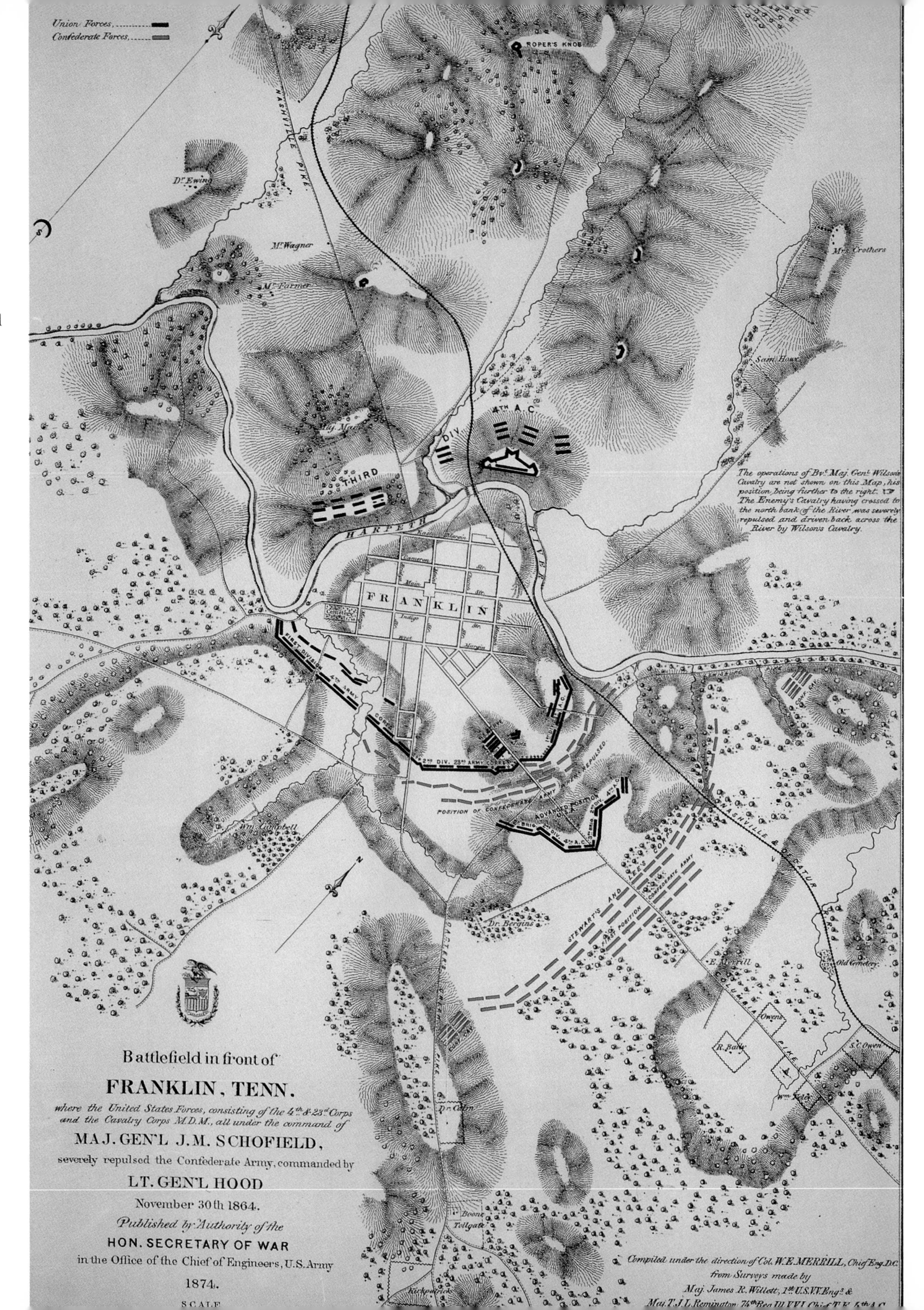

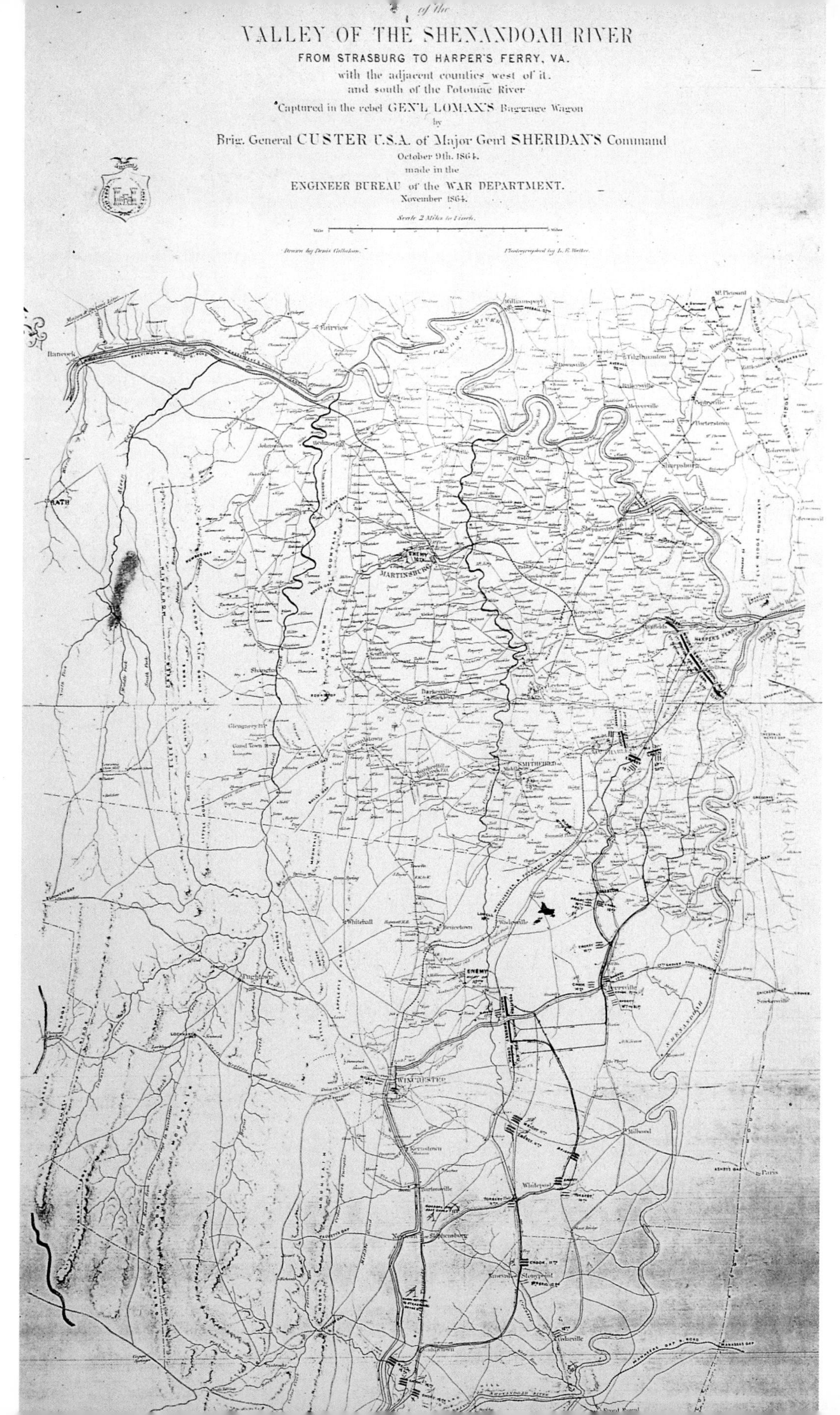

Shenandoah Valley, Fall 1864

Left: Annotated photo-processed map showing the routes and positions of the different commands of Wright, Emory, Crook, and Torbett through the Shenandoah Valley during the early stages of the Valley Campaign. The topographical map is a copy of one captured by General George Custer from General Lomax on October 9, 1864 during skirmishing between Union and Confederate cavalry at Tom's Brook and in the Luray Valley.

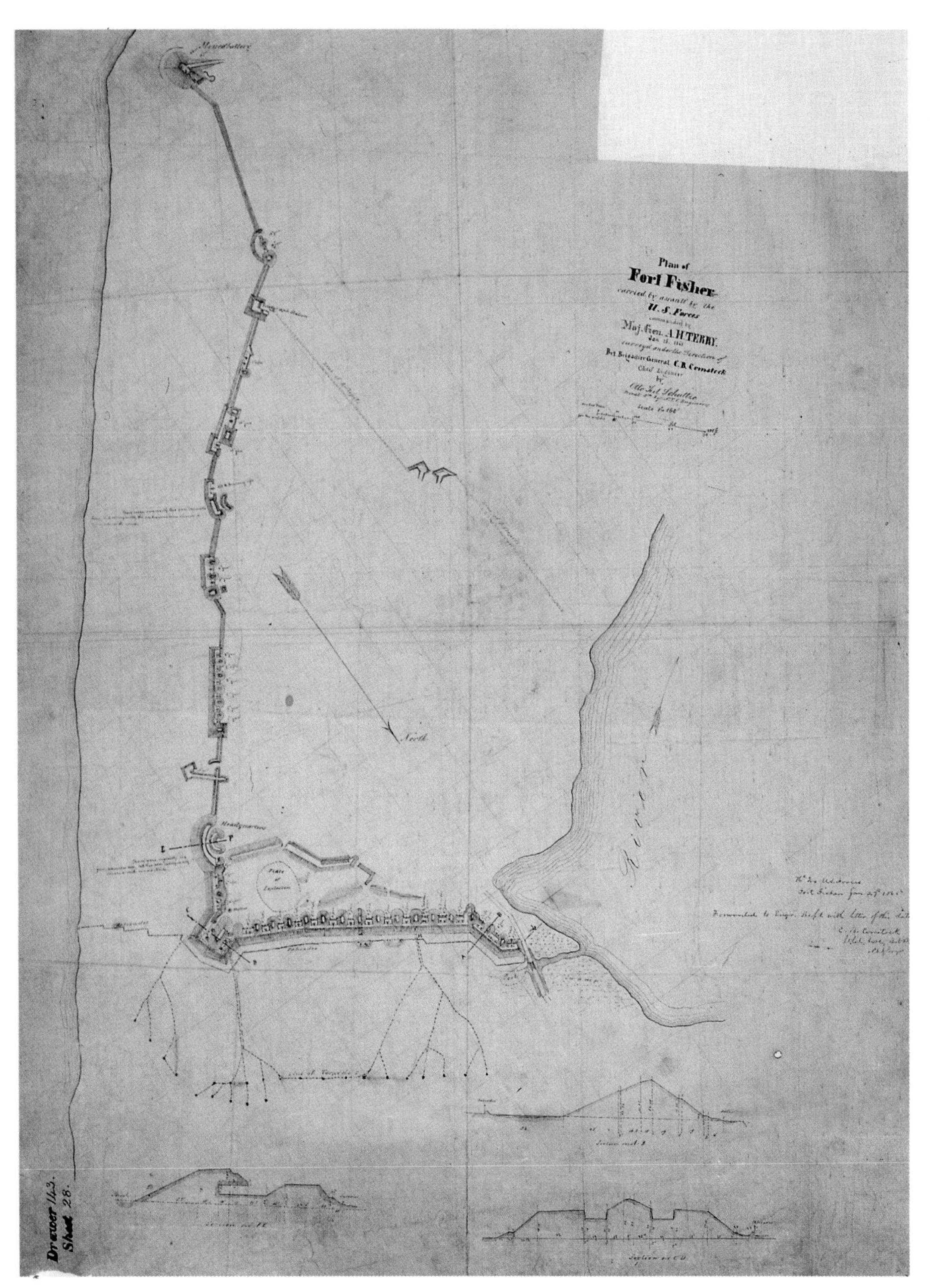

Fort Fisher, North Carolina, 1865

Left: Plan of Fort Fisher surveyed under Brigadier-General C. B. Comstock and drawn by Otto Schulze, a private in the New York Volunteer Engineers. Fort Fisher was taken by a combined Union army and navy force under General Terry and Admiral Porter on January 15, 1865, after a two-day naval bombardment. The line of torpedoes launched by Porter's ships and their "place of explosion" is indicated.

Battle of Nashville, Tennessee, December 15–16, 1864

Map of the battlefield of Nashville signed by Brigadier-General Z. B. Tower showing the positions of the Union and Confederate forces during the action. Photo-reproduction was a common technique, and by 1864 both the Confederate Topographical Department and its Union equivalent had developed means of copying maps in the field.

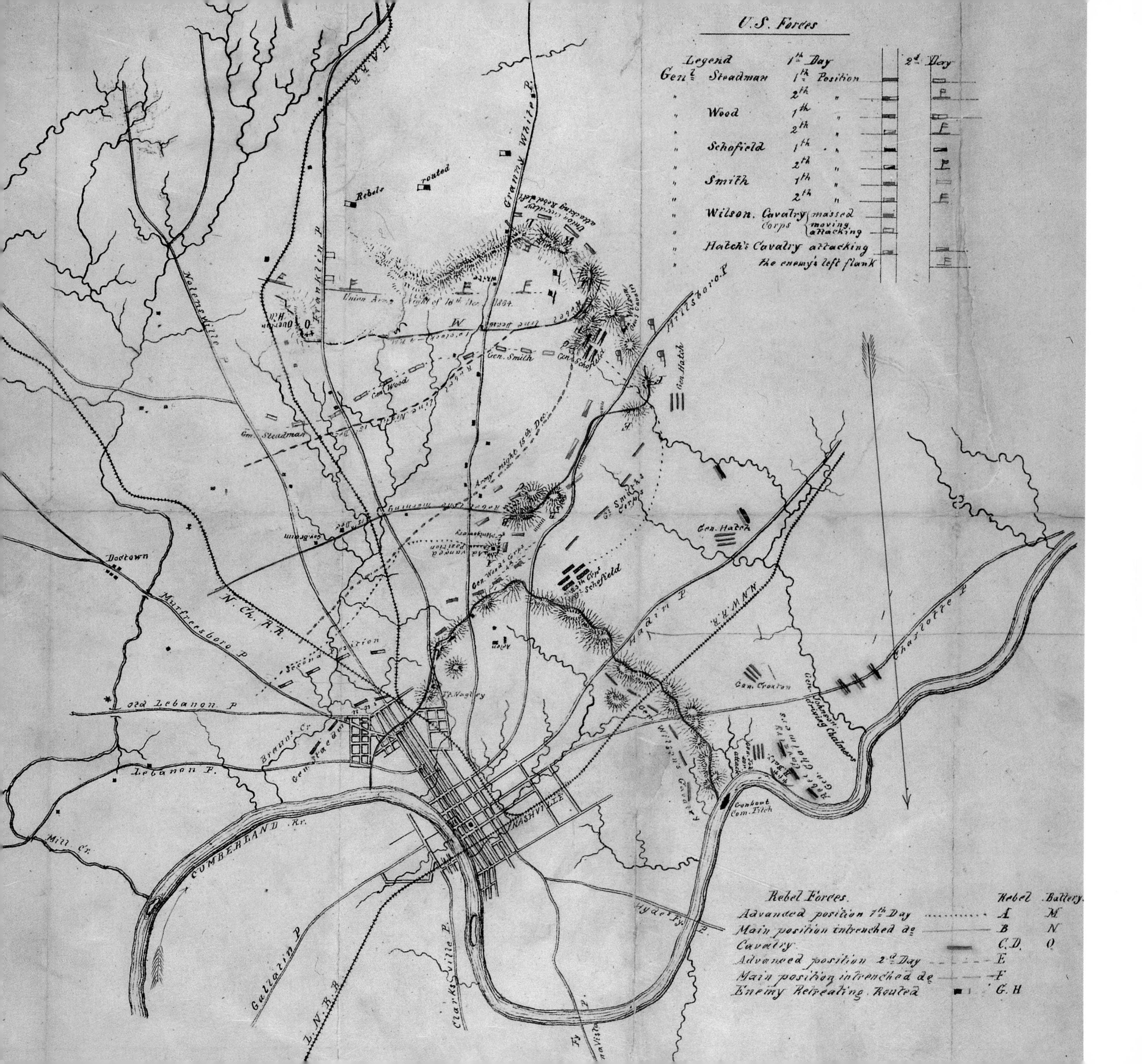
U.S. Forces
Legend 1th Day 2d Day
Genl. Steadman 1th Position
2th
Wood 1th
2th
Schofield 1th
2th
Smith 1th
2th
Wilson. Cavalry Corps massed moving attacking
Hatch's Cavalry attacking the enemy's left flank
Rebels routed
Union Army Night of 16th Dec. 1864
Gen. Smith
Gen. Schofield
Gen. Wood
Gen. Steadman
Gen. Hatch
Gen. Croxton
Smith's Corps
Army night 15th Dec.
Second position
Ft. Negley
Wilson's Cavalry
Gunboat Com. Fitch
NASHVILLE
CUMBERLAND R.
Dogtown
Murfreesboro P.
N. Ch. R.R.
Old Lebanon P.
Lebanon P.
Mill Cr.
Browns Cr.
Nolensville P.
Franklin P.
Granny White P.
Hillsboro P.
Hardin P.
N.N.W.R.R.
Charlotte P.
Gallatin P.
L.N.R.R.
Clarksville P.
Hyde Fy. P.
Rebel Forces.
Rebel Battery
Advanced position 1st Day A M
Main position intrenched do. B N
Cavalry C.D. O
Advanced position 2d Day E
Main position intrenched do. F
Enemy Retreating. Routed G. H

Appomattox, April 1865

Right and Far Right: Two very different maps of the court house at Appomattox, scene of General Lee's surrender on April 9, 1865. The first (**Right**) is a pen and ink sketch, whose author chose to remain anonymous. The map was submitted to the Library of Congress after it was discovered in the "back closet of a desk." It has clearly been executed in some haste, perhaps by an eyewitness to the historic events, who also provides notes in the margin. The more detailed commercial map (**Far Right**) published by Henderson and Co. shows the positions of Union and Confederate troops in red and blue respectively, houses, names of residents, roads, relief by hachures, drainage, and vegetation. There are also "historical notes" to accompany the map.

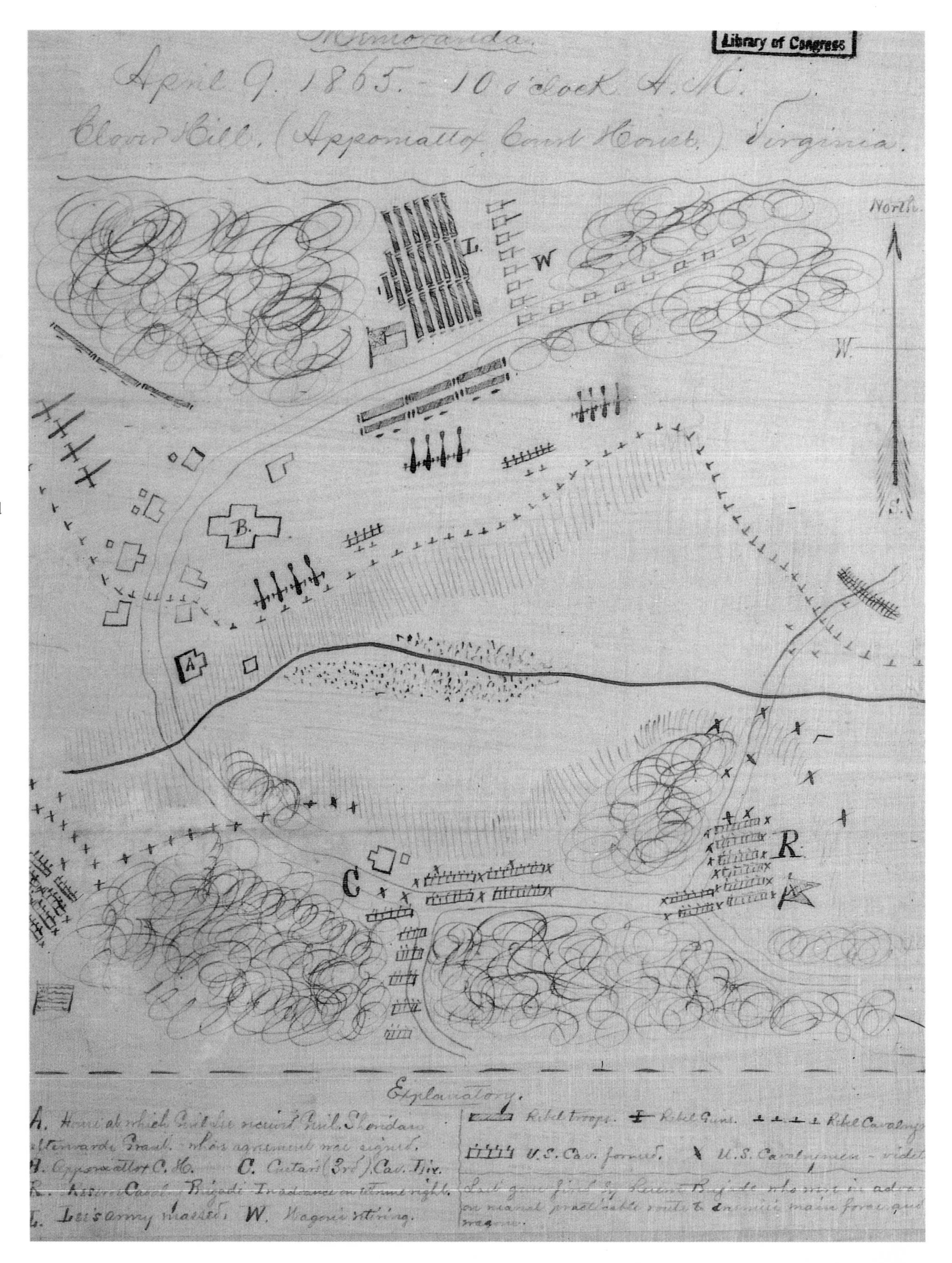

Lee's Head-Quarters.

MAP OF APPOMATTOX COURT HOUSE AND VICINITY.

Showing the relative positions of the Confederate and Federal Armies at the time of General R. E. LEE'S Surrender, April 9th 1865.

Grant's Head-Quarters.

Historical Notes.

On Sunday, the 2d of April 1865, General Lee was holding at Petersburg a semi-circular line south of the Appomattox River, with his left resting on the river, and his right on the South Side Rail Road, fifteen miles from the city. The Federals were pressing his whole line. Sheridan with his cavalry on the right. To save his right flank, General Lee telegraphed to Richmond, that during the night he would fall back to the north side of the river, and ordered that Richmond be evacuated simultaneously.

On the morning of the 3d the retreat commenced in earnest, General Grant hurrying up to get possession of Burkesville—the junction of the South Side and Danville Railroad—in hopes of cutting off General Lee from Danville or Lynchburg. On the 5th a portion of the Federal forces occupied Burkesville, Sheridan with his cavalry being in advance at Jetersville on the Danville Railroad. General Lee at Amelia C. H., 6 miles north of Sheridan's advance. In this situation General Sheridan telegraphed:—"I feel confident of capturing the entire Army of Northern Virginia, if we exert ourselves. I see no escape for Lee." On the evening of the 6th some heavy fighting took place between the Federal advance and Lee's retreating column. Sheridan again telegraphed: "If the thing is pressed I think Lee will surrender." Lee continued to press for Lynchburg—his men probably anticipating the result, daily leaving him by thousands,—until on the morning of the fated 9th of April, 1865, he confronted the overwhelming forces of Gen. Grant with a little less than 8,000 muskets.

The position of the Confederate army was briefly this: occupying the narrow strip of land between the South Side Railroad and the James River; the only road on which it was possible to retreat, was that marked Lynchburg road on the map. Sheridan with his cavalry having struck the railroad at Appomattox Station, obtaining possession of the Lynchburg road, thus effectually cutting off Lee's retreat. Gen. Lee now had the choice of either cutting his way directly through the Federal forces, or immediate surrender. In view of the immense disparity of forces between the ranks of the half starved Confederates and the overwhelming army of General Grant, he chose the letter alternative.

Generals Lee and Grant met at the house of Wilmer McLane, Esq., and after a brief interview, at 3½ o'clock p. m. on the 9th of April 1865, the Articles of Capitulation were signed by General Lee. While negotiations were being conducted by the two Commanders-in-Chief, the General officers of either army were mingling socially together in the streets of Appomattox C. H., and drinking mutual healths. Gens. Ord, Sheridan, Gibbon, Michie and others of the Federals, Gens. Longstreet, Heath, Gordon and others, of the Confederates.

At 4 o'clock p. m. the announcement of Lee's surrender was made to Grant's army. The wildest enthusiasm immediately broke forth, and all seemed mad with joy.

As the great Confederate General rode past his gallant little band from his interview with Gen. Grant, whole lines of battle rushed to the beloved old chief, and breaking ranks, each struggled with the other to wring him by the hand. With tears rolling down his cheeks, General Lee could only say, "Men, we have fought through the war together. I have done the best that I could for you."

On the morning of the 12th April the Army of Northern Virginia marched by divisions to a point near Appomattox Court House, and stacked arms and accoutrements. Maj. Gen. Gibbon representing the United States authorities.

On the afternoon of the 12th, with an escort of Federal cavalry as a guard of honor, attended by a portion of his staff, General Lee returned to Richmond.

Thus quietly passed from the theater of the most desperate war of modern times the renowned Commander of the Army of Northern Virginia, and the remnants of that once invincible army were quietly wending their way to their long forsaken homes.

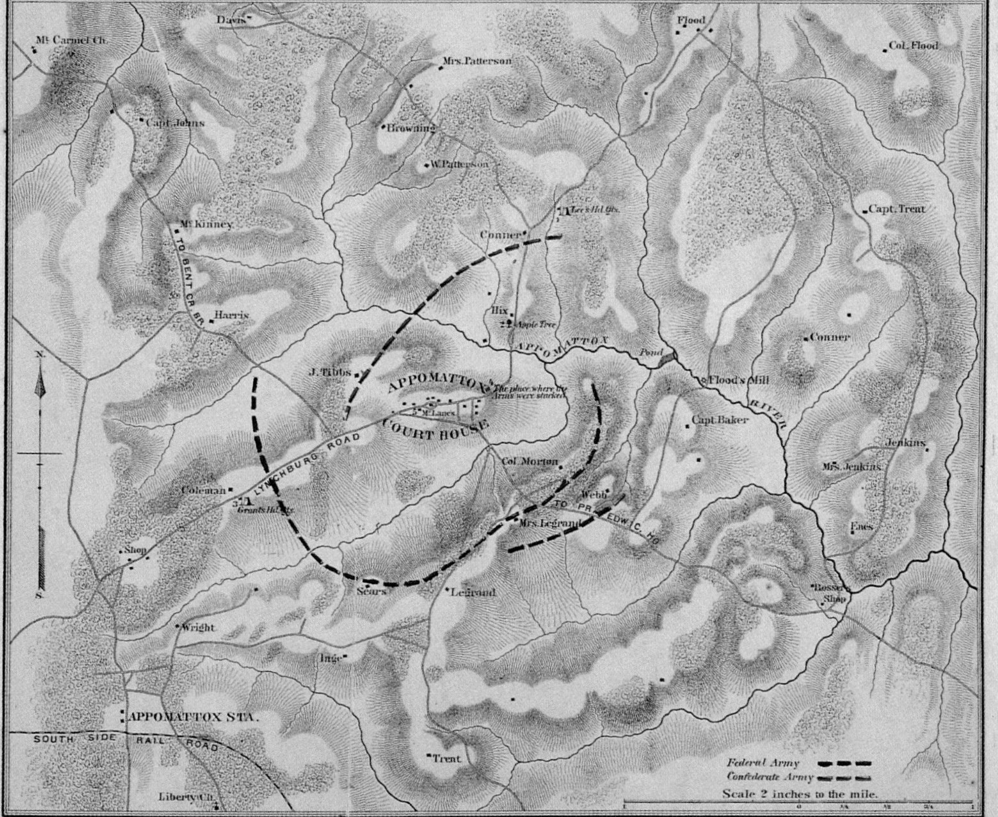

LIST OF ENGRAVINGS.

Gen. Lee's Head-Quarters near Conner's House.—Position marked by a flag and No. 1 on the map.

View of Appomattox Court House.

General Grant's Head-Quarters near Coleman's House.—Position marked by a flag and No. 3 on the map.

Place where the arms were stacked. The exact spot is marked No. 4 on the map. In this picture may be seen the famous apple tree, (position marked with a tree and No. 2 on the map,) near Hix's house, where the first meeting between the Commanders was generally, but incorrectly, supposed to have taken place.

McLane's House, in the village of Appomattox Court House, where the articles of capitulation were signed. The signing took place in the front room, on the right of the door, entering from the porch.

McLane's House.

GEN. LEE'S FAREWELL TO HIS ARMY.

HEAD-QUARTERS ARMY NORTHERN VIRGINIA,
APRIL 10TH, 1865.

After four years of arduous service, marked by unsurpassed courage and fortitude, the Army of Northern Virginia has been compelled to yield to overwhelming numbers and resources.

I need not tell the survivors of so many hard-fought battles, who have remained steadfast to the last, that I have consented to this result from no distrust of them; but feeling that valor and devotion could accomplish nothing that could compensate for the loss that would have attended the continuation of the contest, I have determined to avoid the useless sacrifice of those whose past services have endeared them to their countrymen.

Appomattox Court House.

By the terms of agreement, officers and men can return to their homes and remain there until exchanged.

You will take with you the satisfaction that proceeds from the consciousness of duty faithfully performed; and I earnestly pray that a merciful God will extend to you His blessing and protection.

With an unceasing admiration of your constancy and devotion to your country, and a grateful remembrance of your kind and generous consideration of myself, I bid you an affectionate farewell.

R. E. LEE, *General.*

Place where the Arms were Stacked.

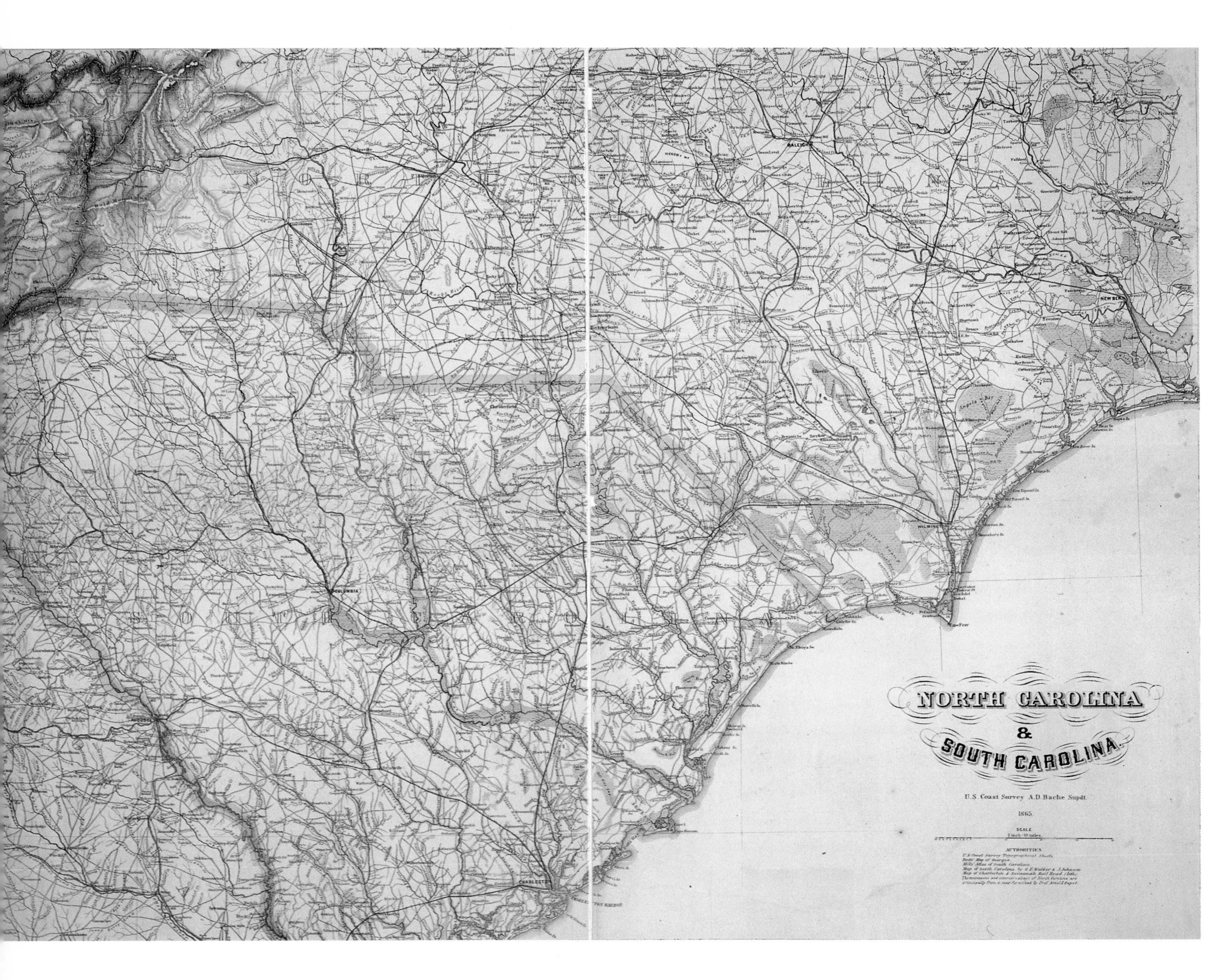
NORTH CAROLINA
&
SOUTH CAROLINA.
U.S. Coast Survey A.D. Bache Supdt.
1865.
SCALE
AUTHORITIES
RALEIGH
NEW BERN
WILMINGTON
COLUMBIA
CHARLESTON

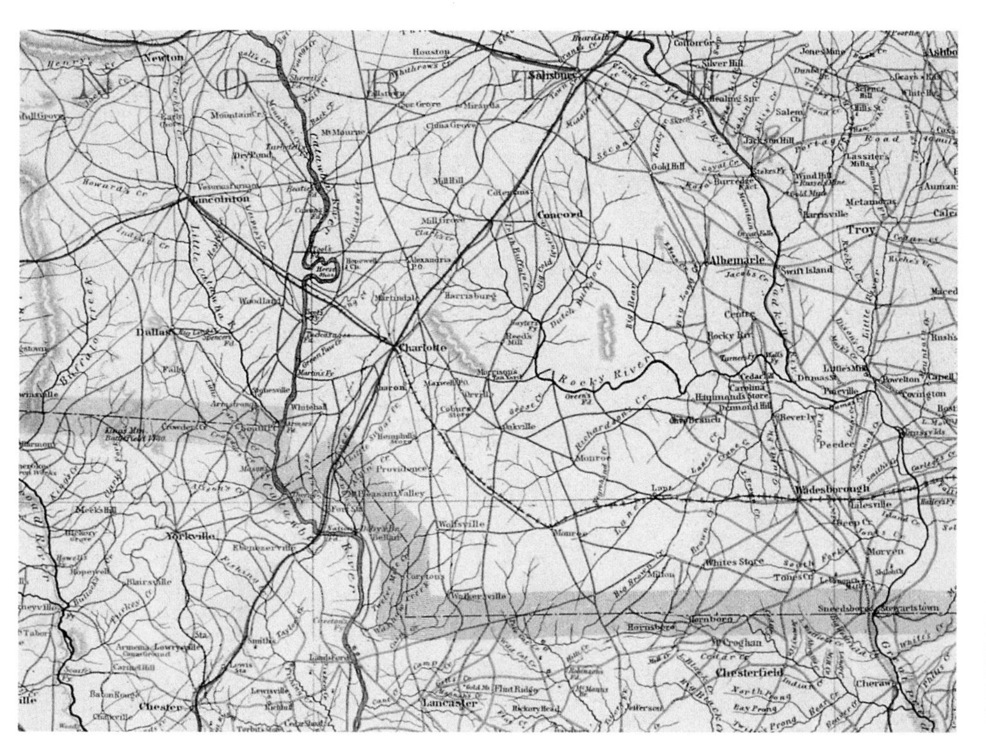

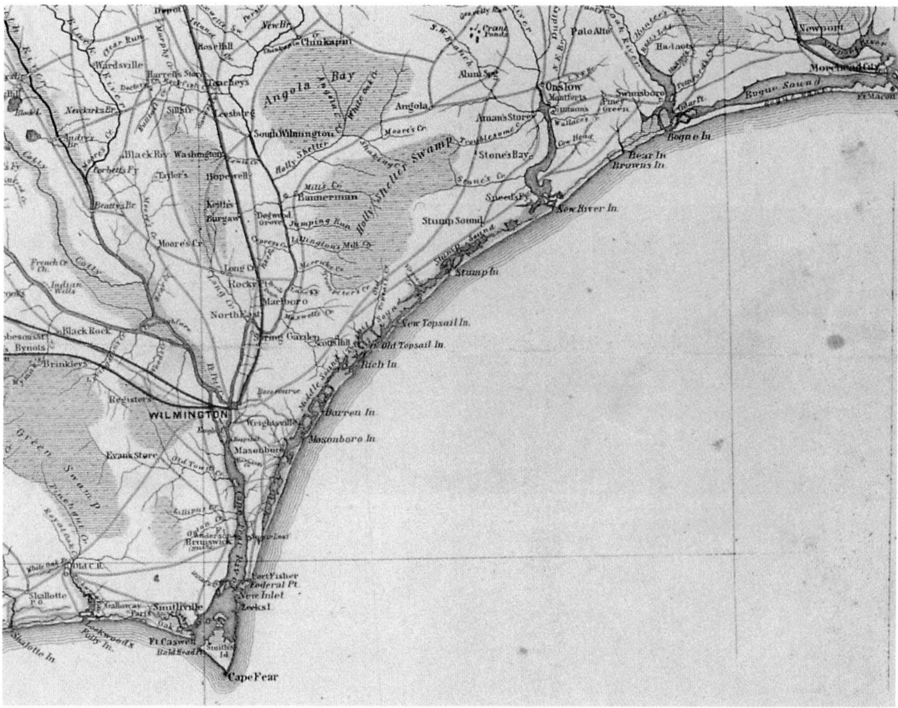

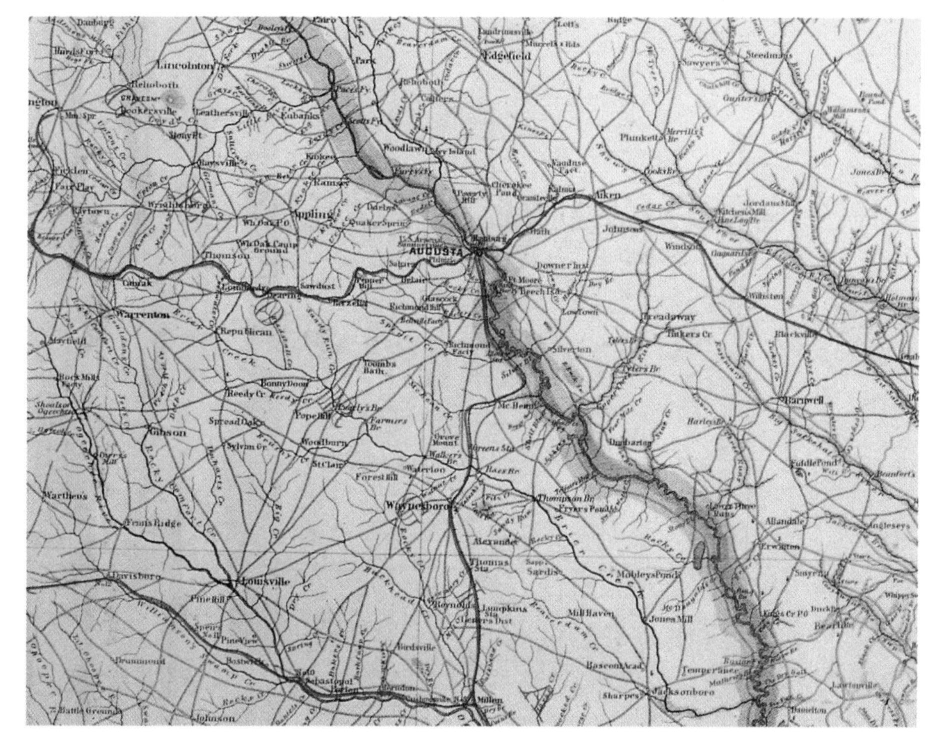

North and South Carolina, 1865

Left and This Page (details): North Carolina and South Carolina, originally drawn by Adolph Lindenkohl in February 1862 for the U.S. Coast Survey. This edition was colored and updated, and published in 1865.

Soldier's Rest, Virginia, 1865

Right: Plan of the convalescent camp at Soldier's Rest, Fairfax, Virginia, mapped in 1865 by a colonel with the 13th Massachusetts Volunteers. This camp was one of several at which soldiers could rest and recuperate.

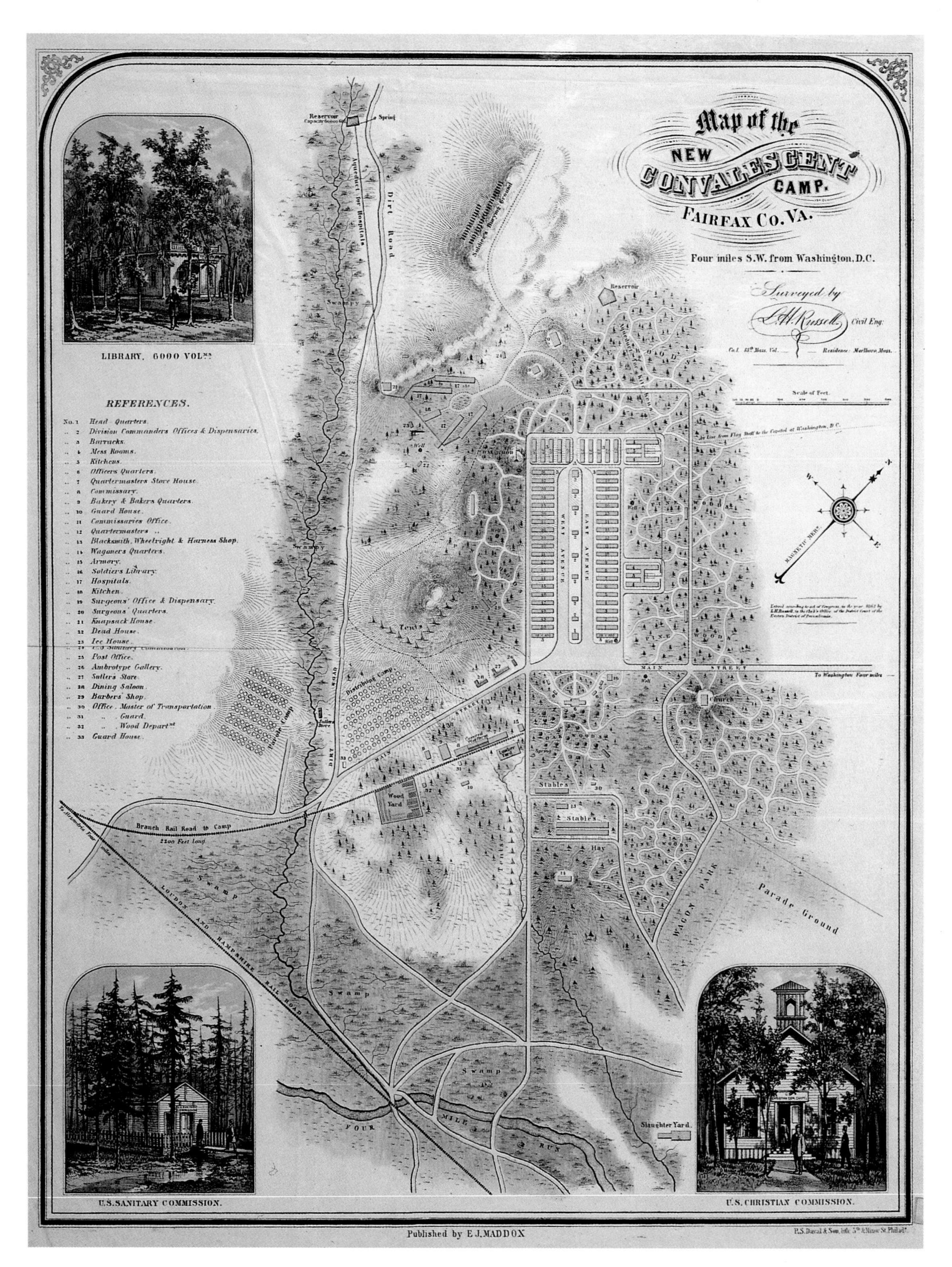

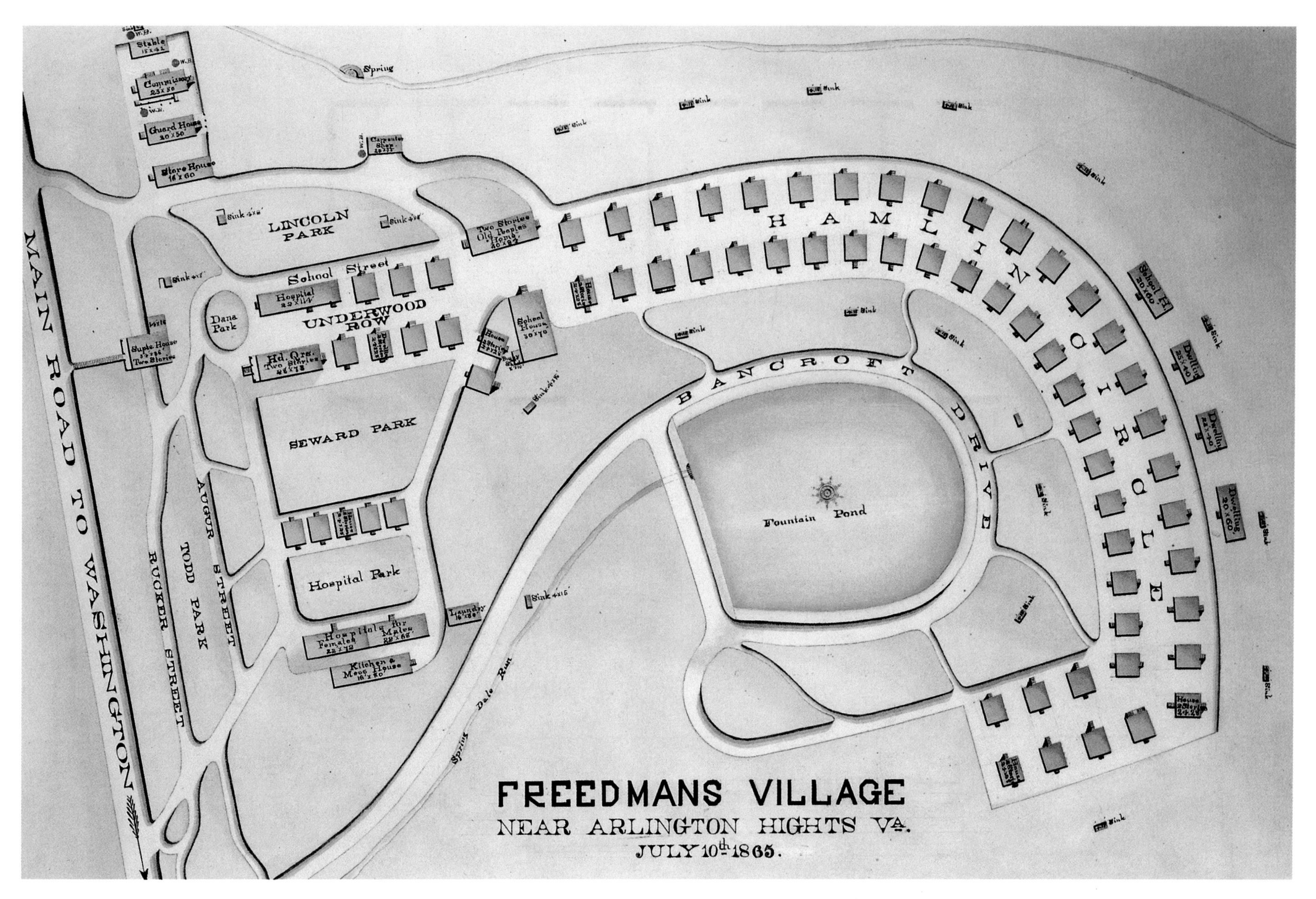

Freedman's Village, Virginia, July 10, 1865

Above: Freedman's Village near Arlington Heights, Virginia. The Freedman's Bureau was charged with the welfare of freed black slaves, and from May 12, 1865 the care of Southern refugees. The Bureau was also given responsibility for extensive tracts of land confiscated by the Federal government during the war.

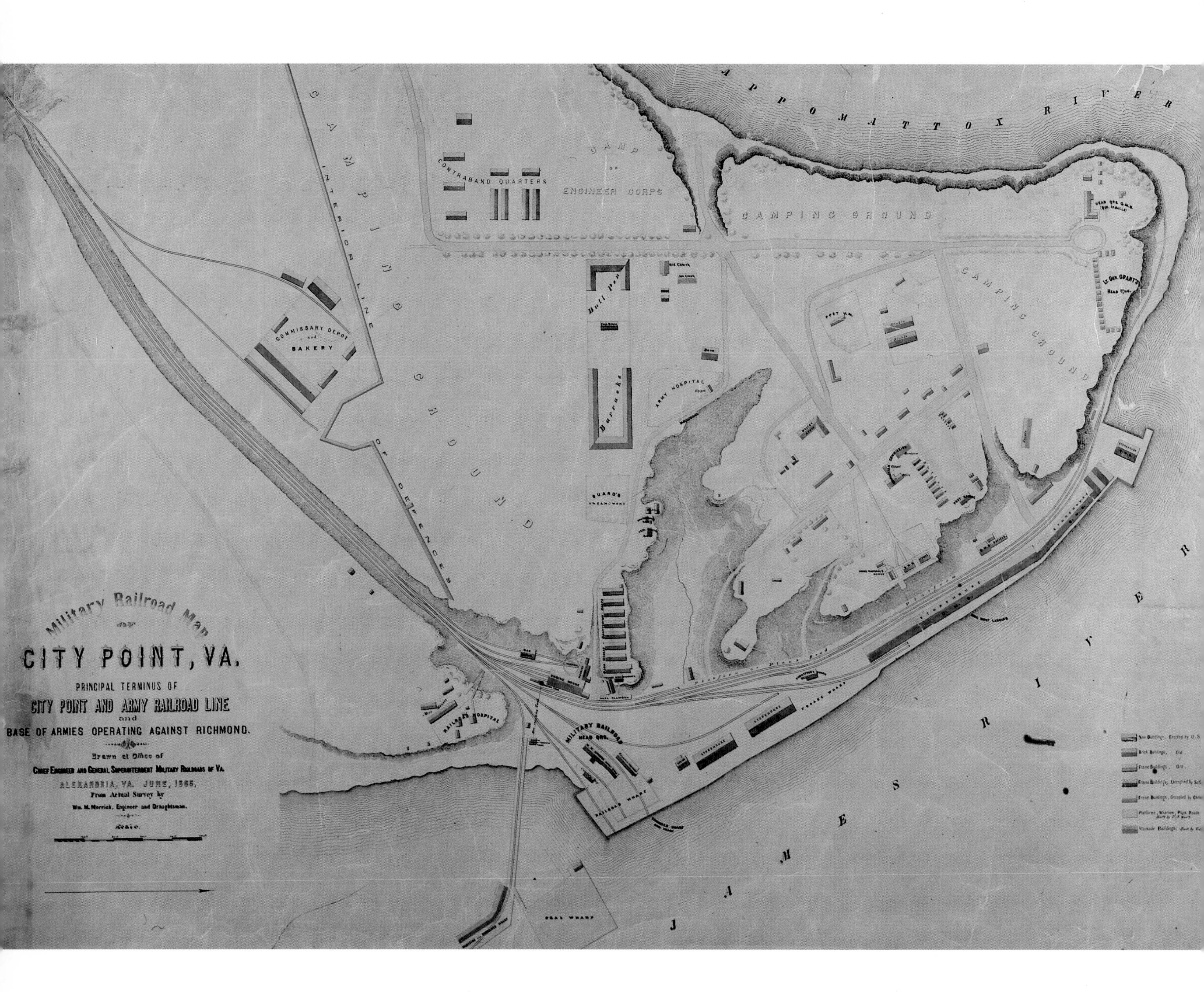
Military Railroad Map
of
CITY POINT, VA.
PRINCIPAL TERMINUS OF
CITY POINT AND ARMY RAILROAD LINE
and
BASE OF ARMIES OPERATING AGAINST RICHMOND.
Drawn at Office of
Chief Engineer and General Superintendent Military Railroads of Va.
ALEXANDRIA, VA. JUNE, 1865,
From Actual Survey by
Wm. M. Merrick, Engineer and Draughtsman.
Scale.
APPOMATTOX RIVER
JAMES RIVER
CAMPING GROUND
INTERIOR LINE OF DEFENCES
CONTRABAND QUARTERS
CAMP OF ENGINEER CORPS
COMMISSARY DEPOT and BAKERY
Bull Pen
Barracks
ARMY HOSPITAL
GUARD'S ENCAMPMENT
Lt. Gen. GRANT'S Head Qrs.
RAILROAD HOSPITAL
MILITARY RAILROAD HEAD QRS.
RAILROAD WHARF
STOREHOUSE
COAL WHARF

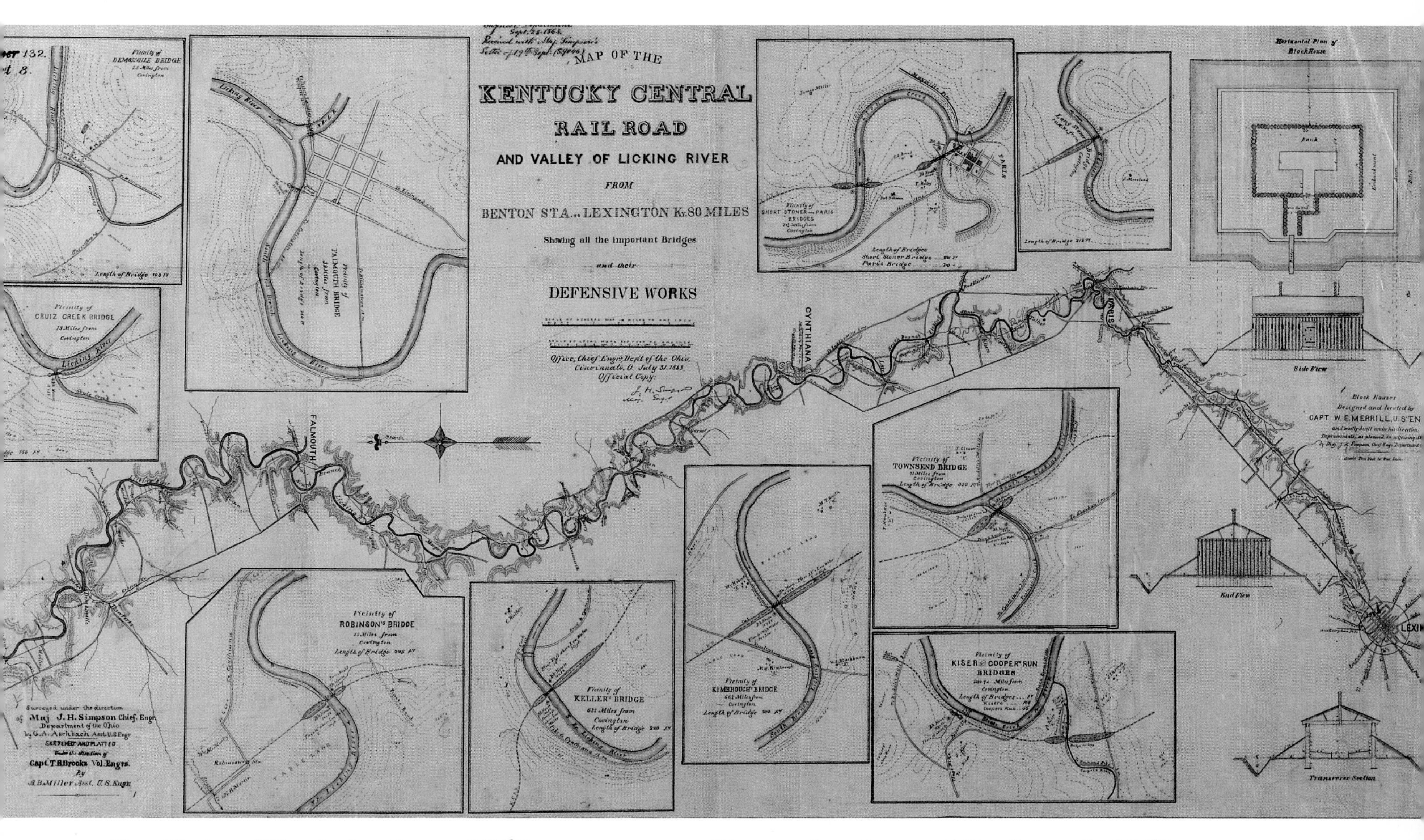

City Point, Virginia, June 1865

Left: The Civil War was the first war in which railroads played a major role. The two maps on these pages show elements of this importance. The first is a map prepared from surveys by William M. Merrick of the railroad systems in Virginia. A manuscript map of June 1865 it shows the railhead at City Point, Virginia. Colors distinguish new buildings erected by the Federal Government during the period when City Point was used as a base for operations against Richmond. Supplies were off-loaded at the various wharves and sent up the railroad to Grant's army. Note the bakery at center left and contraband quarters, where confiscated Confederate supplies were stored.

Kentucky Central Railroad, 1863

Above: The second map is an 1863 manuscript map of the Kentucky railroad system through the valley of the Licking River as surveyed by Major Simpson, Chief Engineer of the Department of the Ohio. The river is shown in blue and the railroad in red. Insets show the defensive systems around important bridges and a ground plan of a blockhouse, which formed part of the defenses. These were designed, located, and mostly built under the direction of William E. Merrill. Many soldiers were tied down by the need to defend the logistics and resupply corridors provided by the railroads.

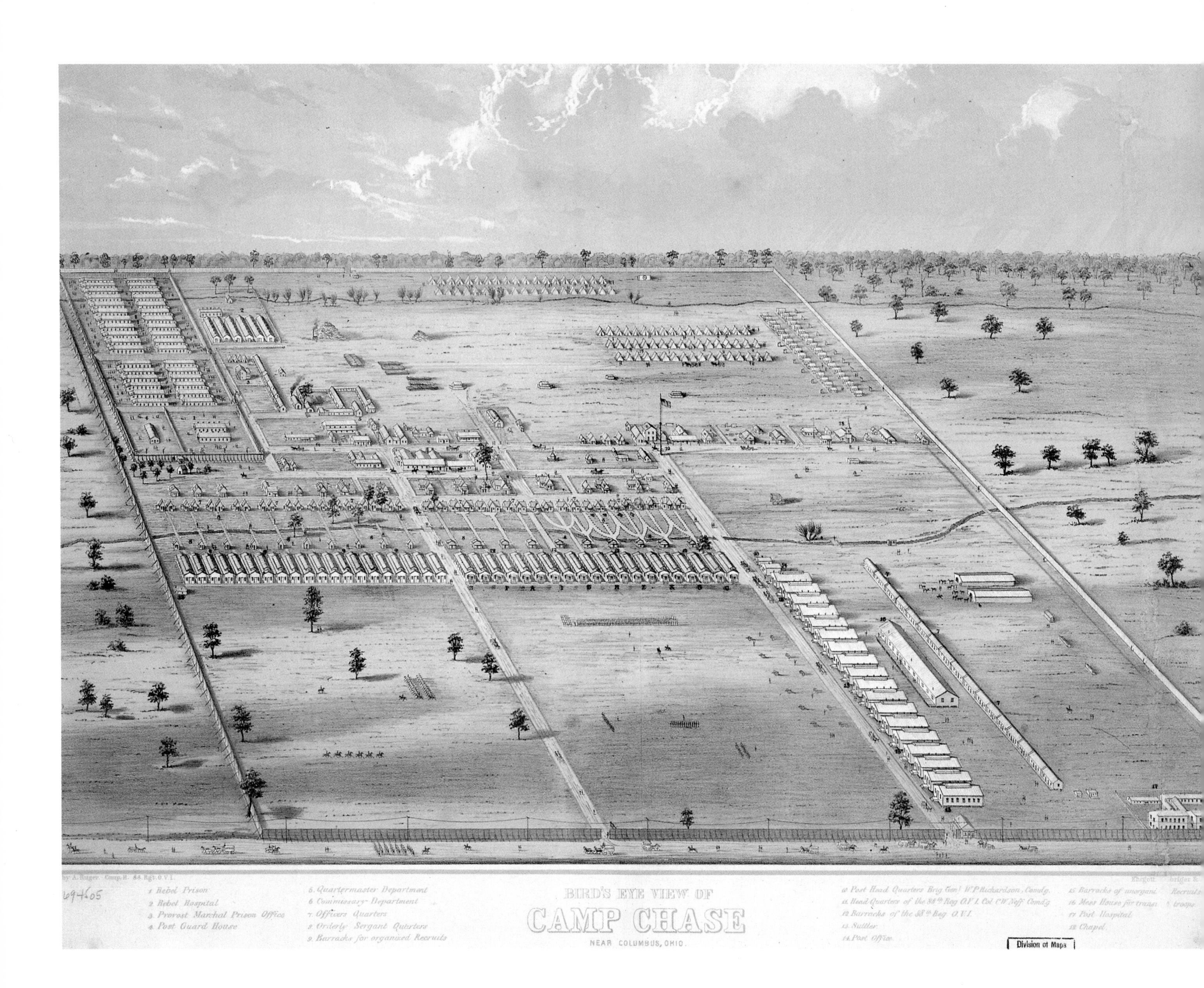
by A. Ruger. Comp. H. 88. Rgt. O.V.I.
694605
1 Rebel Prison
2 Rebel Hospital
3 Provost Marchal Prison Office
4 Post Guard House
5. Quartermaster Department
6 Commissary Department
7. Officers Quarters
8. Orderly Sergant Quirters
9. Barracks for organized Recruits
BIRD'S EYE VIEW OF
CAMP CHASE
NEAR COLUMBUS, OHIO.
10 Post Head Quarters Brig. Genl W. P. Richardson, Comdg.
11 Head Quarters of the 88th Reg O.V.I. Col C.W. Neff Comdg
12 Barracks of the 88th Reg O.V.I.
13 Suttler
14 Post Office
15 Barracks of unorgani Recruits
16 Mess House for transi troops
17 Post Hospital
18 Chapel
Division of Maps

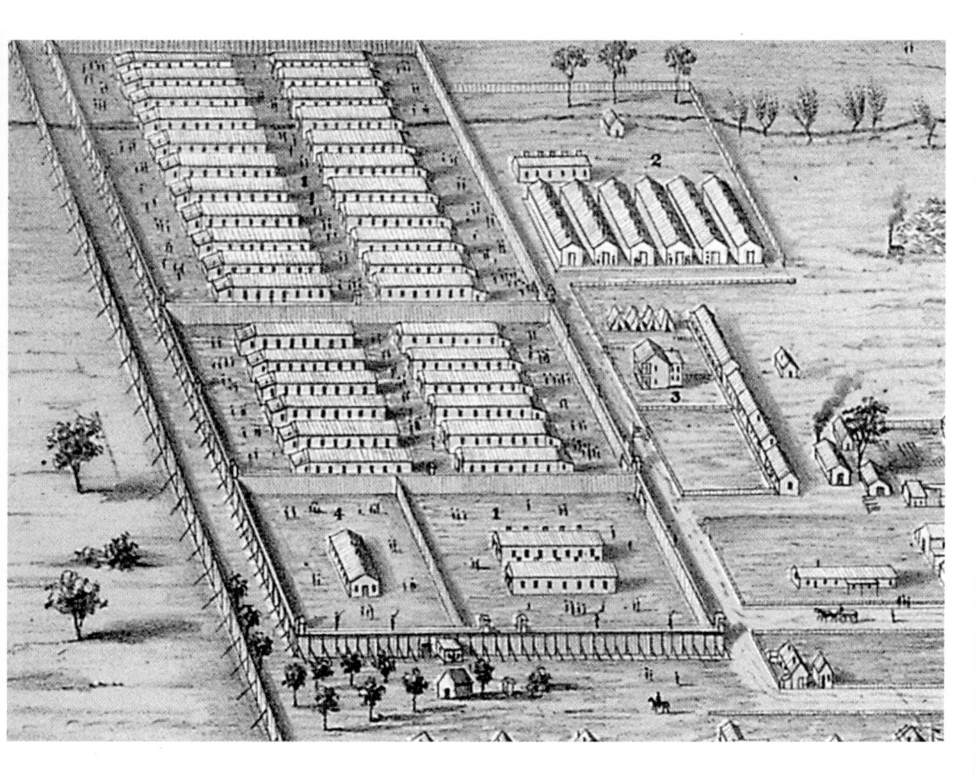

Camp Chase, Columbus, Ohio, 1865

Left and This Page (details): Albert Ruger's panoramic view of Camp Chase, near Columbus, Ohio. Ruger—at the time in Company H of the 88th Regiment, the Ohio Volunteer Infantry—pursued a career as an artist after the war and published a large number of panoramic views of American cities and towns. A collection of 213 of Ruger's bird's eye views are held at the Library of Congress. Principal buildings are keyed to a list in the bottom margin.

*IN*DEX OF MAPS